W9-ASQ-057

PLANNING NEIGHBORHOOD SPACE WITH PEOPLE
Second Edition

ENVIRONMENTAL DESIGN SERIES

Series Editor: Richard P. Dober, AICP

I define the term "environmental design" as an art larger
than architecture, more comprehensive than planning,
more sensitive than engineering. An art pragmatic,
one that preempts traditional concerns. The practice of
this art is intimately connected with man's ability to
function, to bring visual order to his surroundings, to
enhance and embellish the territory he occupies.

Richard P. Dober
Environmental Design

PLANNING NEIGHBORHOOD SPACE WITH PEOPLE

Second Edition

EDS/3

Randolph T. Hester, Jr.
University of California, Berkeley

VNR VAN NOSTRAND REINHOLD COMPANY
NEW YORK   CINCINNATI   TORONTO   LONDON   MELBOURNE

UNIVERSITY LIBRARIES
CARNEGIE-MELLON UNIVERSITY
PITTSBURGH, PENNSYLVANIA 15213

711.5
H58 (v.2)

Dedicated to Marcia, Mattie, and Nate,
and to the memory of my friend, Donald.

Copyright ©1975, 1984 by **Van Nostrand Reinhold Company Inc.**
Environmental Design Series, Volume 3
Library of Congress Catalog Card Number: 83-18437
ISBN: 0-442-23223-3

All rights reserved. No part of this work covered by the copyright hereon
may be reproduced or used in any form or by any means—graphic,
electronic, or mechanical, including photocopying, recording, taping, or
information storage and retrieval systems—without permission of the publisher.

Manufactured in the United States of America.

Published by Van Nostrand Reinhold Company Inc.
135 West 50th Street
New York, New York 10020

Van Nostrand Reinhold Company Limited
Molly Millars Lane
Wokingham, Berkshire RG11 2PY, England

Van Nostrand Reinhold
480 Latrobe Street
Melbourne, Victoria 3000, Australia

Macmillan of Canada
Division of Gage Publishing Limited
164 Commander Boulevard
Agincourt, Ontario MIS 3C7, Canada

15 14 13 12 11 9 8 7 6 5 4 3 2 1

Library of Congress Cataloging in Publication Data
Hester, Randolph T.
    Planning neighborhood space with people.
    (EDS/ Van Nostrand Reinhold Company Inc.; 3)
    Rev. ed. of: Neighborhood space. c1975.
    Includes bibliographical references and index.
    1. City planning.   2. Neighborhood.   3. Open spaces.
I. Hester, Randolph T.   Neighborhood space.   II. Title.
III. Series: Environmental design series (Van Nostrand
Reinhold Company Inc.); v. 3.
HT166.H47   1984   307'.12   83-18437
ISBN 0-442-23223-3

Contents

v

UNIVERSITY LIBRARIES
CARNEGIE-MELLON UNIVERSITY
PITTSBURGH, PENNSYLVANIA 15213

Series Editor's Foreword

Randy Hester's approach to environmental design reflects good faith, optimism, and a strong commitment to improving our beleaguered urban areas. The second edition of his timely work is thus welcomed on many accounts; not the least of which is that he has produced a professional reference work that, as demonstrated by time and utilization, makes a difference in the day-to-day tasks of all those involved in planning and designing neighborhood space.

RICHARD P. DOBER, AICP

Series Editor's Foreword
First Edition

Neighborhoods are beleaguered, especially in central city. Yet for a significant population group they survive, change, even grow, continuing to serve as vital micro-communities, larger than the home, smaller than the city.

Complex, dynamic, filled with conflicting interests, neighborhoods challenge designers and planners who arrive with preconceptions and canned solutions. At issue, too often, is not the quality of awareness and good will, but the quality of response. Foundering and failure often seems to be rooted in a lack of technique for arriving at distinctions that make a difference.

Getting on with the task of designing is never easy when dealing with group clients. A pragmatic reference work, *Neighborhood Space* seems as timely as it is informative in dealing with the issues of process *and* product. The concepts, evaluations, ideas, and critiques therein will truly help improve man's habitat.

RICHARD P. DOBER, AICP

Preface

Last summer I visited a neighborhood playground that I had designed three years earlier in Cambridge, Massachusetts. As I turned down Elm Street, I had an image of parents sitting in the shade of trees reading and watching their children; of children climbing, running, and playing house; of teens playing street hockey, hanging around in a space we had designed together. But at Fletcher School, I stopped and walked into the neighborhood playground and my image was destroyed. There were no children climbing, no parents reading, no teens hanging around. There was no one. All that was left was the hulk of a swing frame, a charred wood climber, twisted basketball goals, and dead trees with their bark stripped and limbs broken. I asked myself, "What's going on here?" and then, "What went wrong?"

It was then that I began seriously comparing this experience with other neighborhood open-space designs. Why had some of the spaces I had designed become significant parts of the neighborhood, while Fletcher had been trashed and gutted? Hadn't the residents there been just as involved? Hadn't they worked with Model Cities to locate all the recreation sites in the neighborhood? And hadn't the Department of Housing and Urban Development praised the process?

SOCIAL SUITABILITY OF NEIGHBORHOOD SPACE

In retrospect, it seems that a number of factors had contributed to the trashing of Fletcher, some of which I as a designer could not have controlled. The general hopelessness and antisocial behavior caused by widespread poverty were beyond my control. But I could have dealt with some factors. The residents had told me a lot that I had not heard or had misunderstood; as a result, the designed space was not socially suitable for their neighborhood. It did not take into account the adults' special patterns of neighboring, the unique concept the children had of recreation, or the sometimes violent interactions between groups. Because the adults depended heavily on their neighbors to share limited material goods, they interacted frequently in the spaces adjacent to their apartments. Because of this pattern of neighboring, the most important neighborhood spaces for the adults were the front porches, sidewalks, and front steps. They never went to Fletcher School and would have preferred sitting areas dispersed throughout the neighborhood. Since the adults' limited recreation time was spent near home, the older children played anywhere but at home. Their favorite places, I learned too late, included streets with limited access, alleys, rooftops, street corners, and forbidden places—the more dangerous the better. Since their concept of fun included a great deal of danger, the children seldom used Fletcher School except during school hours. Smaller children who did enjoy the playground facilities were afraid to go there because of frequent violence between groups of teenagers fighting for "turf" or simply expressing anger at a repressive world. Their violence was often directed at the playground, resulting in broken equipment, broken glass, and broken tree limbs. In short, I had not synthesized the unique wants and needs of the residents.

USER WANTS AND NEEDS

Although the residents had been involved in the design process, I had relied on my elitist criteria rather than on their needs, and my criteria for designing the space were quite different from the criteria the residents used in deciding whether or not to use the space. Whereas I was concerned about "hardware"—how the forms looked, how materials connected and weathered, and how circulation worked—the users were concerned about being safe, being with their friends, expressing anger, or controlling their turf. Simply stated, whether or not a person went to the park depended much more on who else was there than on the physical design of the park. It was this fact that I had misunderstood.

DESIGN RESPONSIBILITY

In addition to misreading social factors that could have led to a better design, I had not worked with the neighborhood responsibly. Although I had fulfilled my legal design responsibility, *I had not been responsive to the needs of the neighborhood residents.* The residents viewed the design process as a means of developing neighborhood power to accomplish other ends. They wanted to preserve their neighborhood, they wanted better jobs, and they wanted to improve the environment for their children. These goals required a long-term commitment to grass-roots community development, not just a flashy, expensive design for one playground. And by not making such a commitment, I had short-circuited their goals. I had said, in effect, that the product was more important than the process, yet the process of grass-roots community development was far more important to the residents than any single product.

I think the design at Fletcher School Neighborhood Playground is the rule rather than the exception, not because designers are ill intentioned but, rather, because we have given too little attention to meeting basic user needs and to fostering community development. Concentrating on aesthetics, we have ignored those factors that make a space suitable and usable. And now, just as the designer is being called on by the public to lend assistance at the neighborhood level, there is impatience with the design professsion because of high cost, elitism, the hardware approach, and debatable results.

The public clearly needs well-designed, socially suitable, livable urban neighborhoods that allow for the growth of individuals and the change of neighborhoods in a context of holistic community development. But can designers assist in meeting this need with their traditional skills, standard methodology, and current policies? I think not. Many of our skills, methodologies, and policies are appropriate; but many more are not.

THE PURPOSE

With these concerns in mind, a decade ago I wrote a book called *Neighborhood Space.* Today, in contemplating the revision of that book, I realized that my own concerns were largely the same. I still believe that we need new skills, methodologies, and policies for designing socially suitable, livable neighborhoods.

The objective of this second primer on planning neighborhood space is to introduce design students in architecture, landscape architecture, and urban planning to neighborhood space, user needs, and appropriate design processes. It is meant to help those who seek appropriate skills and methods make real their dreams and to help others realize their own ideals through the design of neighborhood space. Although I have written with students in mind, certain sections may be useful to professionals, policy makers, community psychologists, and concerned citizens.

Much of the original book remains intact, only updated. I have included more recent examples of neighborhood designs that reflect current patterns, and I have tried to be more explicit in showing how to incorporate social factors into site planning. To that end, I have added Chapter 5 on designing by archetypes and idiosyncrasies, several new case studies to Chapter 6, and exercises for students at the end of each chapter.

ACKNOWLEDGMENTS

I would like to offer special appreciation to Sandy Wendel, who rewrote a draft of this edition from the user's perspective; to Marcia McNally, Mark Francis, Donald Appleyard, Richard P. Dober, and Chuck Hutchinson, who sorted out the purpose and content; to Clare Cooper Marcus, Bob Twiss, Dick Bender, Barbara Gunderson, Bernice Pettinato, and Mary Dorian, who supported and helped produce this book; and to Debbie Phillips, Donna Palmer, Ed Schweitzer, Coleman Long, Marge Smith, and Judy Christopher Hester, who were largely responsible for production of the first edition.

RANDOLPH T. HESTER, JR.

PLANNING NEIGHBORHOOD SPACE WITH PEOPLE
Second Edition

1

Neighborhood Space

RENEWED INTEREST IN THE LOCAL ENVIRONMENT

As poor and disenfranchised urban Americans, uprooted by urban development over the last thirty years, made their plight known, concern about neighborhoods increased. Although interest was spurred by the poor through the civil rights movement and the accompanying advocacy movement, today concern is widespread.[1] People in both middle-class and poor neighborhoods that are threatened by highways, lack of services, and development pressure, are saying that a good, clean, livable environment begins at home, at the neighborhood level. They are demanding neighborhoods that are well designed, or redesigned to be socially suitable, and that meet the needs of the people living there.

Mike Royko of the *Chicago Daily News* put this renewal of neighborhood concern in perspective when he editorialized about his own community. He described the mundane things that make a neighborhood convenient, inexpensive, diverse, and human. He noted that you do not have to own a car. You can walk to the grocery and drug stores and to all sorts of specialty shops and services. You can walk to the schoolyard to fly a kite, play football, or hang around. Royko lamented that the urban neighborhood became obsolete in the rush to suburbia, "There wasn't any sense in walking someplace close by to buy something when you could just as easily take on twenty-four monthly payments and full-coverage insurance, fill up a gas tank with ethyl, and drive 6 miles to buy the same thing."[2] Now the city neighborhood may be the model of the future.

Royko points out, with tongue in cheek, that one of the primary reasons for the resurgence of interest in neighborhood space was a result of the energy crisis and diminished mobility. But other factors contributed to the renewed importance of neighborhood. For one, the public fiscal instability of a slow-growth economy brought a decentralization of city functions and more neighborhood control. Meanwhile, contemporary social issues such as continued anomie, urban isolation, rootlessness, and the threat of global annihilation, fueled the desire for neighborhood security. The rise of neighborhood preservation may indeed be tied to recent declines in national certainty and a new regard for local self-reliance and self-preservation mechanisms.

Today people are consciously seeking "roots" in their neighborhoods. They are recreating lost rituals and creating new ones, becoming more dependent on neighbors, promoting neighborhood self-reliance, and volunteering time and resources towards the reclamation of neighborhood spaces. However, this

high level of neighborhood commitment did not always exist. Many early efforts to preserve neighborhood space were little more than isolated confrontations between poorly organized local groups and city governments.

Grass-roots Efforts

In the 1960s, more successful examples of neighborhood-space preservation emerged. In Berkeley, California, citizens began to fear that their neigh-

Neighborhood groups are organizing all over the country to improve the quality of their daily lives. Here, in Manteo, North Carolina, Lions Club volunteers construct a waterfront park that saved their community nearly $100,000. (Photograph by Eve Rowland)

borhoods were seriously threatened by high-density construction, automobile traffic, and a lack of recreation space and social services. A grass-roots effort reversed the trend.[3] The citizens passed a referendum that provided for "the establishment of a new planning process to achieve the preservation and enhancement of the neighborhoods of the city."[4] They contended that the quality of Berkeley's neighborhoods was a resource that should not be sacrificed. Through rezonings, a special recreation-facilities bond issue, and traffic diverters, substantial neighborhood improvements were effected.

Today there is widespread, highly organized neighborhood involvement in Berkeley. The citywide Council of Neighborhood Associations acts as a watchdog for neighborhood interests. In 1982, the citizens passed a referendum to protect sacred neighborhood stores through commercial rent control. One neighborhood group closed local streets to create pedestrian plazas. And, although state courts have ruled illegal the traffic diverters that protected neighborhoods from crosstown traffic, local groups vow to save them. Perhaps most significant is a council-adopted policy developed by the citizens, empowering local groups with a legal role in the design, management, and maintenance of neighborhood parks.

Another early neighborhood success story took place in the west side of St. Louis. The Jeff-Vander-Lou community was "down and out" in the mid 1960s. It had the worst of everything—unemployment, crime, substandard housing, and absentee ownership—yet local residents managed to form an independent 19th Ward Beautification Committee that included everyone in the neighborhood. The determined community then created its own management corporation to produce affordable housing. Although initial efforts at housing rehabilitation were hindered because established institutions redlined the area, by 1981 the neighborhood had rehabilitated 350 housing units and constructed an equal number of apartments. The group also persuaded the Brown Shoe Company to not only build a new

plant in their neighborhood, but to employ local residents.[5]

In Raleigh, North Carolina, a citizens group, Goals for Raleigh, proposed a policy for the future that reaffirms "the importance of the neighborhood as the basis for community development, maintaining a high quality of life in both old and new neighborhoods." Pointing out that the neighborhood can be planned and implemented in accordance with the wants and needs of the neighborhood residents themselves, Goals for Raleigh urged strategies for both old and new neighborhoods:

Goals for Raleigh urges that a continuing effort be made to increase the physical and social quality of existing neighborhoods. In the future, the allocation of resources should reflect a bias towards the preservation and enhancement of these neighborhoods and the downtown area. If public facilities and social services are not available in some neighborhoods, providing them should become the first priority.

New neighborhoods should be planned from the onset to provide a full range of neighborhood services. Neighborhoods should be in harmony with the existing environment; they should anticipate the need for and absorb the cost of new public services such as schools and neighborhood centers; and they should not add to the deterioration of existing neighborhoods. By properly planning new neighborhoods, a high quality of life can more easily be maintained throughout the city.[6]

Advocating these objectives, Goals for Raleigh sought widespread support for neighborhood preservation and rehabilitation. Success was signaled by the election of a city council whose majority endorsed Goals for Raleigh. Neighborhood rehabilitation efforts replaced urban renewal. Neighborhood groups became legal members of the community-planning process, and highways, disruptive to neighborhoods, were scrapped. Neighborhood groups also developed a new thoroughfare plan. Adoption of their plan, over that of the administration, necessitated subsequent adoption of a new overall transportation plan. The plan's reliance on buses and paratransit resulted in further preservation of inner-city neighborhoods.

In Washington, D.C., a group headed by Leila Smith called Don't Tear It Down began an effort to save historic buildings, but quickly realized that a battle to save one building would not win the campaign to create a livable city. The preservationist group gained strength when it agreed that it is not just historic neighborhoods that should be "saved" from the urban demolition derby—it's neighborhoods that generate a sense of belonging and which contain the amenities (a favorite word of urban planners) that make life in the city bearable—corner stores, a trusty shoemaker or dry cleaner, a bar where friends can congregate; in short, all the pleasantries that are now endangered in modern cities and wholly extinct in modern suburbs."[7] This appealed to a wider group of urbanites who were not concerned about historic buildings but were concerned about increasingly unlivable neighborhoods.

Institutional Acceptance

Of equal importance was the planners' reapplication of the neighborhood as the growth unit of several major urban developments in this country. In the 1960s, partly in response to citizen activism, Hartford, Connecticut, initiated a process to overcome typical piecemeal, low-quality suburban development and accompanying urban decay. Based on the Columbia New Town model, the Greater Hartford Process attempted to prove that the neighborhood could be used as the building block in central-city renewal as well as in new towns.[8] Cities as diverse as New York, San Diego, and Dayton, began to use the neighborhood as the key to renewal and growth.

The advocacy of some professional organizations gave additional clout to the neighborhood movement. For example, in 1972 the American Institute of Architects National Policy Task Force proposed that the neigborhood become the national "growth unit," a standard for urban development that emphasizes quality of life rather than quantity of physical improvements. The task force urged the nationwide adoption of a neighborhood growth unit that would range in size from 500 to 3,000 households and offer the services of elementary education, day care, convenience shopping, health care, and recreation. Community centers and open spaces would also be provided to stem the tide that has swallowed up neighborhoods in the growth and change of urbanizing America. This, they said, would necessitate more citizen control and participation at the neighborhood level because no national policy can do without grass-roots support.[9]

Federal policies in the 1970s corroborated the neighborhood movement. Community development funds stressed a new localism and meaningful citizen participation. Many local officials interpreted the Community Development Act to require that cities establish neighborhood councils to qualify for federal funds. This created the most widespread, institutionalized neighborhood movement in the history of the country. In addition, government emphasis on rehabilitation and historic preservation, instead of urban renewal, reinforced the federally mandated citizen involvement in neighborhood affairs. The neighborhood and citizen decision making were accepted as serving national purposes and were institutionalized by legislation.

In spite of the widespread acceptance of the neighborhood movement, local control created several problems. Although the early federal legislation directed toward neighborhood involvement sought to rectify inequities by providing technical assistance and funding to poor neighborhoods, the federal policy of the early 1980s shifted toward volunteerism and self-help programs. There was a marked reduction in public funds for neighborhood programs and consequently, in many low-income communities, local groups ceased to function altogether. Meanwhile, wealthier, better educated neighborhood groups maintained their political clout exacerbating the disparities that earlier neighborhood programs had sought to remedy.

Another drawback of the neighborhood movement also emerged as neighborhood control, originally the tool of liberal and egalitarian efforts, was used by some for conservative and reactionary causes: segregation, racism, and exclusion. There are charges today that neighborhood control has allowed local self-interest to supercede community well being and holistic, ecological thinking.

In any case, today the neighborhood movement has become an acceptable vehicle for a broad spectrum of values and action. Hardly a day goes by that the neighborhood is not posited as a panacea for crime control, drug rehabilitation, political and fiscal revitalization, energy conservation, and educational innovation. Planners have to respond by seeking approaches to design more consistent with neighborhoods as the residents define them. Central to such approaches are a definition of the important components of a neighborhood, a description of how neighborhood space is used, and an understanding of the importance of increased user expectations that neighborhood space be socially suitable. This chapter explores the role of designers and establishes for them a user-oriented approach to neighborhood planning.

THE IMPORTANT COMPONENTS OF A NEIGHBORHOOD

There has been much discussion of what a neighborhood is.[10] In 1915, Robert E. Park and E. W. Burgess introduced the idea of neighborhood as an ecological concept with planning implications.[11] Their work stressed the physical features of a neighborhood environment: land use, density, street patterns, "natural" boundaries, condition of dwelling units, and amount of open space. Although the work of Clarence Stein, Walter Gropius, Le Corbusier, and Frank Lloyd Wright was flavored with social idealism, it still reflected a physical concept of neighborhood by defining it in terms of desirable features. A neighborhood needs a focal point like an elementary school and recreation area. Residential streets should be laid out in short loops and culs-de-sac. Each house should adjoin planned open space. There

should be neighborhood facilities like an auditorium, senior-citizen areas, and a local shopping center.[12]

On the other hand, social planners and sociologists stressed with equal singularity the social dimensions of a neighborhood. They viewed the neighborhood in terms of its symbolic and cultural aspects and emphasized shared activities and experiences, the resulting social groups, and common values and loyalties. The physical environment was taken for granted. P. H. Mann concluded that the physical aspects of neighborhood were sterile, unrelated to the social aspects, and therefore not useful.

A few planning theoreticians pled for a unified definition that combined both the social and the physical aspects of a neighborhood. In England, Ruth Glass recognized both an area with physical characteristics and a territorial group with primary social interaction. Terence Lee proposed that the urban neighborhood be defined as a sociospatial schema, a definition that most clearly combined the social and physical components of a neighborhood into a unfied schema. The work of Glass and Lee signaled the beginning of a serious effort to define "neighborhood" more comprehensively. Many planners, designers, and social scientists have since tried to define neighborhood by relating human behavior and geography, land development and social predictions, and city planning and social change.

At the same time, another group of sociologists contended that the neighborhood did not need to be defined; rather, it needed to be discarded as a planning unit. This group claimed that neighborhood planning was security-seeking nostalgia, a desire to reconstruct the simplicity of the days when the New England town meeting symbolized the urbanites' rootedness in local territory. R. R. Issacs and Louis Wirth, among others, sought to show that man's behavior was no longer oriented to the local area but to the city, nation, and world. Therefore, a definition of the neighborhood was irrelevant.

In spite of controversy, the application of the neighborhood unit to planning continued. The concept reached an apex of popularity after World War II

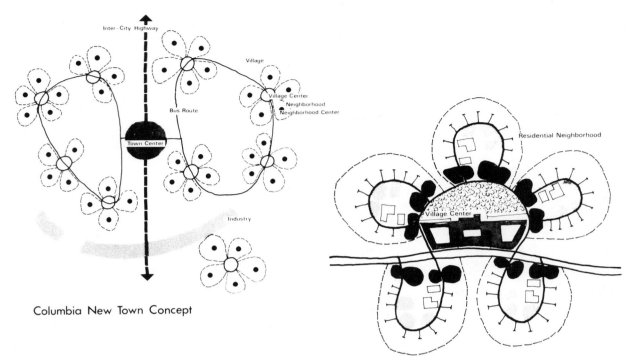

Columbia New Town Concept

Columbia New Town Village Concept

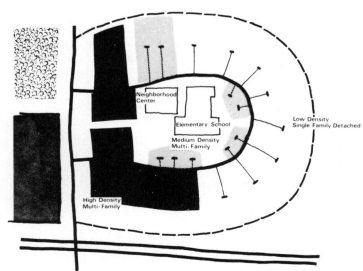

Columbia New Town Neighborhood Concept

In Columbia, Maryland, the neighborhood unit has been successfully employed as the unit of growth in a new-town development. The town is comprised of a number of separate villages, each of which is subdivided into a number of neighborhoods providing a range of housing styles and prices, an elementary school, and a neighborhood center.[13]

and then declined. Planners found many theories impracticable, and other theories simply failed because they were applied in a physically deterministic manner or neglected the user's point of view. In addition, theoretical definitions largely ignored the political aspects of local communities. This situation became painfully clear in the 1960s when planning proposal after planning proposal was opposed by neighborhood groups.

What is needed, then, is a practical definition that embraces the interest of residents in their neighborhoods, recognizes the unique social, spatial, and political aspects of a neighborhood, is user defined, acknowledges the importance of local relationships, and is useful in planning.

Milton Kotler proposed such a definition. "The neighborhood is a political settlement of small territory and familiar association, whose absolute property is its capacity for deliberative democracy."[14] But what does Kotler mean by "small territory" and "familiar association"? These concepts formed the basis of many earlier neighborhood theories, but few planners were able to combine them in a sociospatial schema.[15]

Kotler's acceptance of these concepts within a political context suggests that the size of a small territory depends on the political issue. The specific issue results from the number and geographical range of citizens affected. If the location of a minipark will affect only a block, that is a small territory. If the location of a thoroughfare will affect several thousand people in an area of several square blocks, that is also a small territory. A sixth grader once told me, "A neighborhood is when you get 150 people to protest at city hall against a highway proposed to go through a residential area."

The idea that a neighborhood changes in the minds of the residents according to the nature of the political crisis or issue is basic to a functional definition, but it does not deal with the nonpolitical aspects of daily human activity and interaction, which are just as important to many residents. A small child was not concerned about any political issue when she remarked, "A neighborhood is when your friend lives on the same block." There are many people who would define a neighborhood similarly, without political overtones. It is appropriate, then, to view the small territory as the area close to home that, because of frequent use and familiarity, is considered one's own. This aspect of Kotler's definition is particularly relevant to heavy users of the area close to home—the young, the old, the poor, the homebound, and the deviant. It still suggests that neighborhood boundaries are not fixed but vary from person to person, depending on life-cycle stage, life style, ethnicity, and personal preference. Planners, when referring to this dynamic quality, say that the small territory "roves." For a child, it might be centered around home, school, a friend's home, and a park; for a father, around home and work.[16]

Inasmuch as these personal patterns overlap with others within the territory close to home, familiar associations develop. These associations may be with people using the same facilities or seeking the same services, with the place itself, or with events that have occurred in the place, all of which contribute to a sense of familiarity and ownership.[17] Such shared spaces can be mapped, and neighborhood boundaries can be drawn around these commonly used places.

Underpinning the whole of Kotler's definition was his recognition of the unique political nature of neighborhoods, evidenced by renewed citizen demands to shape and control their own neighborhoods. Previously, planners clung to the idea that the neighborhood planning unit fostered grass-roots democracy and local loyalties. Kotler suggested that the opposite was true—that because of local concerns and shared problems, local loyalties and common values developed. These are expressed through grass-roots democracy, and a feeling of neighborhood results.[18] Thus, a neighborhood is defined by the residents, not the planners, and is expressed in the political actions taken by the residents. This suggests acceptance of what has been called a "collective responsibility," which arises from the people

Spaces where territories overlap

① Home
② Friends & Neighbors
③ School
④ Church & Clubs
⑤ Shopping

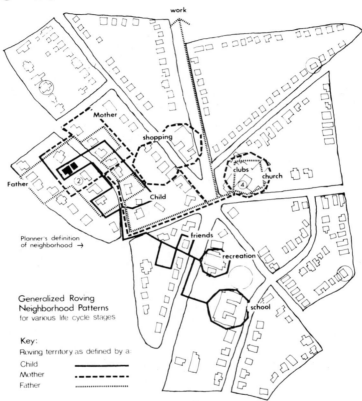

Generalized Roving
Neighborhood Patterns
for various life cycle stages

Key:
Roving territory as defined by a:
Child
Mother
Father

Although planners defined the neighborhood as a large area with strict boundaries, each resident of the Five Points Neighborhood in Raleigh defined his community in terms of his own use patterns. But only when use patterns overlapped did people have a sense of shared neighborhood.[19]

The capacity for deliberative democracy is one unique property of the neighborhood. Residents are able to meet face to face, debate issues that affect their environment, and accept a collective responsibility for the outcome. (Photograph by Marge Hackmann)

Some people view the neighborhood not in political terms, but as a small territory of familiar associations in which the important aspect is informal interaction.

of an area because of shared values, use patterns, and common problems. To facilitate collective responsibility it makes sense that the planned "neighborhood should be small enough to encourage participation of all families in common neighborhood concerns."[20]

In summary, the neighborhood as a political settlement of small territory and familiar association that allows for deliberative democracy, provides an umbrella definition that is both relevant to the people who make up a neighborhood and useful to the designers who must plan change for a quality neighborhood environment. By including the concepts of small territory and familiar association, the definition echoes the social and spatial concepts of neighborhood that were central to the earlier literature. Kotler asserts that the political view of the neighborhood supercedes the importance of either the spatial or social aspects, and it is this emphasis in Kotler's definition that speaks most directly to the renewed interest of lay people in their neighborhoods. But most importantly, the definition provides the context for discussing an approach to socially suitable neighborhood design.

NEIGHBORHOOD SPACE

Having defined neighborhood in political terms, we shall now examine the concept of neighborhood space. Neighborhood space is that territory close to home, including houses, churches, businesses, and parks that, because of the residents' collective responsibility, familar association, and frequent shared use, is considered to be their "own." But in this discussion, the concept of neighborhood space will be limited to public,[21] outdoor territory close to home. For designers seeking to design socially suitable neighborhoods, two questions must be answered. First, what territory is considered the residents' own, and second, how do designers delineate those spaces that residents consider their own?

The concept of "own" refers to a sense of

Frequently, a sense of neighborhood arises when all the residents of an area are threatened by an outside force such as a disruptive beltline expressway, and they must act collectively to save their home environment. (Photograph courtesy of Peter Batchelor)

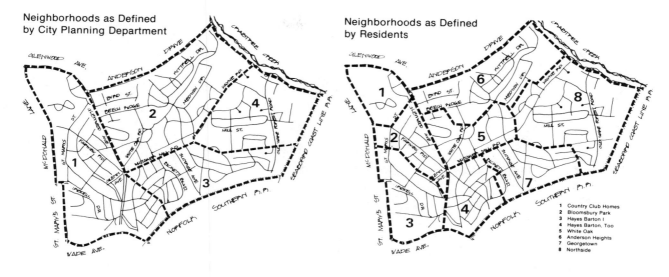

Neighborhoods as Defined by City Planning Department

Neighborhoods as Defined by Residents

1 Country Club Homes
2 Bloomsbury Park
3 Hayes Barton I
4 Hayes Barton, Too
5 White Oak
6 Anderson Heights
7 Georgetown
8 Northside

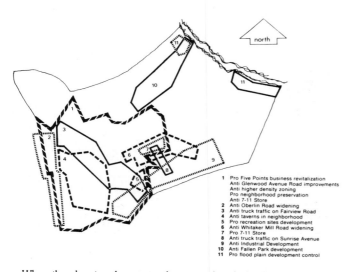

Boundaries of Sub Neighborhoods Based on Issues

1 Pro Five Points business revitalization
  Anti Glenwood Avenue Road improvements
  Anti higher density zoning
  Pro neighborhood preservation
  Anti 7-11 Store
2 Anti Oberlin Road widening
3 Anti truck traffic on Fairview Road
4 Anti taverns in neighborhood
5 Pro recreation sites development
6 Anti Whitaker Mill Road widening
7 Pro 7-11 Store
8 Anti truck traffic on Sunrise Avenue
9 Anti Industrial Development
10 Anti Fallen Park development
11 Pro flood plain development control

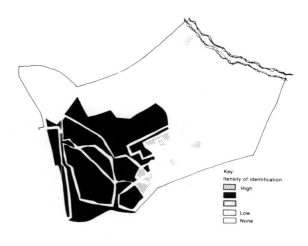

Intensity of Identification with the Five Points Community Based on Issues

Key
Itensity of identification

High

Low
None

When the planning department began work with the Five Points Community, the professional planners divided the area into four neighborhoods. The residents attending a community meeting indicated that there were eight neighborhoods instead of four, and they named each. However, as issues arose in the communi-ty, even the right neighborhood boundaries were incorrect because the issues often affected residents of several neighborhoods. It was also found that the more crises the residents had faced together, the more identification they had, not only with the neighborhood but also with the Five Points Community.

Alternative 1

This is a projection of present trends if they continue.

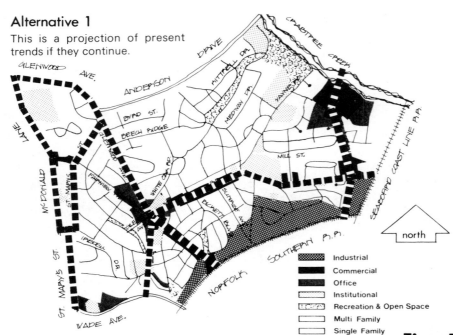

Industrial
Commercial
Office
Institutional
Recreation & Open Space
Multi Family
Single Family
Thoroughfare

ASSUMPTIONS

LAND USE
1. Wake Forest Road, Glenwood Avenue, Fairview Road, and Whitaker Mill will have strip commercial, industrial and office and institution.
2. Residential lots along major thoroughfares and near commercial areas may be utilized as parking lots.
3. Industry will expand from the railroad tracks into Georgetown and Hayes Barton Too.
4. Development may continue in the floodplains if the City's Flood Ordinance is not upheld.
5. Office and institutional will increase behind Wade Avenue.
6. Single family residences will become rental units.
7. Apartment complexes will be developed on vacant land.

ZONING
1. Office and commercial rezoning will be established along major thoroughfares.

TRANSPORTATION
1. The Thoroughfare Plan will be implemented.
2. Mass transit will be via the present bus routes.

Five Points Community

Alternative 2

This plan makes an effort to preserve the present eight neighborhoods while allowing for some expansion of commercial and industrial uses.

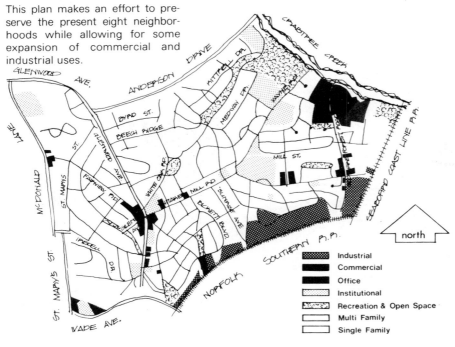

Industrial
Commercial
Office
Institutional
Recreation & Open Space
Multi Family
Single Family

ASSUMPTIONS

LAND USE
1. There will be little or no expansion of parks.
2. Some multiple use will be encouraged.
3. Homes north of Five Points along Glenwood Avenue will be converted to office and institutional use.
4. There will be some expansion of the Five Points Commercial District.
5. Wake Forest Road lot on the corner of McNeil will become offices.
6. The neighborhoods along industrial areas will be stabilized to stop any more industrial encroachment.
7. Multi-family residences will be encouraged in scattered sites throughout the community rather than concentrated in certain areas.

ZONING
1. The Flood Ordinance will be enacted to protect the area around Crabtree Creek.
2. Down zoning will occur in appropriate areas to correspond with present land use density.

TRANSPORTATION
1. Mass transit will be via the proposed bus routes.

Alternative 3

This plan is an interpretation of the Action Group's Goals.

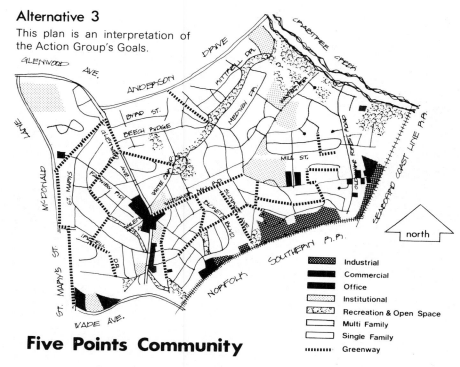

Five Points Community

Industrial
Commercial
Office
Institutional
Recreation & Open Space
Multi Family
Single Family
Greenway

north

In the Five Points Community, planners worked with the residents to develop three alternative plans that the planners were able to describe in terms of land-use changes and impacts on the neighborhoods. Alternative 3, which best reflected the goals the residents had articulated in a survey, was the overwhelming community choice when the alternatives were presented to the residents.

ASSUMPTIONS

LAND USE
1. Open space will be maximized to supplement the community's recreational facilities.
2. There will be a Greenway system to connect residences with businesses, institutions, parks, and to provide safe bicycle routes. Greenways will also be given priority for the maintenance of sidewalks and street trees.
3. There will be a general pedestrian orientation for business areas.
4. Street trees will be planted along major arteries.
5. Buffers will be encouraged along non-residential land uses and traffic arteries.
6. Multi-use of institutional and parking facilities will be maximized.
7. Commercial uses will be clustered to use the land more efficiently.
8. Parking lots behind the stores in Five Points will be established.
9. Neighborhood oriented businesses in Northside Shopping Center will be encouraged.
10. Where possible, residences along Wake Forest Road will be focused inward away from the street.
11. Areas of Georgetown and Hayes Barton Too will be preserved for small homes.

ZONING
1. Compatable land uses for the Flood Plains will be zoned to minimize runoff.
2. The lot at Wake Forest and McNeil will be zoned for apartments.

TRANSPORTATION
1. New bus lines and mini-bus routes will be established.
2. Bicycle routes will be built in conjunction with the greenway.
3. The Thoroughfare Plan will be replaced with a transportation plan

collective-symbolic ownership. It is similar to the sense of turf that urban street gangs demonstrate in their guarding of certain city areas; no member of the gang owns the area legally, but the entire gang, as a group, has a sense of owning it symbolically. On the other hand, a resident may actually have legal ownership of his home, but it is less likely that it will be symbolically owned by the remaining residents. However, if there is a vacant lot in the neighborhood whose private ownership is unclear to the residents, it is frequently used as their own.

In other words, public and ambiguously owned private spaces lend themselves to collective-symbolic ownership more than clearly privately owned properties. Public and ambiguously owned properties include such spaces as parks, street corners, storefronts, alleys, rooftops, sidewalks, schoolyards, playgrounds, parking lots, streets, paths, junkyards, yards, front porches, streams, abandoned lots, undeveloped lots, secret niches, plazas, churchyards, trash dumps, woods, bus stops, front steps, gardens, outdoor cafes, phone booths, forbidden places, favorite places, utility spaces,

Neighborhood space may include places like streets and forbidden places as well as traditional open spaces.

floodplains, ponds, greenways, conservation ease-ments, beautification areas, and transportation-cor-ridor spaces.

Aside from a space being publicly or ambiguously owned, other factors influence the residents' sense of collective-symbolic ownership. Residents frequently share the use of these spaces and can be involved together in acquiring, planning, and changing them. As frequency of use and intensity of involvement increase, collective-symbolic ownership increases. Sym-bolic ownership also increases as the users perceive that the space meets their special needs, as it increases in value as a status object to outsiders (especially to outsiders of high status), or as it increases in value to one's peer group. All the above factors contribute to a sense of collective ownership of outdoor spaces.

Designers need to know how to delineate those spaces that residents collectively consider their own that thereby constitute their neighborhood. A good way to start is to designate the natural boundaries such as streams, undeveloped lands, major transportation corridors, ethnic and social-class boundaries, and historic districts. Although the area designated by such general boundaries is usually larger than the territory that residents consider their own, the designer can use a number of techniques to delineate the smaller areas after he defines the natural boundaries. He can attend political meetings in the area to determine what the issues are and where the concerned people live, review the minutes of neighborhood organization meetings, talk to political leaders, or review newspapers for issues in the area. Another technique is to observe outdoor spaces in the area and ask people why they use them and where they live. This approach should provide an overview of the important spaces and of the users; both the spaces and the home location of the present users can then be mapped. When this information points out new boundaries within the natural boundaries, the areas can be considered to constitute a neighborhood. Places where these areas overlap most frequently are the neighborhood focal points. The designer may consider the people living in that delineated area as the potential users or he may expand the boundary if the neighborhood space he is planning can accommodate more people.

Use of Neighborhood Space

Generally, public outdoor space near the home is used for work and leisure activities, political gatherings, educational projects, and movement from place to place within or through the neighborhood. How the space is used obviously depends on the activity occurring there: work (delivering mail, repairing the automobile, keeping shop); leisure activities (taking a walk, playing football, jogging, bicycling, hanging out, sitting on the front porch, swinging, playing checkers, throwing a frisbee, dancing); political gatherings (protesting a city policy, planning a park, closing a street); educational projects (showing a class the effects of soil erosion, identifying trees); and movement from place to place (walking to work, driving to the grocery). Although it is easy to predict these theoretical uses of neighborhood space, the actual specific use is much more difficult to predict, as a number of studies have shown.

In their study of children's behavior in a Turnkey III housing development in a southern city, Henry Sanoff and John Dickerson found that much more activity occurred in the streets and sidewalks than in the central playground and open field designated for activity. "The site plan provided a 'large open space' for multiple activities, yet it accounted for less than 3 percent of all the people observed . . . the predominant activity in the field was ball play where young children and adolescents were the major participants."[22] Similarly, it would have been difficult to predict that the major pattern of activity clusters would occur in the five culs-de-sac where young children were frequently observed cycling, playing ball, and engaging in random play. Sanoff and Dickerson explained that this clustering of activity was due to traffic patterns and the design of the streets. The culs-de-sac were free from car traffic, allowing uninterrupted ball playing. They also served as meeting places since they were easily identified and described by children.[23] Even though there was a lot of activity in the culs-de-sac, it was all of the same type. Sanoff and Dickerson observed that the shape of the culs-de-sac encourages more organized group activities than the street where the activities are more predominantly cycling and walking.[24] The design of these spaces resulted in a use pattern that the designers did not expect. Although more space was available in the field, the specific qualities of the streets and culs-de-sac made them most attractive to residents.

Another study of the use of neighborhood space

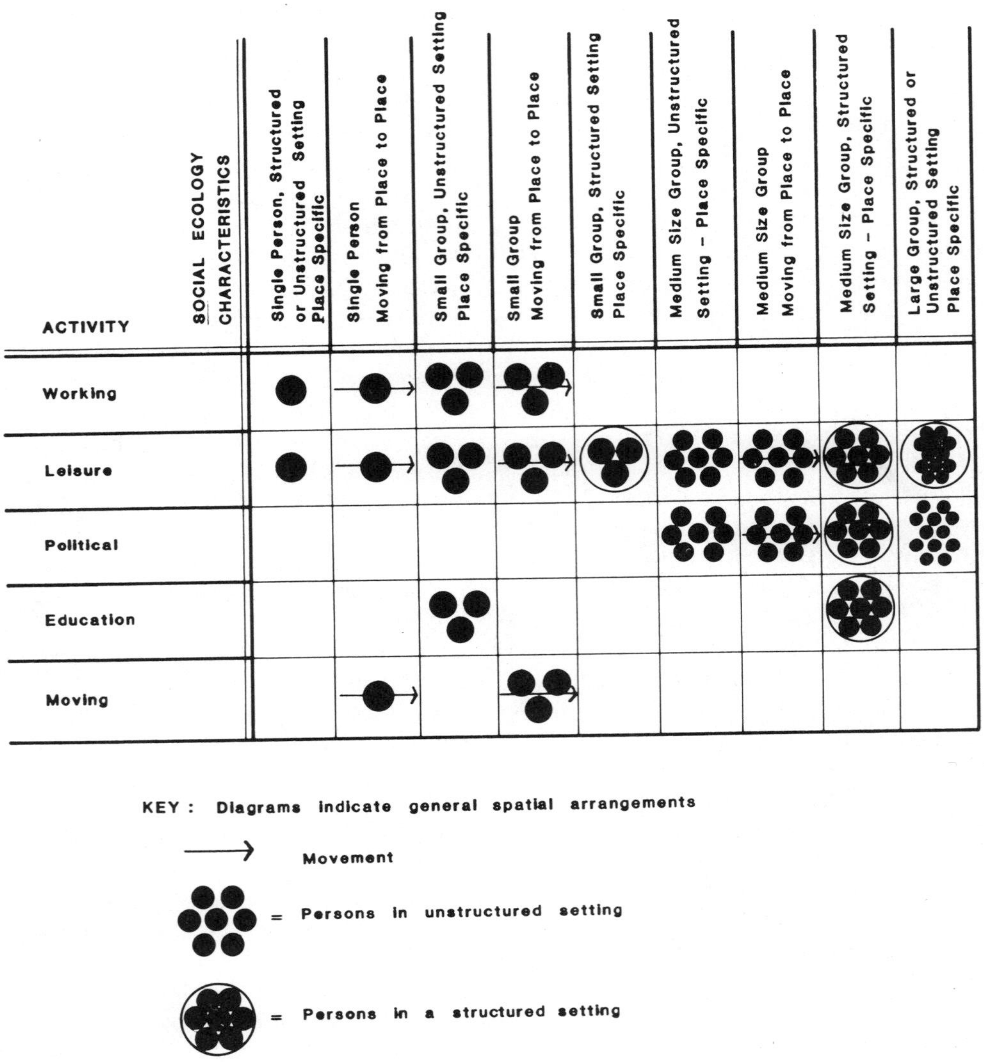

SOCIAL ECOLOGY CHARACTERISTICS

ACTIVITY

Column headers:
- Single Person, Structured or Unstructured Setting Place Specific
- Single Person Moving from Place to Place
- Small Group, Unstructured Setting Place Specific
- Small Group Moving from Place to Place
- Small Group, Structured Setting Place Specific
- Medium Size Group, Unstructured Setting – Place Specific
- Medium Size Group Moving from Place to Place
- Medium Size Group, Structured Setting – Place Specific
- Large Group, Structured or Unstructured Setting Place Specific

Rows: Working, Leisure, Political, Education, Moving

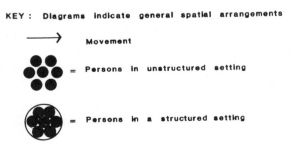

KEY: Diagrams indicate general spatial arrangements

→ Movement

= Persons in unstructured setting

= Persons in a structured setting

GENERALIZED NEIGHBORHOOD SPACE USE :

Activity Social – Ecology Potentials

The different activities that occur in neighborhood spaces require different types of spaces, depending on the characteristics of the social interaction of each activity.

TYPES OF PLAY	Foot Stoop	Driveway	Front Yard	Back Yard	Street	Public Sidewalk	Cul-De-Sac	Community Center	Open Field	Central Play Ground
Random Play			●					○		
General Play			●						○	○
Biking	○		○	○	●					
Non-Active	●	○			○				○	○
Walking	○					●	○			
Basketball	○	○		●		○			○	
Ball Play	○	○			●					
Object Play			●		○				○	
Skating	○		○		●			○	○	
Active Play	○							●		

KEY: ● Indicates highest number of observed activity
○ Indicates lowest number of observed activity

PHYSICAL ELEMENTS AND ACTIVITY TYPES IN APOLLO HEIGHTS

In a study of children's behavior in a Turnkey III housing development in a southern city, it was found that much more recreational activity occurred in the streets and sidewalks than in the central playground and open field designated for play.[25] (Photograph by Marge Hackmann)

in low-income housing projects, by the Committee on Housing Research and Development at the University of Illinois at Urbana, again demonstrates how difficult it is to predict the specific use of neighborhood space. The study found that designers had misjudged the use of circulation routes through the site. Central sidewalks designed to be the major pedestrian collectors were rarely used. The residents were observed walking parallel to the sidewalks through small courts or green spaces, and they often took shortcuts through the existing playground. The study concluded that the mistakes could have been prevented by a more socially sensitive design.

In spite of the difficulty in predicting specific use of neighborhood space, a number of studies began to reveal how people use the space near their homes. A study done by the Department of Planning in Baltimore, Maryland, indicated that neighborhood space was used for outdoor leisure activities in two distinct patterns: in home-based (dispersed throughout the neighborhood) and in recreational facilities (concentrated in areas such as playgrounds). Of these, the home-based spaces accounted for the major portion of recreational time.[26] In addition, those spaces that could be used while retaining visual access to the home tended to be used more. This was corroborated by the Herbert P. Bangs and Stuart Mahler study of rowhouse open space use in Baltimore County. They found that "most people will not regularly use a local open space if it is further than 400 feet away from their homes," but that if good pedestrian and visual access exists, use will not drop off abruptly as distance increases.[27]

In a similar study, Pamela Dinkel found that use of open space within the neighborhood was higher in black than in white neighborhoods, and that use of open space outside the neighborhood was consistently higher in the white neighborhoods. Park use in general was considerably higher in black neighborhoods. There also seemed to be significant differences in informal neighboring and the resulting use of space, and the study indicated this was more dependent on the socioeconomic status of neighbors than any other variable.[28] Low-income blacks interacted with their neighbors more frequently near home resulting in greater use of home-based spaces. The Baltimore Department of Planning Study similarly found a difference in the use of open space based on socioeconomic class. "In the low-income sites studied, most outdoor leisure activities occurred in the front of the house, on porches, steps, sidewalks, or streets.[29] Conversely, in the upper-middle-income sites studied, socializing and playing most often took place in the controlled setting of private yards."[30]

These studies do not offer a complete picture of how neighborhood space is used, but they do indicate that there are a number of important observable factors that influence the use of the neighborhood space:

1. The qualities and quantity of the space
2. The social makeup of the potential users—especially socioeconomic class and life-cycle stage, but also sex, ethnicity and region
3. The psychological factors influencing personal preference
4. The accessibility of local versus nonlocal spaces, facilities, and services

The same idea was stated by Suzanne Keller: "The concentrated use of local services and facilities varies widely according to the economic and cultural characteristics of the residents, the types of facilities and their adequacy, the accessibility of nonlocal facilities and their adequacy, and the degree of isolation of the area, economically, ecologically and symbolically."[31] The important point is that the use of neighborhood space depends on many factors other than the design of the space and varies significantly from neighborhood to neighborhood.

In addition to factors previously mentioned, there is a significant general increase in the use of neighborhood open space for leisure activities.[32] As well as serving for circulation space and children's play space, those places close to home are increasingly perceived as work space, political gathering space, and

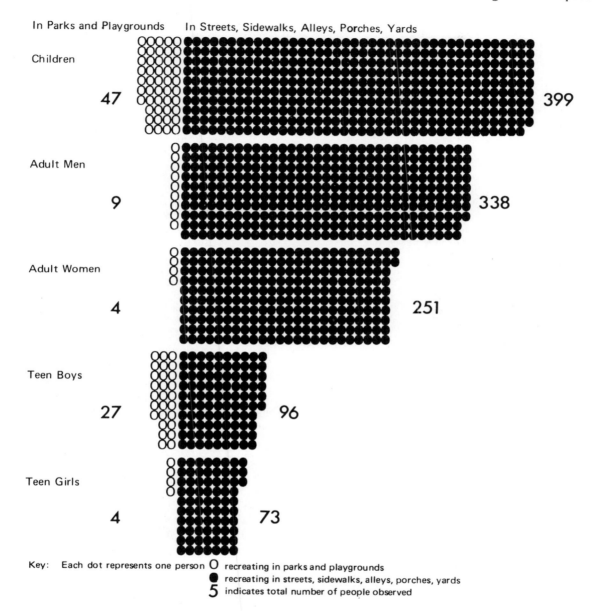

In Parks and Playgrounds   In Streets, Sidewalks, Alleys, Porches, Yards

Children

47   399

Adult Men

9   338

Adult Women

4   251

Teen Boys

27   96

Teen Girls

4   73

Key: Each dot represents one person O recreating in parks and playgrounds

● recreating in streets, sidewalks, alleys, porches, yards

5 indicates total number of people observed

AVERAGE NUMBER OF PEOPLE OBSERVED RECREATING PER DRIVING CENSUS IN VARIOUS NEIGHBORHOOD SETTINGS

A study in Baltimore indicates that home-based activities rather than park activities account for the major part of recreation time.[33]

LEISURE IN MODERN AMERICA: NATIONAL TIME
DIVISIONS OF LEISURE 1900, 1950, 2000

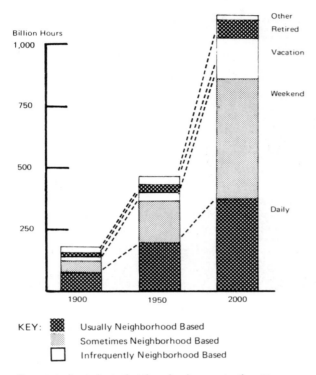

KEY:
▨ Usually Neighborhood Based
▨ Sometimes Neighborhood Based
☐ Infrequently Neighborhood Based

Recent studies indicate that there has been a significant increase
in the use of neighborhood space for leisure activities.[34]

leisure-activity space for all age groups. Recent trends
toward qualitative life-styles, energy and resource
conservation, and grass-roots governments have
increased home dependence and neighborhood-
space use.

To summarize, it appears easy to describe how
neighborhood space is generally used: for work activities, leisure activities, political gatherings, educational
projects, and movement from place to place. It is
more difficult to predict the specific use of outdoor
space near one's home. Studies indicate that the
use of neighborhood space is influenced by important political, social, and psychological factors that
need to be considered in the planning and design of
the space.

THE ROLE OF DESIGNERS AND PLANNERS

Although the demand for "socially suitable design"
was largely a product of citizen action, many professional planners have played a role in its advocation
and literal execution. With their vision they trans-
form ideals into reality; with technical skill they give
form to society's values. Even the most independent
citizen-initiated and controlled project can usually
benefit from the designer's ability to suggest and
explain form alternatives to problems.

A goal of many civic leaders in early colonial
times was the provision of neighborhood open space
as an integral part of town plans. William Penn in
Philadelphia, William Christmas in Raleigh, James
Oglethorpe in Savannah, and Francis Nicholson in
Williamsburg, Virginia, envisioned plans that would
provide public open space within residential areas;
space that could change in function as user needs
changed and that provided an orderly framework
for future community growth and change.

The form of these neighborhood spaces varied. In
Savannah, growth was planned in increments and
required that open space be provided for each building unit. This guaranteed that dense, urban neighborhoods would have community recreation places.
In Raleigh, four block-sized parcels of developable
land were set aside in the original plan of 1792 as
public plazas. And in Williamsburg, the town was
clustered around a central, common open-space
area. Although a number of plans across the country were later sacrificed to development pressure,
residents of urban neighborhoods still benefit from
earlier planning efforts.

Designer Responsibility

In the mid-1800s, neighborhood open space again
became the focus of a small group of civic leaders
concerned about national social welfare. It was the
period in which Jane Addams, Frederick Law Olmsted, Melusina Fay Peirce, and others combined

Although it is easy for designers to predict the general use of neighborhood space, idiosyncratic social activities must be considered to successfully satisfy user needs.

social considerations with the earlier concepts of neighborhood open space planning. They also laid the foundation for the designer's responsibility to the user based on a simple premise: The designer should respond to the needs of the users, to their collective public good, and individual property rights and private interests should be secondary to these public needs. Their guidelines respected the benefits of earlier planned neighborhood spaces—that of providing overall structure while permitting both long-term flexibility and multiple uses. To these guidelines they appended that neighborhood planning should respond to the needs of users to promote democ-

Public Good   **Private Interest**

Frederick Law Olmsted thought that social reform could be accompanied through social planning, but the public goals for social welfare often conflicted with the desires of individual land speculators.

racy and social harmony and to reduce segregation by class, race, and gender.

Jane Addams's Hull House cooperative settlement in Chicago became the model for egalitarian neighborhood efforts around the country. Olmsted sought to overcome the deterioration of the city and the human spirit by the provision of open space. And Peirce argued for kitchenless homes and shared neighborhood day-care and cooking facilities to free women from repetitive household chores. Such efforts resulted in a number of oustanding open-space projects that responded to national needs of the 1850s. Bold projects resulted from the combined forces of romanticism, the urban-recreation and public-park movement, metropolitan design, commercial interest, conservationist and inner-city concern, and political support for the "City Beautiful."[35] The most notable of these projects, Central Park, projected Olmsted into a position of leadership. He was soon viewed as a creative designer with a solution to an immediate problem shared by many cities. Olmsted's plan designated half of Central Park for outdoor recreation and half for natural landscape. It was an immense success. Within ten years all of the major cities in the United States had begun similar projects. Richard P. Dober noted that "open space and landscape came to play a strong role in giving form and content to city design" as a result of Olmsted's work.[36]

Olmsted became conscious of the problems of American cities while engaged in planning around the country. His conclusion was that design had a direct relation to the social problems of both city and nation, and that neighborhood open space would raise the spirits of users by permitting both recreation and the opportunity to experience nature in the city. These experiences he defined as *needs of the users.* He sought further in his work to reduce competition among groups by encouraging social interaction of all classes. He was also sympathetic to deviant groups and the specific needs of rich, poor, young, and old.[37]

Conflict of Values

In spite of Olmsted's recognition that neighborhood space would be used by all classes who dif-

Known to Designer Known to User	Unknown to Designer Known to User
Known to Designer Unknown to User	Unknown to Designer Unknown to User

It is critically important that the unique social factors in each neighborhood be taken into account in the design process. This requires the exploration of factors previously unknown to the designer.

fered in their essential needs and preferences, the tendency during the later part of the 19th century was to define *the best use of public open space* in upper-class terms. The model of the urban park was the royal hunting park,[38] with emphasis on cultural enlightenment and the greater refinement of manners.[39] It was no wonder that the cultural elite viewed Cental Park as "a kind of open-air museum." According to J. B. Jackson, upper-class citizens suggested that at least 100 acres be set aside for a zoological garden—many times the size of any in Europe—while art critic James Jackson Jarvis proposed a nondenominational cathedral. Earlier proposals already included an arboretum, botanical garden, and museums of natural history and art.[40]

Such facilities defined the most important public open space of the century in terms suitable only for the refined. Similarly, a number of other public open space designs based on upper-class criteria were unattractive to middle-and lower-income residents. The conflict, one of user needs ad preferences, resulted from a lack of common values. While the elite maintained that a park was the only legitimate public open space—but not a street corner, the front of a local bar, or a football field—the poor desired playgrounds, informal meeting spaces, and local hangouts close to home.

Although Olmsted held his own, somewhat elitist, conviction that beauty instead of blight and deterioration would resolve urban ills, he disagreed with designers who felt the park should be nothing more than a work of art,[41] characterized by some as "a three-dimensional landscape painting."[42] He was sensitized to the needs of neighborhood residents as a result of his identification of family as the important group and his use of this group as the basic unit for planning.[43] His plans for neighborhood parks in New

York City reflected this by encouraging family recreation and by including places (especially in his plan for the 23rd and 24th Wards) for families to escape from the confinement of the city.[44] Olmsted's method included "a rigorous analysis of social patterns,"[45] and each of his designs was "accompanied by written reports which stressed social needs" for which he was unable to provide in the planning process.[46]

The Professional Class

A sense of responsibility may have stirred 19th-century designers to produce a positive public landscape,[47] yet the most acclaimed projects continued to be designs for "places of recreation of estates for the rich."[48] One reason was that private clients pre-

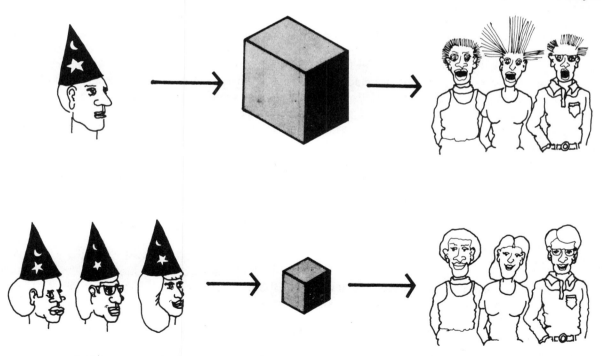

In the community-development process, the creative act remains the same, but instead of the users being awed by the designer-magician, the users are involved in the process and can be expected to understand and appreciate the design process more.

sented environmental problems less complex than clients in urban neighborhoods. Another reason was that private clients had more money to invest. This was coupled with the designer's ability and desire to produce what the private upper class wanted. As a result, Albert Fein reports, the profession of landscape architecture became "a technically oriented profession concerned with the formal design" of the picturesque, wild, remote, and idealized landscape.[49] Such narrow design attitudes isolated many professionals from the majority of society and from peoples' concerns about neighborhood space.

It is not surprising that decades later the role of design was scrutinized against the backdrop of the declining quality of urban life. During the 1960s, designers, as technical fiduciaries of the establishment, were frequently viewed as neighborhood adversaries. The professionals were unprepared to provide the leadership and expertise needed in a more participatory democracy. Theodore Osmundson, then president of the American Society of Landscape Architects, claimed that the American Society of Landscape Architects was a gentleman's club, educated people doing a nice thing. Osmundson felt that an organization that has been treading water since the Olmsted era "is not going to run at full speed into a tough area" like participatory neighborhood design.[50] The alienation of design professionals from neighborhood residents was no doubt accentuated by numerous conflicts brewing between a restless citizenry and the ruling establishment.

New Roles

Hope for amelioration came about with what William O. Douglas, then associate justice of the Supreme Court, described as a rising national commitment "to make the existing system more human, to make the machine subservient to man, to allow the flowering of a society where all the idiosyncracies of man can be honored and respected."[51] For their part, neighborhood designers developed mechanisms to incorporate the social needs of users into the design process and to involve users directly in planning their own neighborhoods. Planners and designers modified existing survey research methods to determine the preferred activities of users. They devised ways to use charrettes, the nominal group technique, and group graphics to do participatory design, and discovered new roles for themselves as group facilitators. At the same time, some of their roles remained unchanged. Designers continued to visualize and draw alternative futures, and they answered technical questions about the efficient use of space, zoning, site planning, materials, and construction costs. In poorer neighborhoods, designers commonly worked through community design centers to provide their services daily and directly to groups in need of such expertise.

In addition, designers were expected to generate useful social research, provide multiple choices instead of single plans, and objectively evaluate the cost and benefits of each plan in terms of the users' perceptions. They were even expected to justify form decisions through an explanation to users of how they anticipated the spaces would be used. For designers, this last cluster of tasks has been the most difficult. The following chapter describes ways in which designers have responded to these problems through the application of social factors in the designing of neighborhood space.

THINGS FOR YOU TO DO

The following exercises will clarify the issues raised in this chapter. Some will check your understanding of the material; others will help you articulate your own values or give you insights into neighborhood-design issues. You may do these exercises alone, but I would suggest doing them with others.

1. Draw a picture of the neighborhood in which you grew up.
2. Write your own definition of "neighborhood."

3. Which of these do you consider unusable neighborhood spaces and why?

back porch
front porch
patio
street corner
pool hall
stoop
teen center
schoolyard
railroad track
park
street

4. Can you recall any neighborhood in which you have lived that became organized around an issue, resulting in the change of neighborhood spaces?
   a. What was the issue?
   b. How was it resolved?
   c. What role did designers play?
5. Give your definition of a neighborhood focal point. List some characteristic neighborhood focal points.
6. Draw an ideal neighborhood from your own viewpoint,
   from the viewpoint of an elderly person,
   from the viewpoint of a child in first grade,
   from the viewpoint of a teenager.
   Be sure to draw what it contains and who else is there.
7. What do you think is the designer's role in a neighborhood-design project?

NOTES AND REFERENCES

1. See Milton Kotler, *Neighborhood Government*, Bobbs-Merrill, Indianapolis, Ind., 1969, for a detailed discussion of neighborhood in the context of today's American political activity.
2. Mike Royko, "Neighborhood on the Way Back," *Chicago Daily News*, Nov. 26, 1973.
3. Ordinance 4641, City of Berkeley, Calif., pp.1-2.
4. Ordinance 4641, p. 1.
5. James Stevens, "Bringing a Neighborhood Back," *The Neighborhood Works*, **4**(15):1-5 (1981).
6. *Goals for Raleigh Technical Report 2: A Policy for the Future*, Goals for Raleigh at North Carolina State University, Raleigh, N.C., 1972, pp. 9-10.
7. Catherine Lerza, "The Block You Save May Be Your Own," *Environmental Action* **5**(5):4 (1973).
8. The American City Corporation, *The Greater Hartford Process*, The American City Corporation, Columbia, Md., 1972, pp. 20-39.
9. *MEMO, Newsletter of the American Institute of Architects*, special issue, Jan. 1972, Washington, D.C.
10. Suzanne Keller, *The Urban Neighborhood: A Sociological Perspective*, Random House, New York, 1968. Many of these discussions are recorded in this work by Suzanne Keller, one of the most complete records of the theories and components of "neighborhood" and "neighboring."
11. For these early writings and studies, see, among others, Robert E. Park, "The City: Suggestions for the Investigation of Human Behavior in the City Environment," *American Journal of Sociology* **20**(5):577-612 (1915).
12. John Ormsbee Simonds, *Landscape Architecture: The Shaping of Man's Natural Environment*, McGraw-Hill, New York, 1961, p. 204.
13. Information provided by Design Workshop, Inc., Raleigh, N.C.
14. Kotler, *Neighborhood Government*, p. 2. The political definition is consistent with the idea of a neighbor being one who is expected to help in time of crisis but otherwise does not intrude. Thus, the sense of neighboring will change as crises arise and dissipate.
15. Terence Lee, "Urban Neighborhood as a Socio-Spatial Schema," in *Environmental Psychology: Man and His Physical Setting*, Harold M. Proshansky, William H. Ittleson, and Leanne G. Rivlin, eds., Holt Rinehart and Winston, New York, 1970, p. 349.
16. From a research project done at North Carolina State University consisting of a survey of neighborhoods. Conducted by Dolly Yarur and Sue Stoffel, 1972.
17. This definition of neighborhood obviously applies to older areas of the city. A "service" neighborhood definition appears to be the most useful concept in planning new towns and new residential areas. At best, however, the services provide only a potential neighborhood environment.
18. Keller, *Urban Neighborhood*, p. 126. Suzanne Keller summarizes the purposes of the neighborhood unit from the designer/planner point of view: Specifically, the neighborhood unit was to do the following: (1) introduce a principle of physical order into the chaotic, fragmented urban aggregate; (2) reintroduce local, face-to-face types of contacts into the anonymous urban society, thereby helping to regain some sense of community; (3) encourage the formation of local

loyalties and attachments and thereby offset the impact of extensive social and residential mobility; (4) stimulate feelings of identity, security, stability, and rootedness in a world threatening such feelings on all sides; and (5) provide a local training ground for the development of larger loyalties to city and nation. Kotler suggests, however, that the neighborhood unit is created by the residents in an area, not by the planners, and the grass-roots democracy fosters the neighborhood unit, not that the neighborhood unit fosters grass-roots democracy. Furthermore, it makes sense that those areas without the information, power, or skills to function as grass-roots democracies must be provided with the elements necessary to function as such, with no strings attached.

19. Yarur and Stoffel, research project.
20. Simonds, *Landscape Architecture*, p. 204.
21. By public, I do not necessarily mean public ownership. A more accurate term would be public and ill-defended private space.
22. Henry Sanoff and John Dickerson, "Mapping Children's Behavior in a Residential Setting," *Journal of Architectural Design* **25**(4):103 (1971).
23. Sanoff and Dickerson, "Mapping Children's Behavior," p. 100.
24. Sanoff and Dickerson, "Mapping Children's Behavior," p. 100.
25. Sanoff and Dickerson, "Mapping Children's Behavior," p. 102. As adapted for use, random play and object play are categories that include activities that the observer could not define, with random play being a situation in which the child seemed to be doing "something." Object play is play in which the object is dominant, like rolling an old tire.
26. Department of Planning and Department of Housing and Urban Development, *Baltimore Community Renewal Program Interim Report: A Progress Report on the First Year of a Two Year Program Study.* Baltimore, Md., May 1972, p. 149.
27. Herbert P. Bangs, Jr., and Stuart Mahler, "Users of Local Parks," *AIP Journal* **36**:330-334 (1970).
28. Pamela Y. Dinkel, "Two Neighborhood Case Studies in Neighboring and Open Space," pp. 1-24. Paper written under the direction of R. Hester at North Carolina State University, Raleigh, N.C., 1972.
29. Department of Planning and Department of Housing and Urban Development, *Baltimore Community Renewal Program*, p. 149.
30. Department of Planning and Department of Housing and Urban Development, *Baltimore Community Renewal Program*, p. 152.
31. Keller, *Urban Neighborhood*, p. 103.
32. Clawson and Knetsch, *Economics of Outdoor Recreation*, p. 20.
33. Department of Planning and Department of Housing and Urban Development, *Baltimore Community Renewal Program*, p. 149.
34. Marion Clawson and Jack L. Knetsch, *Economics of Outdoor Recreation*, John Hopkins, Baltimore, Md., 1966, p. 20.
35. Richard P. Dober, *Environmental Design*, Van Nostrand Reinhold, New York, 1969, p. 32.
36. Dober, *Environmental Design*, p. 32.
37. Albert Fein, "Frederick Law Olmsted and American Landscape Architecture: The Continuing Democratic Challenge," paper given at the Annual Meeting of the American Society of Landscape Architects in Dallas, Tex., June 1964, p. 6.
38. Charles Downing Lay, "Park Design and the Preservation of the Park Idea," *Landscape Architecture* **2**(2):75 (1921).
39. John Brinckerhoff Jackson, *American Space: The Centennial Years 1865-1876*, Norton, New York, 1972, p. 215.
40. Jackson, *American Space*, p. 213.
41. F. L. Olmsted, "Playgrounds in Parks from the Designer's Standpoint," *Landscape Architecture* **7**(3):122-127.
42. Jackson, *American Space*, p. 217.
43. Jackson, *American Space*, pp. 218-219.
44. Fein, "Frederick Law Olmsted," pp. 5-6.
45. Richard Saul Wurman, Alan Levy, and Joel Katz, with Jean McClintock and Howard Brunner, *The Nature of Recreation: a Handbook in Honor of Frederick Law Olmsted, Using Examples from His Work*, MIT Press, Cambridge, Mass., 1972.
46. Fein, "Frederick Law Olmsted," p. 6.
47. Fein, "Frederick Law Olmsted," p. 7.
48. Jackson, *American Space*, p. 218.
49. Albert Fein, *A Study of the Profession of Landscape Architecture*, American Society of Landscape Architects, McLean, Va., 1972, pp. 5-7.
50. Simpson F. Lawson, ed., *Workshop on Urban Open Space*, U.S. Department of Housing and Urban Development, Washington, D.C., ASLA 1, pp. 35-36.
51. William O. Douglas, *Points of Rebellion*, Random House, New York, p. 9.

2

Social Factors in Site Planning: The State of the Art

There is a native American story about a Lakota holy man, Drinks Water, who dreamed that the white man wove a spider web around the Lakotas, forcing them to live in a strange place. According to oral history, Drinks Water said that when that happens, "you shall live in square gray houses, in a barren land, and beside those square gray houses you shall starve." Drinks Water was killed by the sorrow of his dream. Native Americans point to the present box houses and grid streets designed by outsiders as the fulfillment of Drinks Water's dream.[1]

During the past twenty years, designers awakened to the plight of the users of ill-designed spaces everywhere. They have begun to realize that it is critical to design the space near one's home in response to one's idiosyncratic needs, that design and planning must be user oriented, and that the design of neighborhood space must relate to the behavior patterns and values of the people for whom that space is designed, not the values of the designer.[2] Brazilia,[3] the West End Urban Renewal Projects in Boston,[4] and Pruit-Igoe[5] became symbolic of projects that did not respond to the needs of the users.

Probably the worst of the poorly designed areas are the many neighborhood spaces that, for lack of wholesale unsuitability or eloquent spokesmen, have gone unnoticed. Examples include (1) the recreation-center development for an Italian neighborhood that included everything except soccer and boccie, an insultingly inappropriate choice for the users; (2) the many public housing projects with no private outdoor space, often high rises, designed to house rural migrants who are accustomed to a garden and other outdoor spaces as a way of life; (3) a junk playground in Illinois designed by middle-class whites for low-income blacks and painful for both—the whites, because the playground was unused, the blacks because they felt their neighborhood was run down enough without more junk; and (4) many of the neighborhood park and open-space developments created under federal programs. These programs could have been bylined "let them eat cake" for not responding to the many social problems confronted

In Boston's West End lived a tight-knit community of Italian-Americans whose neighborhood was well designed for informal social gatherings and mutual support among neighbors. An urban-renewal project not only destroyed their neighborhood but scattered the residents. Psychologist Marc Fried reported that 46

percent of the women and 38 percent of the men suffered fairly severe grief and that 26 percent of the women remained depressed two years after they had been removed from the West End. High-rent apartments were built where the West End neighborhood had once been.

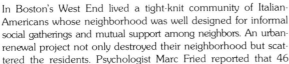

by the users such as neighborhood control, racism, and poverty. This is not to suggest that there were no significant successes in designing neighborhood space to meet the needs of the users. A number of these successes are described in Chapter 6. But the above examples of social failures indicate the need to discover what factors contribute to socially suitable neighborhood environments and what user needs to look for before designing neighborhood space.

A number of recent design movements that viewed

environmental design as a component of social change began to investigate the issue of user needs. Advocacy design and design concerned with neighborhood preservation and human development focused on the human dimensions as well as on the physical and aesthetic aspects. The assumption was that the way people feel about and interact in a space is just as important as what they do in that space. As these designers explored interactions and feelings as determinants of the use of neighborhood space, they developed a list of social factors that can be applied to design.

This chapter describes the state of the art, with special attention to those factors that are useful in the design of socially suitable neighborhood space. These considerations, loosely called *social factors,* include both theoretical proposals and specific applications of nonphysical dimensions. For ease of study, these social factors are categorized under the following headings:

1. The interaction processes continuum from cooperation to competition
2. The specific spatial concepts of the competition process—territoriality, and dominance
3. Symbolic ownership
4. Interaction variations for groups based on regional, ethnic, class, and life-cycle-stage differences
5. Activity variations based on regional, ethnic, class, and life-cycle-stage differences
6. Usable space
7. Comfortable space

SOCIAL FACTORS

Interaction Processes: Cooperation to Competition

Among the interaction processes, the application of design has generally been confined to coopera-

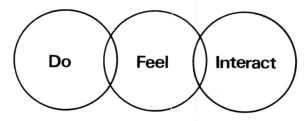

The assumption underlying the design movements to create more socially suitable neighborhoods is that how people *feel* about and *interact* in a space is just as important as what they *do* in that space.

tion, accommodation, and competition. Since neighborhood space is usually quite limited, conflicts arise over its use, as they did in the design process for a neighborhood open space in Cambridge, Massachusetts. During the sequence of meetings to plan Maple Street Play Lot, it became clear to the residents that it was essential for them to develop a compromise plan, one that satisfied the needs of all the users, not just the adults, the teenagers, or the small children:

The meetings produced numerous confrontations between various age groups. The typical ones were parents versus children, parents versus teens, and teens versus children versus tots.

The conflicts between parents and children were centered around parents with young tots who desired to keep their tots safe from the 7-13 year olds' 'malicious rough play.' The parents felt that by excluding the 7-13 year olds from the 'totlot,' the play space could be reserved for parents sitting quietly watching their tots play safely in a danger-free vacuum.

The parents versus teens conflicts were more serious ones, involving teen use of the open space at night for 'hanging' (which usually meant noise, alcohol, drugs, and sex to the parents, and fun to the teens), and vandalism (which the parents said resulted from 'hanging' and the teens said resulted from overuse by smaller children).

The teens versus children versus tots conflicts were natural ones. Since there existed limited play space, the principle of survival of the fittest prevailed. After school the 7-13 year olds played basketball and threatened the tots; then the teens arrived, played basketball, and threatened both the 7-13 year olds and the tots; the teens were threatened by parents and police. Only parents and police had no natural predators.[6]

It became clear that there could be no mutually acceptable design until these conflicts were resolved by the various factions in the neighborhood (an area described by the users as extending only two blocks in either direction from the play lot). But after several chaotic meetings, the Maple Avenue residents succeeded in getting some of the conflicts resolved. The teenagers finally admitted that basketball in the play lot was unfeasible, and an alternative basketball site was sought by the recreation department with the help of the teens.

With the problem of basketball resolved through cooperation, the residents were then able to agree on a program for the open space. They recognized

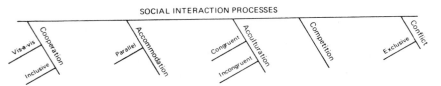

SOCIAL INTERACTION PROCESSES

The consideration of social-interaction processes in the design of neighborhood space has been widespread in the recent design movements; emphasis has been placed on cooperation, accommodation, and competition.

that the space would be used by all ages, regardless of how it was designed. But because of the limited area, they decided it would be best to design a space that would serve the tots and the 7-to 13-year olds. The final plan provided one large open space for action games (not sports), with smaller spaces (tot sized) for construction, fantasy games, and artistic expression. The designer took into account the extreme competition among the various users and attempted to separate the various users spatially, thereby accommodating their needs while reducing their conflicts. An evaluation of the play lot indicated that it is working as intended. This process of accommodation by separating potential user conflicts was observed in most of the case studies presented in Chapter 6.

A similar but more comprehensive application of social interaction processes to the design of neighborhood space has been made in the area of environments for child development. Rather than simply seeking to reduce conflict, provision is made for environments that foster different types of interaction: cooperation, conflict, acculturation, and so on.[7] Designers observed, for instance, that the placement of benches could affect the type of interaction in a neighborhood space. As a result, settings have been designed to encourage (1) inclusive interactions, (2) fact-to-face interactions, (3) exclusive interactions, (4) parallel interactions, (5) congruent interactions, and (6) incongruent interactions.[8]

Inclusive interaction settings[9] provide a small space where a limited number of people can form an in-group, often in a circle. Face-to-face interaction settings provide a space suitable for face-to-face social exchange, as between teacher and student and friend and friend. Both inclusive and face-to-face settings encourage cooperation among the users of the space.[10] Exclusive interaction settings are the leftover spaces that result from an inclusive interaction setting—the exclusive setting being the "out" space. This space is often a conflictive setting, pitting the inclusive group against the exclusive group, as in the situation of the parents and teens conflict at the Maple Street Play Lot. Similarly, a parallel interaction setting is one that does not foster cooperative face-to-face interaction. It generally prevents or discourages social exchange by forcing people to be arranged side by side, as in the long rows of park benches in many urban parks.[11]

Finally, congruent and incongruent interaction settings are those that allow observation of the behavior of a role model and either the acceptance or rejection of that behavior.[12] These settings are directly related to the socialization process, and a number of neighborhood spaces have been designed to allow children to test skills and roles by imitating others, while not being forced to perform the skill or role to the expectation of others.[13] Blair Park in Urbana, Illinois provided small niches where children could safely observe the actions and skills of older children from whom they learn or are socialized.

From these experiments with bench arrangements and simple environments, designers gained insights that were then applied to more complex neighborhood spaces. Julie Graham built play environments in which specific settings encouraged competition, cooperation, acculturation, and accommodation. She provided tower spaces where children could positively compete "to get to the top first" and spaces where they must cooperate to get to the top at all. In addition, there are spaces in Graham's Dennis Chávez Play Environment in Albuquerque, New Mexico, where children must take turns or risk serious falls from the towers. At the same time that these children are sharing limited resources with each other, other children observe and learn in small spaces below.

Territoriality and Dominance

Two specific spatial attributes of the competition process, territoriality and dominance, have been applied to the design of neighborhood space even more than the interaction processes just described. They are often referred to as territorial dominance, a single attribute that reflects an interrelationship between territoriality and dominance. Territoriality, a term bor-

rowed from ethology, refers to the act of defending an area against other specified members of one's species or other species,[14] and has become a popularly discussed social concept and a less widely applied design construct. Robert Ardrey fears what he sees as the deterritorializing of man. He argues that if man is a territorial animal, then as we seek to repair his dignity and responsibility as a human being, we should first search for a means of restoring his dignity and responsibility as a proprietor.[15]

This territorial view of man suggests that he defends a space and dominates[16] that space in much the same way that he seeks to dominate a position of high social status.[17] However, only one example of territorial dominance, as the concept is applied to the design of neighborhood space, fits this strict interpretation of territorial dominance—the idea of turf dominance, the phenomenon often associated with gang wars.[18] This is an extreme form of the processes by which people stake out and personalize the public environments in which they live.

A project with the Dana Park gang provides an interesting example of the application of turf domi-

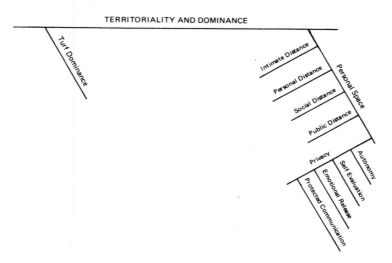

The aspects of territorial dominance that have been most widely applied to the design of neighborhood spaces are turf dominance and personal space.

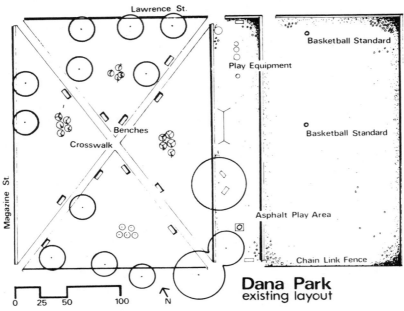

Dana Park
existing layout

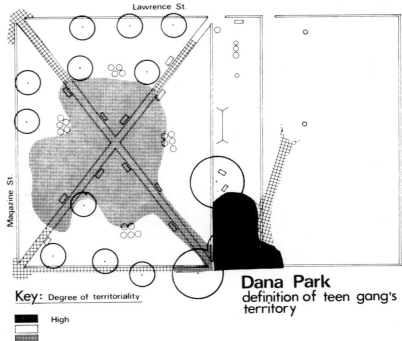

Key: Degree of territoriality

■	High
▦	
▤	Low
□	None

Dana Park
definition of teen gang's territory

The design of the existing Dana Park actually encouraged conflicts among various user groups. The teenagers who dominated the turf conflicted with the elderly because the benches were located in the path of their football games, with younger teens because the play equipment was located near their "hanging" area and basketball courts, and with all users who walked through their hanging area. By moving the sitting areas for the elderly to the side, relocating the play equipment, and adding a basketball court, many of the conflicts were resolved while allowing the teenagers to dominate their turf.

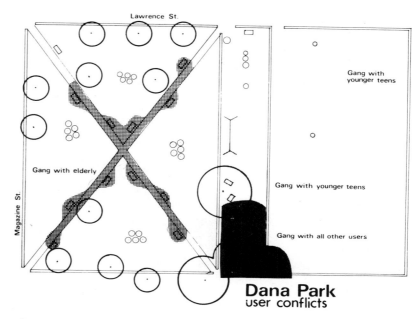

Dana Park
user conflicts

Lawrence St.

Magazine St.

Gang with younger teens

Gang with elderly

Gang with younger teens

Gang with all other users

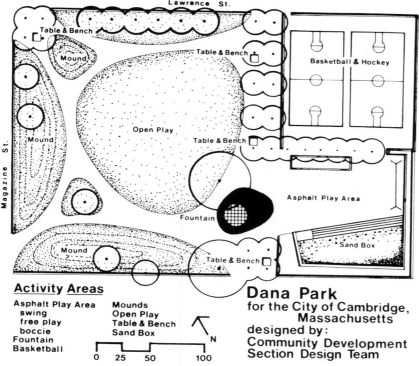

Lawrence St.

Magazine St.

Table & Bench

Mound

Table & Bench

Mound

Open Play

Table & Bench

Mound

Table & Bench

Fountain

Basketball & Hockey

Asphalt Play Area

Sand Box

Activity Areas

Asphalt Play Area
  swing
  free play
  boccie
Fountain
Basketball

Mounds
Open Play
Table & Bench
Sand Box

N

0   25   50   100

Dana Park
for the City of Cambridge, Massachusetts
designed by:
Community Development Section Design Team

nance to the design of neighborhood space. A group of community leaders complained of constant harassment by a teenaged gang in a neighborhood park in Cambridge. The gang members exerted such dominance over their turf that they were able to direct a redesign of the neighborhood park, which reduced long-standing conflicts among the various users. These conflicts, the gang explained, were brought about by intrusions by adults, young teenagers, and elderly people into their space. A careful analysis of their territorial dominance led to the identification of specific turf conflicts centered around the areas most often occupied by the gang. These conflicts were subsequently solved, without violating the gang's territorial needs, by removing the activity settings used by other groups from the gang's turf.[19]

Robert Sommer has identified similar, less hostile, examples of territorial dominance in people as they attempt to control public spaces in parks, libraries, bars, prisons, and classrooms.[20] His findings have influenced neighborhood designers throughout the country. M. Paul Friedberg realized that older children dominated younger children in parks in New York by frequently taking over the "best" equipment. He solved this conflict at Jacob Riis Plaza by providing two of each of the most frequently used "best things," separated by considerable distances. It is interesting that the older children, while dominating the best things, still want younger children around to serve as an audience. Friedberg also noticed this in his design of Carver Houses and later applied the principle at Jacob Riis Plaza in New York City by locating the major play area beside a circulation route that provided a continual audience for child play and heroics. He noted that this play area was the most popular of all the facilities located in Jacob Riis.

Personal Space

Robert Sommer has also dealt with another aspect of territoriality: personal space, the emotionally charged zone around each person,[21] an area with invisible boundaries surrounding one's body into which intruders may not venture.[22] Sommer's experiments in redesigning spaces indicate that violations of personal spatial distances are threatening to people. He records examples of people violently protecting personal spaces like favorite chairs, parks, and benches.

E. T. Hall determined that there were different spaces for different interaction situations. He classified these as (1) intimate distance, (2) personal distance, (3) social distance, and (4) public distance[23] and posited that each distance could be described as a territory or spatial zone, the dimensions of which varied according to cultural, ethnic, life-cycle stage, and personal factors. These ideas have been applied rather intuitively in design through the relation of appropriate scale of spaces to the activities desired. For example, in the design of the Dennis Chávez Park, provision is made for a whole range of spaces from intimate to public distance. There are spaces where children can climb for intimate interactions, spaces where two adults can sit and share a personal conversation, spaces where groups can meet for informal discussions, and spaces where theater groups can comfortably perform to an audience 50 feet away. An evaluation of the park indicates that it is used as the designers expected. Frequently, this concept of personal space is combined with a final territorial concept, spatial privacy.[24]

Privacy

As the urban environment becomes increasingly crowded, the need for privacy is one of the most significant factors in the use of neighborhood space. According to A. F. Westin, privacy functions to protect one's need for personal autonomy, to provide emotional release, to offer the opportunity for self-evaluation, and to offer limited and protected communication.[25] These functions of privacy have long been mentioned in justifying the need for neighborhood open space because only public spaces pro-

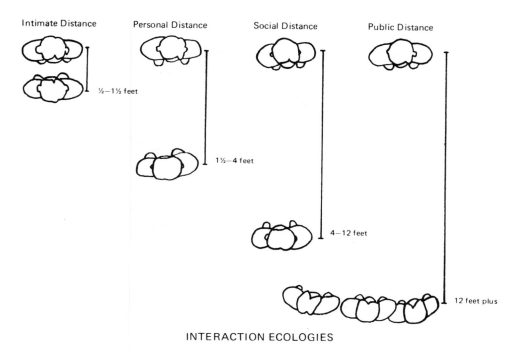

Intimate Distance   Personal Distance   Social Distance   Public Distance

½—1½ feet

1½—4 feet

4—12 feet

12 feet plus

INTERACTION ECOLOGIES

E. T. Hall described the distances required for various interaction situations from intimate to public distance.

KEY: ● Indicates the types of privacy satisfying various functions of privacy, settings for which can be provided by neighborhood space.

| | TYPES OF PRIVACY | | | |
FUNCTIONS	Solitude	Intimacy	Anonymity	Reserve
Autonomy	●			
Emotional Release	●	●	●	
Self Evaluation	●		●	
Limited Communication		●		●

TYPES OF PRIVACY SATISFYING VARIOUS FUNCTIONS OF PRIVACY [26]

Recent research indicates that different types of privacy satisfy various functions of privacy, suggesting that the "simple" problem of providing for private space may be much more complex than originally thought by designers.

vide an opportunity for privacy in overcrowded environments. Recent applications to design are noteworthy because they have recognized the need for privacy among children. Case studies of Jacob Riis Plaza, Putnam Gardens Tot Lot in Cambridge, Dennis Chávez Total Environment Play Area, and Washington Environmental Yard in Berkeley, California, each give special attention to creating spaces where children can escape to be totally alone.

Symbolic Ownership

Another social factor that has been used in the design of neighborhood space is symbolic ownership. More accurately, the term is used here to describe three social factors: ownership, status objects, and symbolic space. Robert Gutman considers the three to be of equal importance as functional aspects of site planning.[27] Symbolic ownership is also valuable as an extension of legal ownership in increasingly crowded urban areas. Sommer discusses this phenomenon, pointing out the necessity for designing public spaces that could be symbolically owned. He notes that by building upward we can guarantee everyone dominion over an enclosure of his own although "man will be spending even more of his life in space he does not own or control."[28]

The awareness that legal ownership may be replaced with symbolic ownership for many urban dwellers spurred new interest in this idea, and the results of several studies helped to clarify the definition of symbolic ownership. Collective symbolic ownership of neighborhood space increases

1. as the space becomes less private and more public;
2. as the residents' use of the space increases;
3. as real ownership becomes less clear;
4. as the residents' collective involvement in acquiring the space or manipulating the space increases;
5. as the users perceive that the space meets their special needs;

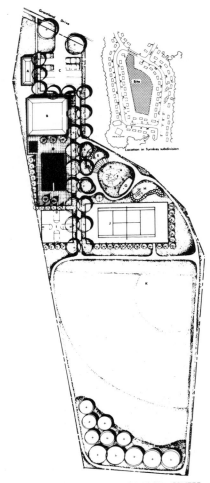

APOLLO HEIGHTS NEIGHBORHOOD CENTER

6. as the space increases in value as a status object to outsiders, especially outsiders of high status;
7. as the space increases in value to one's peer group.

The design applications indicate the recognition of three distinct components of symbolic ownership: ownership, status objects, and symbolic space.

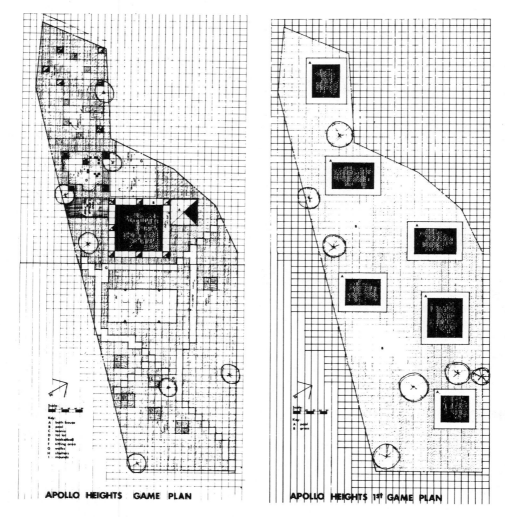

APOLLO HEIGHTS GAME PLAN

APOLLO HEIGHTS 1st GAME PLAN

In the design of the park for the Apollo Heights neighborhood, a game similar to Monopoly was used that allowed residents to buy certain facilities, spaces, and equipment. When the children played with an unlimited budget, each participant wanted a swimming pool located close to his house. The game resulted in six swimming pools, each a status object for the child who lived closest to it. The final plan located a single pool in such a way that it could be seen from almost every backyard to satisfy the residents' desires for the status of having their "own" swimming pool.

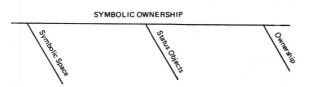

Symbolic ownership refers to three factors that are being applied to design: symbolic space, status objects, and ownership.

Ownership

David Lack said : *"Victory goes not to the strong but to the righteous — the righteous, of course, being the owners of property."*[29]   In an earlier study of neighborhood parks, a widespread feeling of symbolic ownership of local parks was observed. This was most often expressed by children, adults who had been involved in the design process, and people who felt that the parks met their special needs.[30] For instance, The Washington Environmental Yard in Berkeley appeared to be symbolically owned by a majority of the children enrolled in the school. Every child claimed that the space was his own, that he had "jurisdiction" over the space.[31] That the design reflected special considerations for the child-user may have contributed to this response. The designer had attempted to provide settings that the students could own — a child garden, a nature-study area, a mural the children could paint — activity settings that were all unique and met the children's special needs.

Status Objects

A second aspect of symbolic ownership is status objects or status space. I have noticed that the park itself is often viewed as a status object and that users pay close attention to what parks are like in the neighborhoods occupied by people of a higher social status, especially the class to which the users aspire. As a result, the play equipment that people want is often what they have seen in the "better" neighborhood.[32] Friedberg reported that the residents of Jacob Riis Housing Project viewed the completed project as such a high status object that they wanted to keep other people from using it.[33] In the case of Redwood School Playground, Salt Lake City, the architect, Von White, discovered a desirable status object and it came to be a major design determinant. In that city, the higher-income neighborhoods occupy the hillsides while the lower-income neighborhoods, one of which is the Redwood School area, are located in the flatlands. Because the residents involved perceived the hills to be a high status object, they wanted them in the schoolyard.

Similarly, in working with the black lower-income residents of the Elmhurst neighborhood of Oakland, California, we found that the residents wanted their community to look suburban. They rejected proposals that enhanced the existing urban character and opted for the status objects of those middle-class neighborhoods nearby. This pattern is so widespread that some designers refer to it as the "class-above syndrome."

In the design of the park for the Apollo Heights neighborhood of Raleigh, North Carolina, a game similar to Monopoly was used that allowed residents to buy certain facilities, spaces, and equipment. When the children played with an unlimited budget, each participant wanted a swimming pool located close to his home. The game resulted in six swimming pools, each a status object for the child who lived closest to it.[34] The idea of having a swimming pool in their own backyard was viewed as such a strong status object that the children were reluctant to agree on a single location, although they realized they had to agree before a final plan could be developed. The final plan located a single pool in such a way that it could be seen from almost every backyard. This satisfied the children and the parents who wanted the status associated with their "own" swimming pool.

Symbolic Space

A third aspect of symbolic ownership is symbolic space. This aspect is unique because no personal control is necessary over the space for it to be meaningful symbolically. This idea has been indirectly applied to neighborhood space since Robert Park identified "natural areas" of the city that take on symbolic meaning such as good or bad areas, slums, or "areas across the tracks." Anselem Strauss also concluded that the city could be viewed as a complex set of symbolized areas.[35]

An attempt was made to create strong symbolic areas in the new town of Columbia, Maryland. This was quite successful in the village centers, for each had its own readily symbolized shopping and recreation facilities. In another instance, Kevin Lynch identified symbolized images in the neighborhoods of central Boston.[36] In many neighborhoods, historically significant places become symbolically owned. One of the best examples is the Paul Revere Mall in Boston's North End, which is a point of orientation for tourists and residents alike. It is of particular symbolic significance for the North End residents because they use the space every day and take pride in its history.

Certain neighborhood spaces take on social symbolic meaning because of activities that occur there, and it can be difficult to change those activities. Recently, the New Landscape, an advocacy design group, was working with a neighborhood group in redesigning Roanoke Park in Raleigh, North Carolina. The adults wanted to remove the basketball court to create a quiet park for more passive recreation, but the teenagers balked, even though several better basketball courts were offered for their use. Roanoke Park had obviously come to have symbolic meaning as a place to play basketball and in the final design, the basketball courts remained. In another Raleigh neighborhood, Boylan Heights, a park designed to be used by different social groups was used by only the lower-income group. It became symbolic of that group, and over time, the other groups stopped using it.

Jane Jacobs described a similar phenomenon in an area where urban redevelopment had replaced symbolic informal gathering places with more formal meeting rooms, resulting in less public use and a disintegration of the vital neighborhood social organizations. She noted that there were not fewer total places for people to gather in the project, counting places deliberately planned for constructive socializing. Jacobs felt that the problem was a lack of bars, candy stores, hole-in-the-wall *bodegas,* and restaurants in the project.[37] Jacobs puzzled over the reduced use of the planned gathering places. She argued that the institutionalized game rooms, malls, and outdoor benches were dead and useless. She further noted that the public sidewalk and other *informal* places seemed to fulfill purposes that the *planned* gathering places did not. Still she wondered why the informal public sidewalk life bolstered a more formal organizational public life.[38]

A partial answer lies in the process of symbolizing and owning public space. Jacobs pointed out that these formal spaces were difficult to immediately personalize. They clearly belonged to someone else, not the residents. Sidewalks, bars, and alleys, on the other hand, did belong to the residents because they had personalized them, used them daily, cleaned them, and had good times in them. Such spaces are symbolically significant, and designs that have taken symbolic ownership into account tend to be extremely popular and socially suitable, for example, Pike Place Market in Seattle.

Interaction Variations

Another social factor of relevance to design is the interaction and neighboring differences between groups based on regional, ethnic, class, and life-cycle-stage distinctions. The idea that social interaction can be fostered and encouraged by the design of neighborhood space is not new. Community centers have been designed as social focal points;[39] apartment buildings have been arranged to encourage social interfaces;[40] paths, neighborhood stores, open spaces,[41] and playgrounds[42] have been designed to maximize informal interaction; and housing has been planned to increase neighborliness by decreasing the functional distance between neighbors.[43] Wolf Von Eckardt's idea for a "block pavilion" further united the best of the living room and the neighborhood center.[44]

Although these applications of interaction norms are not new, the idea that there are differences in interaction and neighboring patterns is more recent

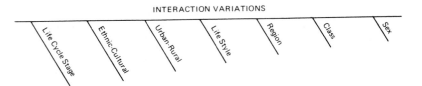

INTERACTION VARIATIONS

Life Cycle Stage   Ethnic-Cultural   Urban-Rural   Life Style   Region   Class   Sex

Interaction variations due to a number of factors, particularly life-cycle stage and class, are being applied to the design of neighborhood spaces.

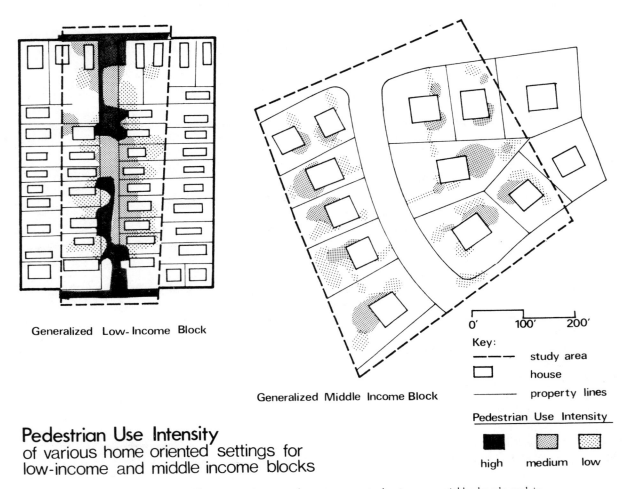

Generalized Low- Income Block

Generalized Middle Income Block

Key:

- - - -   study area

☐   house

———   property lines

Pedestrian Use Intensity

high   medium   low

Pedestrian Use Intensity
of various home oriented settings for low-income and middle income blocks

There is a distinct difference in the use of open spaces in low-income neighborhoods and in middle-income neighborhoods.

to design. Herbert Gans introduced the idea when he advocated acceptance of plural standards for neighborhood quality based on the values, beliefs, and goals of the residents themselves in the West End of Boston. He advanced the notion that different groups perceive, use, feel about, and interact in space differently. But it was Karl Linn who first applied this in his work with low-income blacks in Philadelphia. He learned by experience that white solutions wouldn't work in black neighborhoods and designed their neighborhood commons accordingly. Since then, there have been important research projects exploring these subtleties and numerous attempts to apply interaction variations to design.

Class Differences

Some of the most noticeable variations in interaction and neighboring patterns are attributed to class

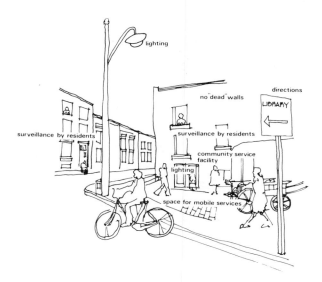

One significant interaction variation is attributed to class differences. Since lower-income residents use the streets, sidewalks, and corners frequently for informal gatherings, a proposal by the Baltimore Planning Department called for the redesign of these spaces to facilitate such interactions.[45]

differences. The observation that lower-income open-space use is oriented to the street and home has guided a number of design proposals. For Baltimore's low-income Reservoir Hill area, a proposal was made to provide suitable spaces "for sitting, congregating, playing street games . . . spaces that serve as stops for fish, fruit, and vegetable vendors, and for ice cream trucks that are such a feature of residential streets in the Inner City . . . stops for certain mobile city services such as book mobiles, health services, etc." Such spaces were to be "suitably paved, well lighted, suitably planted, and equipped with mailboxes, telephone booths, and trash containers."[46] The objective was to enhance the use of those spaces already frequented by low-income residents. In the Chavis Heights redevelopment scheme in Raleigh, a block-by-block rehabilitation plan sought to preserve the street orientation of front porches and informal gathering points at neighborhood stores and churches. These are often the primary spaces in many low-income southern black neighborhoods as they presently exist.[47] This plan retained the basic layout of the neighborhood — the narrow streets, corner shops, and dense single-family housing — thereby demonstrating a positive alternative to urban renewal clearance based on the observed interaction patterns of the residents.

In evaluating Easter Hill Village in Richmond, California, Clare Cooper found among the public-housing residents a desire for privacy without isolation; that is, a desire to have private family places and personal spaces but at the same time to be close enough to neighbors for both friendship and help in time of need. The residents felt a need for closeness, particularly female heads of households who shared the use of cars and telephones. This is a frequent pattern among the urban poor. Cooper suggests that this desirable interaction was facilitated by a network of outdoor walkways, communal parking lots, and yards without high fences. But at the same time, she found that by placing the front doors and housing units too close together the designers had actually produced neighborhood tensions instead of

The Chavis Heights redevelopment plan in Raleigh calls for block-by-block rehabilitation that preserves the street orientation of front porches and play areas and keeps the informal gathering points at neighborhood stores. (Photograph by Marge Hackman)

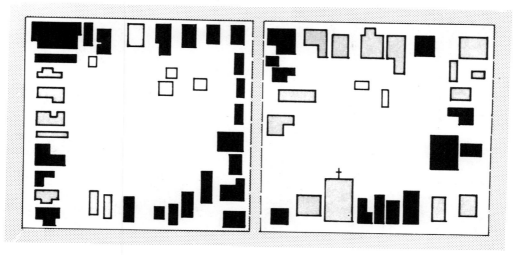

Existing Block Conditions

▬▬ Existing Deteriorated Structures
Existing Repairable Structures
Existing Right-of-Way

Phase 1 Block Rehabilitation

Existing Right-of-Way
New Right-of-Way
Abandoned Right-of-Way
Repairable Structures to Remain
● Turning Circle

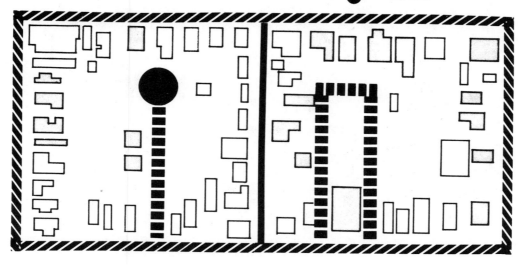

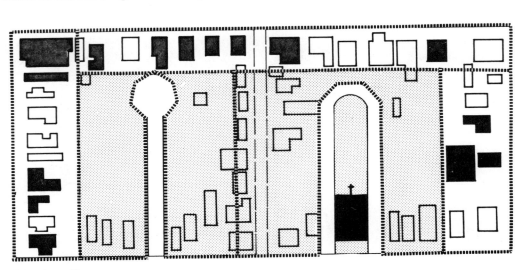

Phase 2
Block Rehabilitation

New streets into interior of blocks. New houses constructed and sold to residents in gray areas

Houses to be replaced

Phase 3
Block Rehabilitation

New Structures

Rehabilitated Structures Moved

Rehabilitated Structures

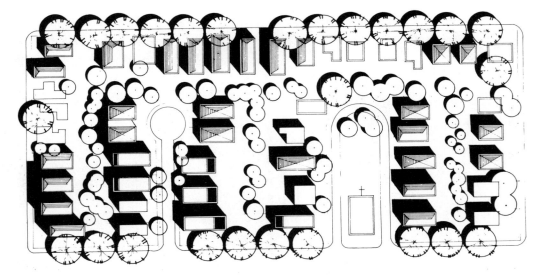

neighborliness. In addition, she saw a need for two other informal interaction settings for low-income public housing residents: preschool play spaces and places for the elderly to sit and talk.[48]

In contrast to these poor neighborhoods, Cameron Park, a middle-income professional neighborhood in Raleigh required a different solution. Since social interaction usually occurs toward the back of the homes, it was proposed that the old alleys be redesigned to be the primary circulation routes serving secret play spaces, private sitting areas, and vegetable and flower gardens. Most suburban developments have taken into account the interaction desires of the middle-class prospective buyers by providing maximum separation and privacy.

Life-Cycle Stage

A second variable in interaction differences is the life-cycle stage. Recognition of this factor led designers to pay special attention to the interaction needs of families whose lack of mobility makes them dependent on neighborhood space — particularly, families with preschool or elementary school children, teenagers, or elderly family members. Attention to the neighboring patterns of families with young children produced a design for Ridgefield Park in Chapel Hill, North Carolina, a low-income housing project in which play equipment was dispersed throughout the project rather than in one concentrated area.[49] This allowed mothers to observe their children's play from inside their apartments while doing household chores. It was a desirable pattern from their point of view. The design is excellent because the designers recognized and applied the home-based interaction patterns of families with young children.[50] Similarly, the design of Putnam Gardens Tot Lot allowed for parental surveillance from the kitchen window by placing the play area in an inner court. Although many residents wanted the tot lot located a block away, the parents of young children knew their neighboring patterns and insisted on an inner-court location.[51]

A more complex interaction pattern of families with young children was a major determinant in the redevelopment of the Jefferson Park Housing Project in Cambridge. The big court was scheduled to become a major play area, and the designer suggested clustering the four separate clotheslines to enlarge the central open space. This idea met with stiff opposition on the part of the residents because the young parents with limited mobility were using the clothesline area not only for drying clothes but also for observing their children's play and for socializing. Four separate friendship circles existed, based on the clotheslines as a socializing space for families with young children. Even the fathers met there to drink beer after work, and they, too, saw the design proposal as interrupting their home-oriented meeting place.[52] The design was changed to reinforce these corner areas as four, separate, semiprivate interaction centers.

With special attention to the interaction patterns of small children, Robin Moore and Mark Francis observed that children's play is entirely linked and not separated into categories such as swings, slides, seesaws, or monkey bars. They have designed and built neighborhood spaces that provide nodes of intense activity within a connecting system that forms a ballet of movement[53] as a child slides, runs, swings, jumps, and learns through the environment. Such environments are not only challenging and open ended but also appear to be consistent with how children interact.[54]

Similar attention to the neighboring patterns of the elderly in a southern city produced a plan for a low-rise public housing project with private outdoor spaces that allowed the elderly to be insulated but not isolated.[55] The people expressed a desire to be close enough to the activity centers to observe the activities but far enough away to be protected from the "crowd." The private outdoor spaces provided for this desirable interaction pattern.

Teenagers are a final group whose interaction patterns are often overlooked, partly because they are more mobile and less bound to the neighbor-

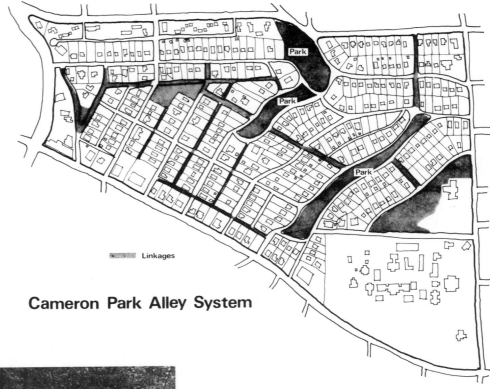

Cameron Park Alley System

In Cameron Park, a middle-income neighborhood, social interaction focused around the backyards. Old alleys are being redesigned to provide primary circulation routes and play spaces. (Photograph by Marge Hackmann)

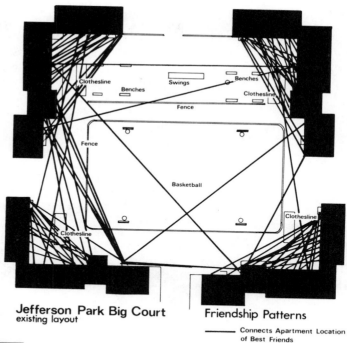

Jefferson Park Big Court
existing layout

Friendship Patterns

Connects Apartment Location
of Best Friends

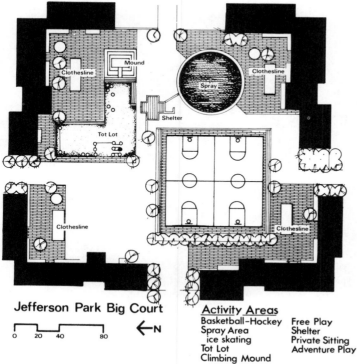

Jefferson Park Big Court

0   20   40   80   ←N

Activity Areas
Basketball-Hockey   Free Play
Spray Area   Shelter
  ice skating   Private Sitting
Tot Lot   Adventure Play
Climbing Mound

When the designer proposed that the clotheslines be clustered at one end of the big court of the Jefferson Park Housing Project, he met stiff opposition. The four clotheslines had become the center of activity and friendships for parents there to work or to socialize. The residents dictated a plan that reinforced the four informal gatherings around the clotheslines but still allowed for children's play areas.

47

LIFE CYCLE CLASSIFICATION	MOBILITY	Extremely Low	Low	Moderate	High	Extremely High
Preschool Child		●				
Elementary School Child			●¹			
Teen-Ager				●¹		
College Student						●
Unmarried Adult						●²
Young Marrieds					●²	
Family with Young Children		●¹				
Family with Older Children				●²		
Middle Aged					●²	
Elderly		●				

¹Significant sex differences in mobility, females generally being lower.

²Most significant class differences in mobility, lower income being generally lower.

GENERALIZED MOBILITY ACCORDING TO LIFE CYCLE STAGE

There is a significant variation in the mobility of people of different ages, with small children, their mothers, and the elderly being particularly homebound and, therefore, heavy users of neighborhood spaces.

hood than the other groups discussed. At the Jacob Riis Plaza, a private sitting garden designed for the elderly was taken over by teenagers because it provided the perfect space for hanging out close to home in an intimate setting without adult supervision.[56] These same characteristics made the space unsafe for the elderly. Of the case studies presented in Chapter 6, both Dana Park in Cambridge, and Kingwood Forest Park in Raleigh, provided specific areas for teenagers to hang out. The increased use of certain outdoor recreation facilities in Cambridge was attributed, in part, to the provision of informal,

unsupervised interaction places near home that teenagers could easily personalize and claim as their own.[57]

Although class and life-cycle stage appear to be the most important of the interaction variations to be applied to the planning of neighborhood space, regional, ethnic, cultural, life-style, sex, and urban-rural interaction variations also are frequently applied today as designers search for authenticity and indigenous solutions. Designer Mark Francis discovered that the residents of Village Homes in Davis, California, wanted a place for children to play that was consistent with their energy-conscious life-styles. The result was an informal network of play spaces, intermixed with vineyards and community gardens, along the walkways from home to community center and a playground entirely user built from recycled materials.

Claire Reiniger has worked with Navaho groups to design new communities based on the groups' traditional social patterns. Most of these communities have used a modernized hogan (a log and mud building) as the housing type since it is preferred by most of the Navaho. This dictates the form of the housing cluster because, traditionally, women use the space to the south of the hogan, men to the north, and medicine men to the west. In addition, Reiniger has proposed a decision-making process for community planning that would include Navaho artists, councilmen, tribal artists and traditional medicine men because they are most familiar with the symbolic interaction patterns of their tribe.

Activity Variations

Samuel Z. Klausner has stated that different groups seek different leisure-time activities. For example, people with higher incomes participate more in picnicking rather than camping; Northeasterners are more interested in swimming than people in other parts of the country;[58] white populations in urban areas want rocks to romp over, zoos, and art museums, but city Negroes are less likely to want these

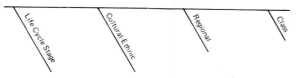

ACTIVITY VARIATIONS

Variations in the activities of people in different social classes, at different life-cycle stages, and of different ethnic and regional groups comprise an important social factor that has been applied to the design of neighborhood space.

activities;[59] bowling attracts more of the working class than of other classes. Some games are related to certain cultures—tennis with the English, baseball with Americans,[60] ice hockey with Canadians, lacrosse with American Indians, and bocci with Italians. Some activities, like street hockey, skin diving, and skiing, says Klausner, are even associated with regions.[61] The recognition of such variations in activities because of class, life-cycle stage, ethnic, and regional differences has produced significantly different designs for neighborhood space.

Class Differences

For many years neighborhood parks followed the standards of the National Recreation Association, which called for a grassed area for informal games, play apparatus, a shelter, a paved court area, landscaping, and fencing. The assumption was that every neighborhood wanted and needed the same activities.[62] But in some cases, for example in upper middle-income communities like Hilton Head, South Carolina, the desire for linear parks for bike riding and walking was greater than the desire for concentrated neighborhood parks. In others, like Southgate, a low-to-moderate income black neighborhood in Raleigh, the City Parks and Recreation Department proposed a standard community park with a lighted baseball field, tennis courts, and a small multipurpose court. The residents insisted, however, that their priority

activity was basketball, and the plan was changed to include two full-sized basketball courts to accommodate this overwhelming preference.

Pamela Dinkel discovered and applied another activity variation, based on class differences, to two neighborhood park designs. She found that the leisure time activities in a low-income neighborhood were more frequent, less organized, and more informal in comparison to a middle-income neighborhood where, although less time was spent in leisure activities, they were well defined, organized, and formal. The resulting designs reflected these differences: the low-income park provided for several areas of play equipment, benches, and a shelter interspersed in an informal way, and the middle-income park provided a single, highly organized tot lot adjacent to tennis courts.[63]

Life-Cycle Stage

Equally significant are the design applications based on activity variations due to life-cycle stage. The most numerous of these have been related to activities children enjoy outside of formal play areas.[64] Peter Sipjkes,[65] Julie Graham,[66] and Robin Moore[67] learned from their studies of environments for children's play that children enjoy activities that are spontaneously made up, that involve building something, that are daring but not dangerous, that combine learning and play, and that are "far out," crazy, new, or "freaky." Their conclusion resulted in the adventure playground or variations thereof, like Joseph Baker's McGill Mushroom in Montreal, Canada. The dislike parents have for such playgrounds attests to the need for activity variations for different life-cycle stages.

In an attempt to meet the needs of the elderly, at least half of the case studies presented in Chapter 6 provided sitting areas, observation places, and other spaces for passive recreation. However, later observations made it clear that the activity needs of the elderly were largely misunderstood. Only one site,

The Devonshire School Playground designed by Peter Sipjkes and the McGill Community Design Workshop, is immensely popular with children because it provides them with a "far-out" place to play. (Photograph by Ted Remerowski)

Dana Park, was used by the elderly as intended. In the other cases, the elderly had wanted less passive activities more conveniently located to their homes and less isolated from other neighborhood residents.

Cultural, Ethnic, and Regional Factors

In addition to class and life-cycle stage, cultural, ethnic and regional factors significantly affect the activities and design of neighborhood environments. In many Canadian-American neighborhoods of the Boston area, street hockey and ice hockey are the preferred activities.[68] Neighborhood landscapes are greatly altered because every available space is suitable for street hockey—one often sees games being played around garbage cans, under clotheslines, and at front door steps. In contrast, special and costly facilities are necessary for ice hockey. In Albuquerque, New Mexico, the redesign of Dennis Chávez Park centered around an amphitheater where Spanish dance and theater could be performed for local residents. And, the repeated preference of low-income blacks for more basketball in neighborhood parks than is provided under current recreation standards, again points to the importance of regional and ethnic activity variations and their potential influence on the design of neighborhood space.

Usable Space

Another social factor that has been applied to the design of neighborhood space is the concept of usable space, the basic physical requirements for a certain social activity in a given place. How much space do you need to stop to talk on a sidewalk, wait for a bus, make love in the woods, play football, have a picnic, go for a swim, sit in a park, fly a kite, hunt lizards, ice skate, ride a bike, play in the sand, hang out, play four square, go for a walk, or commune with nature? Usable space is a setting that satisfies the minimum requirements of size, slope, linearity, light, openness, weather, and compatibility with adjacent activity settings for a given activity. If a setting meets the minimum requirements, it has the potential for use.[69]

Neighborhood designers are expected to make decisions daily about what the basic minimum requirements are for an activity. Notes like "tennis courts paved 120 by 120 feet, amphitheater with 30 percent slope, bike trail must be at least two miles long, needs 30 foot candles at least, retain open field for kite flying, provide all-weather courts for school children, and separate archery from neighborhood activities" indicate frequent design considerations. Although standards exist for many of these basic requirements, many other determinations fall within the subjective domain of the designer.

Someone recently asked me what the usable space requirements are for football. I responded with the standard 120 yards by 160 feet, even 2 to 3 percent grass slope, even lighting, goalposts, and yard markers.[70] Then I thought of a recent football game I had seen being played by first graders in a space 10 yards by 10 feet among giant oak trees. It occurred to me then that I had always given too little attention to the variations from the accepted standards of usable space.

There have been few applications of such variations, but one deserves recounting. In a playground in Cambridge, the small children were frequently chased off the basketball courts by teenagers. The parents suggested that a lower basketball hoop be installed for small children. They made the hypothesis that the "baby" court would not be considered a usable space because the teenagers were accustomed to a 10-foot goal and a standard court layout. The result worked as they expected—teenagers played on the standard courts, and the small goal was always open for small children.

In spite of a few such applications and the critical

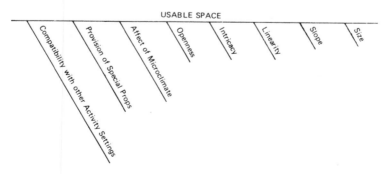

Usable space, the basic physical requirements for a space to be used for a certain social activity, has long been a consideration in the design of neighborhoods.

nature of usable space, there has been little exploration of the variations from the standards that might be necessitated by age or density differences. There is little mention in the literature of such variations,[71] indicating that designers need to conduct more research.

Comfortable Space

A final social factor that has had design application is the concept of comfortable space. In the design of neighborhood space, physical comfort is frequently among the most important design determinants, but psychological comfort, a social factor, is seldom considered. Most of the examples presented by planners appear to be aesthetic factors (trees to soften edges or hard materials) or territorial factors[72] (placing benches in protected places). Also related to psychological comfort and aesthetics is the balancing of order and diversity. It has been hypothesized that in any situation an individual attempts to organize his physical environment to maximize his freedom of choice.[73] Thus, any setting that provides a wide range of alternatives would contribute to one's psychological comfort. But a wide range of alternatives can sometimes produce a feeling of confusion, uncertainty, ambiguity, and discomfort. Humphry Osmond has described the specific need of schizophrenics to reduce ambiguity and uncertainty in the environment.[74]

COMFORTABLE SPACE

Designers have often considered the physical comfort of the users of neighborhood spaces, but only recently have they given much attention to psychological comfort.

Although users need to be able to make choices, in some cases the range or type of choices must be limited. When applied to neighborhood design, this idea is often expressed only in terms of visual unity. The traditional play equipment at Dennis Chávez Park was removed because it did not blend visually with the new play sculpture. This limited the choices but was done mainly for aesthetic reasons. The aesthetic notion of balancing order and diversity plays a critical part in determing psychological comfort, with order providing security and diversity allowing for new experiences.

Jacobs discussed similar concepts, intricacy and centering, as two of four elements of intensely used neighborhood spaces:

Even the same person comes for different reasons at different times; sometimes to sit tiredly, sometimes to play or to watch a game, sometimes to read or work, sometimes to show off, sometimes to fall in love, sometimes to keep an appointment, sometimes to savor the hustle of the city from a retreat, sometimes in the hope of finding acquaintances, sometimes to get closer to a bit of nature, sometimes to keep a child occupied, sometimes simply to see what offers, and almost always to be entertained by the sight of other people.[75]

A place must have intricacy to allow such diverse activities, but there must also be a center, a place where the main circulation routes cross, where people pause and meet. The center is the climax. In this explanation, centering provided the order of psychological security, and intricacy provided the new experiences. The point is that there does seem to be a strong correlation between the idea of visual unity, which designers often apply, and the ideas of activity unity and psychological comfort.

THINGS FOR YOU TO DO

The following exercises will clarify the issues raised in this chapter. Some will check your understanding of the material; others will help you articulate your own values or give you insights into neighborhood-design issues. You may do these exercises alone, but I would suggest doing them with others.

1. List some of the positive and negative aspects of establishing territorial control over neighborhood spaces.
2. What do you perceive as the reasons for vandalism and graffitti in an established neighborhood space? Do you think that design can or should function to minimize it? Describe how.
3. Can you think of a space that you feel you have symbolically owned? Describe the space and the reasons for your attachment to that space.
4. What makes a space feel "crowded" to you? Do you think this varies from person to person?
5. As the mother of two first grade children, where in your neighborhood would you feel safe allowing your children to play? As a first grader, where would you want to play in your neighborhood?
6. Divide a sheet of paper into three columns. In the middle column write down the facilities you would include in the redesign of your own neighborhood. Now, in the other two columns, write down the facilities that you think your next-door neighbors—those living on either side of you—would want. Compare your responses.
7. Imagine yourself a resident of a lower-income neighborhood that is being rehabilitated. What might be your specific concerns in redesigning the neighborhood?

NOTES AND REFERENCES

1. John G. Neihardt, *Black Elk Speaks,* Pocket Books, Inc., New York, 1972, pp. 9-10, 28.
2. Herbert J. Gans, *People and Plans: Essays on Urban Problems and Solutions,* Basic Books, New York, 1968, p. ix.
3. William Mangin, "Squatter Settlements," *Cities: Their Origin, Growth and Human Impact,* W. H. Freeman and Company, San Francisco, 1973, pp. 233-240.
4. Herbert J. Gans, *The Urban Villagers: Group and Class in the Life of Italian Americans,* The Free Press, New York, 1962, p. 367.
5. Mildred F. Schmertz, "Designing the Spaces in Between," *Architectural Record* **143**(3): 128 (1968).
6. Randolph T. Hester, Jr., Susan Grose, and J. Edward Washington, Jr., *Neighborhood Open Space for Political Involvement: A Report of the Community Development Section,* City of Cambridge, Cambridge, Mass., June, 1970, pp. 1-2.
7. The work of Robin Moore has largely been concerned with the provision of a variety of interfaces or settings for different social interactions and man-environment interactions. The Washington Environmental Yard, one of Moore's projects, is included as one of the case studies in Chapter 6.
8. These categories are borrowed from the writings of A. E. Scheflen and Julius Fast, whose efforts in nonverbal human communication well describe the various interaction settings being designed for child-development environments. See Julius Fast, *Body Language,* Simon and Schuster, New York, 1973. Although the categories adequately describe the interaction settings being designed by Robin Moore and others involved in the development of child environments, the categories are my own classification of these settings.
9. The term "interaction setting" is used to describe a space that is suitable for or encourages social interaction. It implies that the environment is perceived not as a setting for an activity, but rather as a setting for social exchange.
10. Humphry Osmond has classified settings such as these that encourage, foster, and even enforce the development of stable interpersonal relationships. He refers to these as sociopetal spaces and offers examples: the tepee, the igloo, and most private homes. See Humphry Osmond, "Function as the Basis of Psychiatric Ward Design," in *Environmental Psychology,* H. M. Proshansky, W. H. Ittleson, and L. G. Rivlin, eds., Holt, Rinehart and Winston, New York, 1970, p. 567.
11. Osmond, *Environmental Psychology,* p. 567. Osmond refers to these settings as sociofugal and states that urban society necessitates such environments, like railway stations, hotels, mental hospitals, general hospitals, and jails. One might add many new urban and most suburban neighborhood spaces to this list.
12. Although the spatial qualities of congruent and incongruent interaction settings seem to be the same, the results of accepting or rejecting the observed role models' behavior are significant enough to discuss them separately.
13. I have applied this principle to the design of children's play environments for a number of years. I find that Albert Rutledge, Julie Graham, and Robin Moore are applying this idea to the design of parks, playgrounds, and environmental yards. This application is significantly different from Scheflen's definition in his application of this classification to body postures.
14. Eugene P. Odum, *Fundamentals of Ecology,* 3rd edition, W. B. Saunders, Philadelphia, 1971, pp. 221-224. Odum clarifies

several points in regard to the natural ecological dimensions of territoriality that seem relevant to this discussion: (1) the idea defended is actually a space in that it is three dimensional; (2) the defense of the space usually does not involve physical conflict but rather symbolic postures or ceremonies; (3) the defense is usually sex specific, often related to mating, feeding, nesting, and breeding; (4) territoriality is most pronounced in vertebrates and certain anthropods; (5) the forces that bring about territorial isolation or spacing of individuals are not as widespread as those favoring aggregation; (6) this isolation is nonetheless important because it reduces competition and tends to conserve energy during critical periods, therefore preventing overcrowding and exhaustion of the food supply.

15. Robert Ardrey, *The Territorial Imperative*, Atheneum, New York, 1966, p. 102.
16. The concept of dominance also originated in natural ecology. Frequently during periods of stress, a vertebrate vigorously defends a home range and comes to dominate the area. This usually does not require physical battle, but the losers are driven out and often die for lack of the basic needs of the species.
17. Samuel Z. Klausner, *On Man in His Environment*, Jossey-Bass, San Francisco, 1971, pp. 161-162.
18. Klausner, *On Man*, p. 163.
19. The territorial-dominance analysis, although done with great care, was the result of informal basketball/hanging sessions with the gang for two months. This process is described in the detailed case studies in Chapter 6.
20. Robert Sommer, *Personal Space: The Behavioral Basis of Design*, Prentice-Hall, Englewood Cliffs, N.J., 1969, p. 177. Sommer's work has had such an impact on the design of socially responsive neighborhood space that virtually all the projects considered for the accompanying case studies took territorial considerations into account.
21. Sommer, *Personal Space*, p. viii.
22. Sommer, *Personal Space*, p. 26.
23. Edward T. Hall, *The Hidden Dimension*, Doubleday, Garden City, N.Y., 1966.
24. Sommer, *Personal Space*, pp. 39-48.
25. Harold Proshansky, "Freedom of Choice in a Physical Setting," in *Environmental Psychology*, H. M. Proshansky, W. H. Ittleson, and L. G. Rivlin, eds., Holt, Rinehart and Winston, New York, 1970, p. 177.
26. Proshansky, "Freedom of Choice," p. 177. Adapted from Proshansky's critique of A. F. Westin's constructs.
27. Robert Gutman, "Site Planning and Social Behavior," *The Journal of Social Issues* **22**(4): 103-115 (1966).
28. Sommer, *Personal Space*, p. 43.
29. Ardrey, *Territorial Imperative*, p. 106.
30. See the case studies in Chapter 6.
31. Philip D. Roos, "Jurisdiction: An Ecological Concept," in *Environmental Psychology*, H. M. Proshansky, W. H. Ittleson, and L. G. Rivlin, eds., Holt, Rinehart and Winston, New York, 1970, pp. 239-246. Roos refers to this idea of authority over a space as jurisdiction, combining the ideas of territoriality and symbolic ownership.
32. From informal discussions I had with Susan Grose and Ed Washington during the design processes of Rindge Field and Glacken Field in Cambridge, Mass. in 1971. We dubbed this phenomenon "the class-above theorem."
33. From a phone conversation with M. Paul Friedberg on Oct. 24, 1973.
34. Wayne Maynard, "Game Simulation and Community Advocacy," *Landscape Architecture* **62**(4): 334-335 (July, 1972).
35. Anselem Strauss, *Images of the American City*, The Free Press, New York, 1981, p. 19.
36. Kevin Lynch, *The Image of the City*, MIT Press, Cambridge, Mass., 1960, pp. 16-25, 78-83.
37. Jane Jacobs, *Death and Life of Great American Cities*, Random House, New York, 1969, pp. 55-73.
38. Jacobs, *Death and Life*, pp. 55-73.
39. "West End Multi-Service Center to Be Built," *City of San Antonio Model Cities News*, Jan. 10, 1972, p. 1ff.
40. Sarah K. Davidson and James L. Curtis, "A Case Study of Behavior," unpublished paper prepared under the direction of R. Hester at North Carolina State University, Raleigh, N.C., 1971. One finding of this study was that the interaction index was higher in apartments clustered around a parking lot than in apartments sharing a common open space. See also Herbert Gans, "Planning and Social Life," *Journal of the American Institute of Planners* **27**(2): 27 (1961).
41. Randolph T. Hester and Pamela Y. Dinkel, "What Rank Open Space?" unpublished paper, Pennsylvania State University, University Park, Pa., 1970. One finding was that the residents of the apartments studied stated that an informal open space was a prime reason for meeting their friends. Only sharing the same work and having children ranked higher as a cause of social interaction.
42. Hester and Dinkel, "What Rank Open Space?" p. 10.
43. William H. Whyte, *The Organization Man*, Simon and Schuster, New York, 1956. Whyte found that the small-scale layout of Park Forest, Illinois, was a major factor in determining friendships. My observation is that, although the courtyards and streets are similar to many others in design, the Oakwood Street closeness is unmatched in personal significance. See also Gutman, "Site Planning and Social Behavior," *Journal of Social Issues* **22**(4): 103-115, and Leon Festinger, Stanley Schachter, and Kurt Back, *Social Pressures in Informal Groups*, Stanford University Press, Stanford, Calif., 1963.
44. Wolf Von Eckardt, "New Ideas for Inner City," *Raleigh Times*, April 27, 1974, p. 5A.
45. Department of Planning and Department of Housing and

Urban Development, *Baltimore Community Renewal Program Interim Report: A Progress Report on the First Year of a Two Year Program of Study*, Baltimore, Md., May, 1972, p. 154.

46. *Baltimore Community Renewal Program*, pp. 115-157.

47. Randolph T. Hester, Jr., "Student Advocacy in Raleigh and the Community Development Process," *Landscape Architecture* **62**(4): 331-332 (1972).

48. Clare Cooper, *Some Social Implications of House and Site Plan Design at Easter Hill Village: A Case Study*, University of California, Institute of Urban and Regional Development, Center for Planning and Development Research, Berkeley, Calif., 1965, pp. 260-263.

49. Henry Sanoff and Gary Coates, "Behavioral Mapping: An Ecological Analysis of Activities in a Residential Setting," *International Journal of Environmental Studies* **2**: 227-235 (1971).

50. Suzanne Keller, *The Urban Neighborhood: A Sociological Perspective*, Random House, New York, 1968, p. 118.

51. From meeting notes of the Community Development Section, Office of the City Manager, Cambridge, Mass., 1970-1971.

52. From conversations with Fred Arsonault during the design process, Cambridge, Mass., 1969-1970.

53. From an interview with Robin Moore at the University of California at Berkeley, May 20, 1973.

54. Robin Moore, Patsy Ford, and Carol Malcolm, *Living Kid City: Alice in Megalopolis*, Department of Landscape Architecture, University of California at Berkeley, Berkeley, Calif., 1973, p. 10. See also M. Paul Friedberg, *Play and Interplay*, Macmillan, New York, 1970.

55. Rebecca Dixon, William Brantley, and Richard Nolte, *Southside Urban Renewal Guidelines* School of Design, North Carolina State University, Raleigh N.C., May, 1972.

56. Phone conversation with M. Paul Friedberg, Oct. 24, 1973.

57. Randolph T. Hester, Jr., "Institutionalized Team Advocacy Design," *Eleven Views: Collaborative Design in Community Development*, John Pearce, ed., Student Publication of the School of Design, vol. 20, Raleigh, N.C., 1971, pp. 135, 139.

58. Klausner, *On Man*, pp. 139-140.

59. Klausner, *On Man*, p. 164.

60. Klausner, *On Man*, p. 165.

61. Klausner, *On Man*, p. 165.

62. Klausner, *On Man*, p. 165.

63. Hester and Dinkel, "What Rank Open Space?" pp. 18-23. A similar combination of tennis and tot lot was built in 1972-1973 in Urbana, Ill., as a landscape architecture class project.

64. Charles Zerner, "Worms, Crabs, and Anchovies," in *Living Kid City: Alice in Megalopolis*, Robin Moore, Patsy Ford, and Carol Malcolm, eds., Department of Landscape Architecture, University of California at Berkeley, Berkeley, Calif., 1973, pp. 24-27.

65. Joseph Baker, *Green Thumbs and Sore Thumbs and Adventure Playgrounds*, McGill University, Montreal, 1972.

66. Robert E. Koehler, "A Genuine Response to the Region," *AIA Journal* **57**(6): 27-34 (1972).

67. Robin Moore, "The Diary of a Volunteer Playground," *Landscape Architecture* **63**(3-4): 216-221 (1973).

68. From meeting notes of the Community Development Section, Office of the City Manager, Cambridge, Mass. Specific projects, which include street and ice hockey, include Rindge Field, Jefferson Park Public Housing Project, and Fletcher School.

69. Gans, *People and Plans*, p. 6.

70. Standard dimensions for organized sports and games are given in a number of design references like *Architectural Graphic Standards*, *Anatomy of a Park*, and *The Nature of Recreation*.

71. Richard Saul Wurman, Alan Levy, and Joel Katz, with Jean McClintock and Howard Brunner, *The Nature of Recreation: a Handbook in Honor of Frederick Law Olmsted, Using Examples from His Work*, MIT Press, Cambridge, Mass., 1972, pp. 26-33. Wurman's description of performance standards based on a number of continuums is a notable exception.

72. Marion Clawson and Jack L. Knetsch, *Economics of Outdoor Recreation*, Johns Hopkins Press, Baltimore, 1966, p. 20.

73. Proshansky, "Freedom of Choice," p. 175.

74. Osmond, *Environmental Psychology*, pp. 563-566.

75. Jacobs, *Death and Life*, pp. 103-105. The four elements are intricacy, centering, sun, and enclosure.

3

User Needs: A Checklist

Everyone shares common needs with each other, but each person also has unique needs and ways of expressing and satisfying those needs. The process of neighborhood design involves balancing common needs and individual ones. Knowing what shared needs to expect is important, but discovering the unique needs of a neighborhood is a key to socially suitable design because it is the "idiosyncratic needs that generate idiosyncratic values, which in turn generate idiosyncratic but appropriate neighborhood spaces."[1]

In this chapter, ways to recognize and apply idiosyncratic neighborhood needs are described and a holistic checklist of user needs, encompassing the social factors presented in Chapter 2, is developed. The checklist is derived from the preferences of users rather than sociologists and designers, but the concepts incorporate sociological findings and are readily transferable into design programs. The chapter includes sections on a user-needs checklist, the relative importance of user needs, the application of user needs to the design process, and user-needs performance standards.

THE USER-NEEDS CHECKLIST

By thinking of an outdoor space close to home and then listing all the reasons why one goes there and what would make one go there more often, an idea of the factors important to one's use of that space emerges. If these answers are combined with the answers of others, a pattern of personal preferences can be derived directly from the users. Such a pattern represents the requirements that residents expect neighborhood space to satisfy. A number of studies over the last decades attempted to uncover these patterns for diverse groups of people, and recurring user needs were identified. Such studies were reinforced by neighborhood-space observation,[2] interviews with open-space users,[3] literature searches,[4] interdisciplinary brainstorming sessions,[5] small group tests, and role-playing sessions[6] in which the same user-needs patterns were recorded. Listed below are the aspects of neighborhood space that people say influence their use of that space:

> People one wants to do an activity with or without
> Settings for the activity one wants to do
> "Relatedness" through interaction with the natural
>   environment
> Safety
> Aesthetic appeal
> Convenience
> Psychological comfort
> Physical comfort
> Symbolic ownership
> Policy on use
> Cost

These aspects are offered as the major components of a checklist of user needs related to the design of neighborhood space. Although these concepts may seem self-explanatory, each must be clearly defined before application to the design process.

People One Wants to Do an Activity With or Without

The concept of people one wants to do an activity with or without is considered by the users to be the most important determinant in neighborhood-space

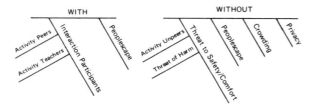

The single most important factor in a person's use of a neighborhood space is who else is there. If people a person wants to be with are there, he is likely to go there, but if a person wants to avoid people who are there, he will not go there.

use. This has repeatedly been the case with various groups representing different classes and life-cycle stages. The "with" component of this concept includes desirable "interaction participants" who may be activity peers or activity teachers and who may be described by life-cycle stage, class, ethnic, or regional characteristics. If there is an appropriate match between these characteristics, the participants could be expected to engage in a certain activity, thereby using a space. When describing their use of neighborhood space, people frequently give responses such as the following: "We go to the lot to hang out with our friends," or "Sometimes my dad teaches me about flowers in the park."

The with component also includes a positive "peoplescape," that is, people whose presence is a positive factor even though one does not interact with them. The following responses characterize the reasons people give for using a neighborhood space because of a "peoplescape" attraction: "I go there because there is always a variety of people," or "We go to look at the hippies."

The "without" component includes getting away from people, seeking privacy, and avoiding overcrowding. It also includes a negative peoplescape aspect, that is, people whose mere presence is a negative factor or a threat to one's safety or comfort. This component indicates that people may be disinclined to use a space if undesirable people are there. A number of user responses reflect this without component: "I go there to get away from my family," or "We don't use the park much anymore because there are always too many people there. . . because there are Negroes there . . . because we are afraid of the rough gang that hangs out there. . . because the grown-ups always bother us there."

The concept of people one wants to do an activity with or without encompasses the bulk of social factors discussed in Chapter 2, particularly the interaction processes of cooperation, accommodation, acculturation, and competition, including territoriality and dominance, and activity and interaction variations based on class and life-cycle stage differences.

Appropriate Activity Settings

The provision of appropriate activity settings is frequently mentioned by people as a determinant of their use of a particular space. Even more frequently, appropriate activity settings are considered by designers as determinants in planning neighborhood spaces. These settings are determined by the physical aspects of neighborhood spaces—the location and the site characteristics.

As to location, people are most often concerned about the compatibility of the surrounding neighborhood with the desired activities. A stream in a quiet neighborhood may be an appropriate location for a family picnic but may not provide a good place for teenagers to hang out late at night. Or a park in an area of college-student housing might be a good location for Frisbee, but a family might be reluctant to go there for a picnic because of the surrounding rundown houses.

But more important to the user are the site characteristics of the space itself. Users frequently ask questions related to appropriate activity settings: "How many tennis courts are there?" "Can you build a fort from that junk?" "Can you play volleyball there?" "Are there woods for a picnic?"

The user often perceives site characteristics differently than the designer. While the designer may consider a swale as a serious drainage problem, a young child may regard it as an excellent place to sled, or the users may want picnic facilities in a wooded area that the designer wants as a nature preserve. In such cases the designer has to be careful not to impose his site-planning expertise and ruin an appropriate activity setting. In other cases, however, the user may not be concerned about soil conditions except when grass does not grow in the outfield; about the water table except when the ground is too soggy to play football; or about the sun angle except when a tennis ball is lost in the afternoon sun. Obviously, the designer needs to intervene in these cases to explain to the users the site constraints. Professionals may have difficulty distinguishing

between the two. The former are conflicts over values with no overwhelming technical constraints. The latter have technical constraints that only the designer may be aware of prior to construction. A good rule of thumb is for designers to ask themselves, "Is there a technical reason for this?" If there is, the designer needs to say so. If it is only a matter of values, then the user should prevail.

Site planners have the difficult task of determining what activity settings the users want, what activities the site is capable of supporting,[7] and how to communicate this to the users. This requires translating data about soil, water conditions, slope, vegetative cover, climate, and other factors into a form on which users can base decisions. Then the designer has to describe the desired activities in terms of alternative guiding principles that combine the users' preferences and the character of the site. For example, a site might be organized around a theme of ecological awareness, active-versus-passive sports, or commercial-development opportunities. From there, the users may choose or suggest new themes.

On the basis of the selected theme, the designer must describe the activities in terms of the necessary site factors, including size and quantity,[8] openness, slope,[9] domination by microclimate,[10] linearity,[11] compatibility with other activities, variety, and the need for props. Each of these factors forms a continuum. Activity spaces may be small-to-large, enclosed-to-open, flat-to-sloped, microclimate unaffected-to-microclimate dominated, linear-to-nodal, or simple-to-intricate. Activity spaces may be compatible with other activities or with no other activities; they may require props or no props. By categorizing the desired activities according to the site characteristics needed, the planner can match the desired activity settings with the site capability. This is a technical process, but the designer also has to make these technical limits of size and compatibility clear to the users. Thumbnail sketches can show these spatial constraints or qualities to the users.

Also, I find it useful to encourage users to think about activity settings as being fixed or adaptable.

SETTINGS FOR THE ACTIVITY ONE WANTS TO DO

LOCATION   SITE CHARACTERISTICS

Peoplescape   Fixed Space   Adaptable Space

Appropriate activity settings, including both location and site characteristics, are frequently mentioned by designers as determinants in planning neighborhood spaces.

When the designer is asked what are the spatial requirements to make a place an appropriate setting for an activity, he must consider the users. A 50-by-50-foot corner may be excellent for small children to play baseball, but adults may require a regulation-sized field.

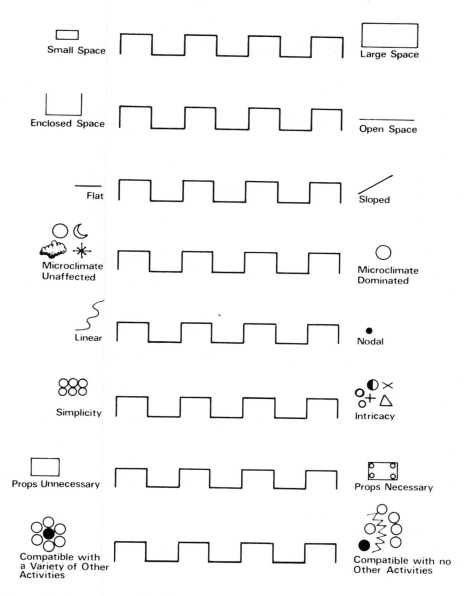

Small Space — Large Space

Enclosed Space — Open Space

Flat — Sloped

Microclimate Unaffected — Microclimate Dominated

Linear — Nodal

Simplicity — Intricacy

Props Unnecessary — Props Necessary

Compatible with a Variety of Other Activities — Compatible with no Other Activities

Continuums of Characteristics of Fixed and Adaptable Spaces

The site characteristics, although standardized by designers, often will be perceived differently by users. For instance, a space the designer considers small may be monstrous to a young child.

Another aspect of appropriate activity settings is the peoplescape—the part of a space that is enhanced by the presence of people with whom the user has no personal interaction.

Fixed space limits the use of that place to appropriate activities. For example, tennis requires a special space, 60 by 120 feet with a hard surface appropriately lined, and special props—a net, balls, and rackets. A space so defined dictates its use. Adaptable space does not dictate its use. As an example, a field with a pile of wood on the edge may be used to fly a kite, build a fort, play volleyball, or do a variety of other activities. The dichotomy between fixed and adaptable space is somewhat misleading if taken at face value, because fixed space does not mean fixed and restricted as in an architectural structure; rather, the user is given direction in the use of the space. This

clarification is necessary because neighborhood open space allows people to act more freely than architectural spaces,[12] and the terms "fixed" and "adaptable" are simply ends of a continuum within that definition. As an example, although a tennis court is considered a fixed space, more open-ended activities can occur there than in a building that has a single purpose. In comparison to buildings, both fixed and adaptable neighborhood open spaces are "adaptable." As a general rule, outdoor neighborhood spaces are most successful when they are as adaptable as possible yet still accommodate the highest priority activity settings of users.

In sum, when considering the appropriate activity settings the designer needs to:

1. Help the users give priorities to their most desired activity settings;
2. Be careful not to impose activity settings that only he wants;
3. Clearly describe guiding principles, or themes, for the site from which users can choose;
4. Show the users which activity settings are incompatible with the site for technical reasons;
5. Offer new ways to organize the activity setting that users have not considered;
6. Describe the important spatial characteristics of the activity settings so the users can make decisions about what can be included.

Relatedness Through Interaction with the Natural Environment

Of the essential reasons that determine people's use of neighborhood space, being able to relate to the natural environment emerges as an important concept. Students continually make remarks like this: I go there to get myself together, to see ducks flying, to watch clouds, to relax, to see what is real after a hectic day, to chase butterflies, to sit in the same grassy spot everyday and watch the sun set. I come away with a better feeling about myself and others. Such relatedness has historically been a major consideration in the design of open spaces since landscape architecture is grounded in a reverence for a oneness betweeen man and nature.[13] But psychologists support the concept as well, formulating theories that incorporate both the natural and the human environment.[14]

To accommodate both the physical and psychological aspects of relatedness, Harold F. Searles suggested a concept that included both landscape design and applied psychological theory. He defined this concept as "relatedness through interaction with the natural environment." Searles said that related-ness involves a sense of intimate kinship with nature and a sense of personal identity apart from nature, and he implied a dynamic balance between them. He identified four components of this concept that he described as the "benefits of positive relatedness" with the natural environment: easing painful and anxiety-laden states of feeling, fostering self-realization, deepening perceptions of reality, and fostering appreciation and acceptance of one's fellowmen.[15] His research indicated that "relatedness with the non-human environment is critical in fostering healthy child development"[16] and adult mental health.[17] This is corroborated by the frequency with which people, especially elementary-school and college students, mention this concept as being important in their use of neighborhood space.

Safety

People also choose to use neighborhood spaces on the basis of safety factors. These include both physical and social dimensions. Physical safety includes "facility" considerations such as the proper location of activity settings to prevent dangerous situations from arising and special settings like barriers and signs. The improper placement of a tot play area next to a baseball field would prevent its use when a baseball game was being played; or the lack of a guardrail around a lake might prevent a handicapped person from enjoying a walk by the water. In addition, maintenance to prevent harmful accidents is a critical part of physical safety.[18] People will be disinclined to use a space if there is trash or unrepaired equipment, as the following response indicates: "We never go there because there is broken glass where the kids want to play."

Other typical responses concerning physical safety include: "I never take the kids there because I'm afraid they will get hit by a baseball" and "That's a nice safe place; there are fences separating the fields from the children's play equipment. . . yes, we go there often."

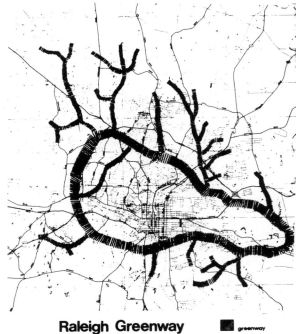

Raleigh Greenway   ■ greenway

Many cities have recognized the importance of relatedness through interaction with the natural environment and have set aside large greenways, not for active recreation but for quiet contemplation.

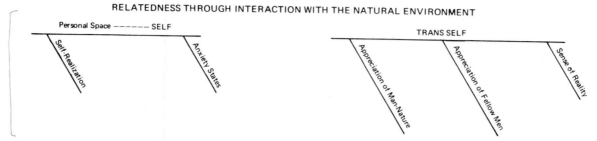

Relatedness with the natural environment fosters self-realization, relieves anxiety states, and enriches an appreciation of man and nature, an appreciation of one's fellow men, and a sense of reality.

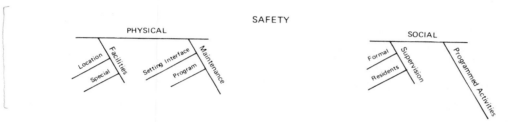

People often choose to use neighborhood spaces on the basis of safety factors, including both physical and social dimensions.

For some people, the social aspect of safety has become their overwhelming concern. Due to the steady increase in crime, it is now a key factor in the use of open space in large, city neighborhoods,[19] especially for lower-class and elderly people. Both supervision and programmed activities affect safety. In some cases formal supervision by park leaders or police is used to guarantee safety. In other cases, as in the North End of Boston, informal supervision by local residents from windows above the street is more conducive to safety.[20] In addition, special events or programmed activities that bring people into neighborhood spaces throughout the day and night tend to increase the feeling of safety because the presence of others acts as a deterrent to crime. The need for security seems to be greater "in the ill than in the well, in the unpropertied than in the propertied, in the omega fish than in the alpha, in the unstable society than in the stable."[21]

In spite of the need for safety, the provisions necessary for safety may impede some activities. Teen hanging out,[22] private conversations, and solitude may be discouraged by supervision or programmed activities, and adventure play may be discouraged by over-maintenance. Therefore, conflicts can be expected between various users over what is a safe environment. It is important to remember, especially in conflict situations, that safety incorporates the social-interaction processes of territoriality and dominance, and interaction and activity variations. Attention to these will help determine the appropriate balance of supervision and programmed activities.

In the North End of Boston, informal supervision by local residents from windows above the street helps create a safe neighborhood.

Aesthetic Appeal

Aesthetic appeal is another quality that may invite people to use neighborhood space. Aesthetics has long been a fundamental consideration for designers, who frequently assume they must train the layman to see beauty by shaping his "powers of awareness."[23] The designer often resorts to selling his personal or

professional taste or style with the idea of winning a design award.[24] (Style is what is considered fashionable in a culture at a given time; taste is an individual or group preference for a certain aesthetic quality.) In addition, many designers have decried the loss of grace and beauty as neighborhood space has become more practical, functional, and user oriented. These changes, in fact, show that users have their own ideas about what is beautiful and useful, for instance: "What do you mean, we need art like a hole in the head. We want a fence."[25] Such a statement may more crudely, but accurately, typify the feelings of neighborhood users. How a place looks is certainly important to users, but on their terms.

Another aspect of aesthetic appeal is visual unity, that is, a clear sense of the whole, sequence compatibility, stimuli balance, and cleanliness. These components of visual unity are dicussed at length in other sources,[26] so the terms need only to be defined here. A sense of the whole exists when the user perceives that the spaces, colors, forms, and textures are complete, in harmony, and balanced.[27] Sequence compatibility extends this sense of harmony to the three-dimensional linear manner in which a neighborhood is viewed;[28] it is not one pattern by itself but a pattern developing into other patterns viewed in various sequences. The balance of stimuli among new and old visual experiences is important because some of the security of the familiar is necessary for a person to enjoy new visual stimuli, although different people and groups prefer different degrees of visual arousal at different times.[29] Recently, the residents of the Inman Square neighborhood in Cambridge, Massachusetts, were confronted by a design proposal that was inconsistent with their aesthetic views. A designer proposed a sculpture for the square that he said reflected the chaos of the intersection. The residents wanted something more subdued and in harmony with the neighborhood. A public debate ensued.

Finally, the visual aspect of cleanliness refers to the lack of the negative stimuli of trash and clutter. A number of studies indicate that reducing trash and

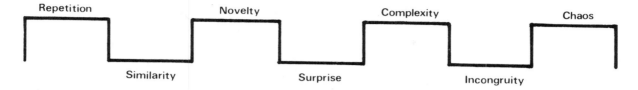

Repetition		Novelty		Complexity		Chaos
	Similarity		Surprise		Incongruity	

Continuum of Stimuli Balance

The balance of visual stimuli is important to users; repetition of stimuli is boring, and overly complex stimuli create chaos in the mind's eye.

What may be the apple of a designer's eye may not appeal at all to the users of a neighborhood space.

AESTHETIC APPEAL

APPROPRIATENESS
Taste   Style

VISUAL UNITY
Sequence Compatibility   Stimuli Balance   Sense of Whole   Cleanliness

Users identify six components of aesthetic appeal: taste, style, sequence compatibility, stimuli balance, sense of the whole, and cleanliness.

clutter eliminates negative tensions that interfere with a person's visual enjoyment of a space.[30]

In general, designers seldom relate the concept of aesthetic appeal to the needs of specific users. We have assumed that good aesthetics was within the domain of our professional expertise and was not a matter for users to decide. Recent experiments indicate that users do want to make aesthetic decisions, and a new challenge for designers is to objectively show users the choices rather than imposing one style.

Convenience

Convenience is another factor that people consider in their use of neighborhood space. It is a balancing of availability and desirability. A 5-minute walk to the corner drugstore may be considered convenient; a 10-minute drive to play tennis may be considered convenient; a 3-hour train trip to snow ski may be considered convenient. A person may say that each is near because he is balancing his

CONVENIENCE

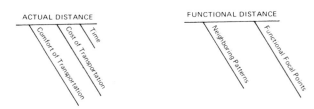

ACTUAL DISTANCE   FUNCTIONAL DISTANCE

There are two dimensions of convenience that are important to users: actual distance and functional distance.

desire to do the activity with the availability of that activity. Typical user responses in regard to convenience include:

The gasoline crisis has made us aware of how convenient it is to go to the neighborhood park; we can walk. We bike to the store because it is so close. It's near our friend's house and it costs us nothing. I never go to Chávez Park because it's on the edge of the neighborhood, far away from everything.

The major consideration is the distance from one's home. Distance is a function of time and mode of transportation and can be described in actual or functional terms. Actual distance is measured in feet or blocks or miles from home; functional distance is measured in relation to neighborhood focal points or neighboring patterns.[31] To illustrate, although one picnic place may be closer to home in terms of blocks, another will be used because it is located on a pedestrian greenway that is frequented on trips to the corner shopping area. Similarly, a playground located three blocks from home may be used more often than one located one block away because of proximity to a funtional focal point like a friend's house. In both of these examples, functional distance determines convenience. Also, considerations of *actual* time, comfort, and cost are replaced by

perceived time, comfort, and cost. Because convenience includes these individual perceptions, this concept incorporates the social factor of psychological comfort. It also incorporates interaction variations and physical comfort.

Psychological Comfort

In choosing to use neighborhood space, people are also influenced by the psychological comfort that they experience in that space. The users surveyed indicated at least three components of psychological comfort: emotional release, social reinforcement, and balance between old and new choices.

People frequently describe their use of a neighborhood space for emotional release in these terms: "I need to get away from it all sometimes, otherwise I would lose my mind." "I go there to blow off steam." "The park is a place where I can get out a lot of hostilities that build up in the office." These appear to be needs that neighborhood open space in some measure satisfies. In a similar manner, neighborhood space provides many users with a chance for the informal, peer-group reinforcement that is necessary for the feeling of belonging to a group, of being loved and accepted, and of being respected as a unique individual. Such reinforcement is also required for a person to develop a sense of social safety. These feelings contribute to a person's psychological comfort and reinforce the desire to use a certain neighborhood space:

I go to the playground to play basketball. The guys respect me; I'm the best on the block.

We hang out there. You know we're a real close gang, and we take care of each other.

I feel comfortable in the park. Some of the people there are friends, and that makes me feel completely safe.

In addition, there appears to be a need for a balance of old, secure choices and new experiences for a person to feel psychologically comfortable in a

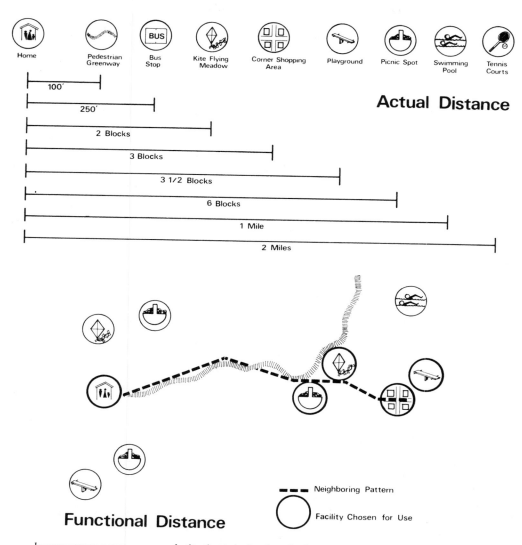

Actual Distance

100'

250'

2 Blocks

3 Blocks

3 1/2 Blocks

6 Blocks

1 Mile

2 Miles

Functional Distance

- - - Neighboring Pattern

◯ Facility Chosen for Use

In many cases, a person uses a facility that is farther from his home than a similar facility because it is located on the pathway he frequently walks. In such cases, the functional distance to that facility is shorter.

neighborhood space. This is similar to the concept of visual security and new experiences discussed earlier in this chapter under aesthetic appeal, except in this case, the discussion focuses on activity choices rather than on visual experiences. The following responses are often mentioned: "We go there to picnic but we always discover something new," "I feel uncomfortable because there are so many things to do," and "The kids don't like to go to that park because there is nothing to do except swing."

PSYCHOLOGICAL COMFORT

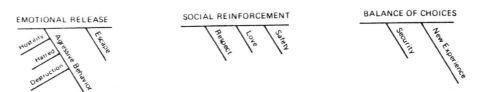

Users indicate that there are at least three important components of psychological comfort: emotional release, social reinforcement, and balance of choices.

Want

Need

Continuum of Want - Needs

Designers are constantly confronted with the problem of distinguishing between wants and needs. Is the provision for a shelter in a park a need of the users, or is it simply a physical comfort that is desirable but not necessary?

PHYSICAL COMFORT

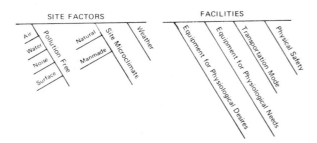

To provide for the users' physical comfort, the designer can manipulate both the site factors and special facilities.

Physical Comfort

Physical comfort, another factor in one's choice of neighborhood space, involves both site factors and facilities and incorporates the social factors of comfort and usable space. One crucial site factor is the weather. Weather considerations such as solar angle, temperature, humidity, precipitation, and wind direction and force are typically studied in the planning of a space because favorable conditions will increase use. In spite of an extreme climate in a particular region, the comfort range for people may be met by the "microclimate" of a specific space. Lynch describes

The designer can make a place comfortable to sit in by careful attention to materials, orientation, and surroundings.

how within a given general climate there may be surprising variations from site to site due to vegetative cover, water, and topography. He notes that wind speed, solar access, noise, and temperature may vary markedly within a few feet of elevation, and that a site planner must pay close attention to these effects because they are not recorded in official data.[32]

Just as the natural variations in topography, cover, wind speed, and temperature can alter a microclimate, so can man-made modifications improve the climatic conditions of a space. People often comment on the value of shelters, trees, and building orientation:

> We need a shelter to get out of the sun and rain and to break the wind. That would be a big improvement.
> I go to the nature trail because it's cooler there since the city planted trees along both sides of the stream.
> In winter, the kids play in that little pocket that gets sun because it warms up when the playground is freezing cold.

In these examples, special provisions for physical comfort are added incentives to use a space.

A second site characteristic that contributes to physical comfort is the lack of pollution, including surface, water, air, and noise pollution. Each factor must be kept below a certain threshold for physical comfort. By preserving a natural vegetative buffer to prevent the siltation of a swimming hole, providing trees to remove air pollution, increasing maintenance to remove park litter, or building mounds with shrubs to screen out noise, a designer can produce a more comfortable space. If he does not, people frequently will not use the space as planned.

Physical comfort can also be enhanced by adequate facilities for transportation and safety as well as equipment for basic physiological needs. Potential users may be disinclined to go to a space if the means of transportation are uncomfortable. Hot, overcrowded buses or narrow, unshaded sidewalks may prevent use of neighborhood space in the summer. Also, certain people will be more inclined to use a space if safety facilities such as warning signs, guard rails, rounded edges, and soft surfaces are appropriately placed. Furthermore, people will choose spaces that meet their physiological needs through the careful placement of drinking fountains, toilets, food stands, benches with backs, and ramps.

Symbolic Ownership

A survey of users has indicated that symbolic ownership of neighborhood space will increase the

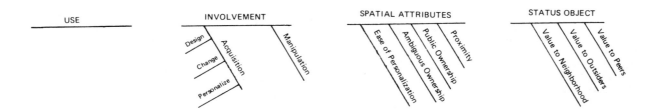

Users indicate that the more one uses a space, the more one comes to consider the space his own. And if a person participates in acquiring or changing the space, his sense of owning it increases. Symbolic ownership will also increase if the space has appropriate physical traits and is viewed as a status object by other people.

use of that space. The factors that tend to increase such a sense of symbolic ownership are identical to those discussed in Chapter 2, which described design application of various aspects of symbolic ownership. A review of this concept, from the user's point of view, indicates that symbolic ownership increases:

1. When one uses a space frequently. The more one uses the space, the more one comes to consider it one's "own";
2. When one participates in the acquisition, design, or redesign of a space;
3. When the space is perceived as a status object by others;
4. When legal ownership is ambiguous and public;
5. When the space is personalized by the user;
6. When a person lives close to a neighborhood space.

Responses such as the following are typical of those expressing symbolic ownership:

The park is ours because we use it all the time. It's our turf.

We worked hard to get them to close that street. It was a year before the city agreed and another year before the parks' people put in the equipment. Now they want to tear it down.

It's a keen playground. The mayor came to cut the ribbon. Architects come all the time. People from the other side of town come on weekends. It's the best playground in the city. I'm glad it's ours.

Policy on Use

Frequently, a person is confronted in neighborhood spaces with signs such as these:

No ball playing
No soliciting
No alcoholic beverages
No parking
No bike riding
No swimming
No dogs

No entrance
No loitering
No littering
Keep out
Private property
No pedestrians beyond this point
No entrance after dark

Signs like these are somewhat less frequent:

Basketball tournament June 10, 11, 12
Street dance Saturday night
Neighborhood craft fair, October 8, 9
Supervised play from 10 A.M.-3 P.M.
Mixed volleyball every Sunday

Such official rules and regulations regarding the use of neighborhood space affect residents both by enabling policies that permit and encourage activities and restrictive policies that prohibit activities. Equally important are the informal policies established by various neighborhoods themselves: "The puppet man and the lady on the corner always run the teenagers off the courts at night," "Thursday nights the grown-ups play softball," or "Kids aren't allowed when the old folks are meeting at the corner."

Although policy on use is seldom mentioned by people as the most important consideration in their use of neighborhood spaces, rules and regulations indirectly influence safety, convenience, symbolic ownership, the people one wants to do an activity with or without, and cost.

POLICY ON USE

Rules, regulations, and other policies affect the use of spaces not only by permitting and encouraging certain activities but also by prohibiting other activities.

Cost

In the minds of people using neighborhood spaces, the cost consideration is simple: the cost that is lowest is best. There may be costs for transportation and admission to the facility, but from the users' point of view these costs are relatively minor because neighborhood space is usually within walking distance and free of charge. Although the major costs related to neighborhood space are for acquisition and construction, these are not normally reflected in a direct user cost.

COST

ADMISSION   TRANSPORTATION

In the minds of people using neighborhood spaces, the cost consideration is simple: the lowest cost is best.

Summary

By continually asking the question, "Why do people use neighborhood space?", we have derived a checklist directly from user needs. Since the user-needs checklist includes the major social factors, the checklist can be applied in neighborhood planning to the extent that the social factors have been. More complete applications can be expected since the user-needs checklist is more inclusive than the social factors that are being applied to design.[33]

RELATIVE IMPORTANCE OF USER NEEDS

After identifying the user needs, the designer is faced with uncertainty about which user needs are the most important in various situations. Is the concept of people one wants to do an activity with or without more important than aesthetics? Is psychological comfort more important than appropriate activity settings? The safest answer is that the designer must discover the idiosyncratic priorities in each separate situation. However, a few preliminary observations can be reported.

Studies indicate that the importance of various user needs varies according to life-cycle stage and class differences. Elderly people give major consideration to the people with or without whom they desire to do an acitivity, but safety is almost as important to them. The actual physical setting is clearly secondary to the elderly. Middle-class college students say that people to do an activity with or without, relatedness through interaction with the natural environment, and symbolic ownership are the most important factors influencing their use of neighborhood space. Lower-class college students likewise consider "people" important, but rank safety—a concern on the part of women—and psychological comfort higher than middle-income college students. Elementary school children say that people, appropriate activity settings, and relatedness are their highest priorities, whereas preschool children consider

CONCEPTS	RANK	General Users	Designers
People one wishes to do an activity with or without	1	6
Settings for the activity one wants to do	2	1
Relatedness through interaction with the natural environment	3	4
Safety	4	3
Aesthetic appeal	5	2
Psychological comfort	6	7
Symbolic ownership	7	9
Physical comfort	8	5
Convenience	9	8
Policy on use	10	12
Cost to use	11	----
Cost of construction	----	10
Definition of space	----	11
Construction methods	----	13

Designers and users frequently do not consider the same factors in planning and using a space. Although designers give careful attention to the cost of construction, the definition of space, and the construction methods, these are almost never considered by users.[34]

appropriate activity settings the most important by far. For all groups, safety, symbolic ownership, convenience, and physical comfort appear to have a stronger latent than direct influence on use. For the lower-class college students, aesthetic appeal has a similar latent effect.[35] These studies indicate that there

CONCEPTS	RANK	Elderly	Middle Class College Students	Lower Class College Students	Elementary School Children	Day Care Children
People one wants to do an activity with or without	1	1	1	1	3
Settings for the activity one wants to do	3	6	4	2	1
Relatedness through interaction with the natural environment	6	2	6	4	2
Safety	2	7	2	5	6
Aesthetic appeal	5	5	5	6	5
Convenience	9	9	10	10	4
Psychological comfort	10	4	3	3	---
Physical comfort	7	8	7	8	---
Symbolic ownership	4	3	8	7	---
Policy on use	8	10	9	9	---
Cost	11	11	11	11	---

The needs of various users vary according to life-cycle stage and class differences.[36]

is considerable variation in the importance of the user-needs concepts from situation to situation. The designer, simply by knowing that his own values may be different from those of the users, can be more sensitive and open to such differences in the planning and design process.

APPLICATION OF USER NEEDS TO THE DESIGN PROCESS

After a designer has decided that it is important to use a checklist of user needs, he is confronted with the task of fitting this new information into his design

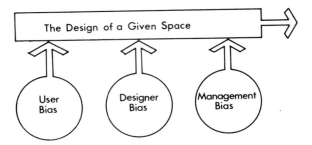

In the design of any space, the opinions or biases of many participants are incorporated; the needs of the users, although a primary consideration, are only one set of factors that may conflict with other factors.

process. One step-by-step approach for site planning with people is described in detail in Chapter 5. Here we are concerned, however, with the general ways of applying user needs.

User needs, when considered as design criteria, will often conflict with the manager's or owner's criteria or the designer's own criteria, complicating the design process. For example, the user-needs criteria may suggest that closing a street would solve a particular neighborhood recreation problem. The designer discovers that the city manager thinks an additional policeman would solve the problem, and the city traffic engineer opposes closing any streets. The designer himself would like to design a park to solve the problem. He faces a personal dilemma as well as the responsibility of resolving the conflicts.

Conflicts also arise because residents often view the neighborhood design process as part of an ongoing, user-oriented community-development process. Although the design of a particular neighborhood space may have a clear beginning and end point in the eyes of the designer, no such distinction exists for the users. For them, the designed space is just as dynamic after it is finished as was the problem that originally led to the design of the space. The designed space has to be maintained, policed, and changed to accommodate changing users. To consider such

complex and dynamic long-term needs adds difficulty to the design process. In addition, the design of a neighborhood space may be only a means to another end and not an end in itself. For instance, residents may consider the acquisition of a neighborhood park as a transition strategy to achieve neighborhood support for an expressway fight.

Many conflicts can be avoided if the designer can discover the relevant user needs at the appropriate times in the design process. Such information is an important consideration in the steps of problem definition, data gathering, program formulation, site selection, and form giving. The user needs of people, appropriate activity settings, convenience, safety, and policy on use are necessary considerations in defining the problem. In combination with these, symbolic ownership needs to be considered prior to programming. All these factors, in addition to aesthetic appeal, relatedness, psychological comfort, and physical comfort, should be considered in writing the design program. These same factors become part of the site-selection process; the form-giving synthesis step is influenced by cost in addition to the above-mentioned user needs.

A special consideration, the need for long-term flexibility, complicates the design process for new neighborhoods. In the design of new communities, neighborhood open space is only one of many components to be provided for; housing, open space, transportation, commercial facilities, and other neighborhood services must also be considered. Because no residents are present, it is impossible to ask the users what will be socially suitable. One design solution is to provide a flexible framework of neighborhood space that the new residents can then change to suit their needs. Potential user needs must be anticipated and weighed against the capability of the land unit being developed.

Several new town plans have dealt with this complex process and serve as excellent models for such neighborhood open-space development. Columbia, Maryland provided both a front- and back-door, linear, open-space system that links the entire community.

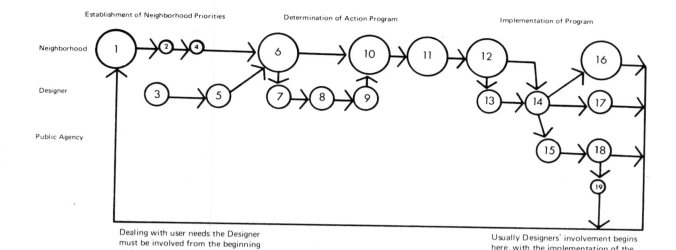

Establishment of Neighborhood Priorities

Determination of Action Program

Implementation of Program

Neighborhood

Designer

Public Agency

Dealing with user needs the Designer must be involved from the beginning and continually throughout the process

Usually Designers' involvement begins here, with the implementation of the program (see the generalized neighborhood space design process, all of which fits under implementation of the program)

1. Neighborhood organizes around problem
2. Neighborhood defines its want needs
3. Neighborhood requests design-planning assistance
4. Neighborhood establishes priorities
5. Designer-planner commits self to problem
6. Neighborhood expands organization
7. Designer-planner inventories priorities
8. Designer-planner makes social analysis
9. Designer-planner makes ecological analysis
10. Designer-planner presents alternatives

11. Neighborhood defines plan of action
12. Neighborhood communicates action
13. Designer-planner determines specific program
14. Designer-planner designs facility
15. Public agency administers plan
16. Neighborhood expands action
17. Designer-planner evaluates action taken
18. Public agency constructs facility
19. Public agency programs facility

THE DESIGN OF NEIGHBORHOOD SPACE AS A PART OF AN ONGOING COMMUNITY DEVELOPMENT PROCESS

When the designer considers the idiosyncratic needs of the users, he must be involved from the beginning and continually throughout the problem-solving process.

A. Problem Definition

B. Data Gathering
    1. Activity and Interaction Sets
    2. Land Unit Capability Sets (In terms of housing, neighborhood
        open space, transportation, neighborhood shopping and other
        neighborhood services)
    3. Economic Constraint Sets
4. Land Unit Suitability Sets (in terms of housing, neighborhood open
    space, transportation, neighborhood shopping and other neighborhood services)
5. Land Unit Feasibility Sets (in terms of housing, neighborhood open
    space, transportation, neighborhood shopping and other neighborhood services)

C. Data Analysis
    6. Activity and Interaction Sets
    7. Land Unit Feasibility Sets (in terms of housing, neighborhood
        open space, transportation, neighborhood shopping and other
        neighborhood services)
    8. Economic Constraint Sets

D. Program Formulation (Criteria for activity, interaction, land unit
    feasibility and economic sets)
9. Regulatory Constraints
10. Designer's Aesthetic Bias
11. Designer's Functional Creativity

E. Form Giving Synthesis
    12. Form Alternative Rejected
    13. Form Alternative Rejected
    14. Form Alternative Chosen
15. Client Acceptance and Financing Commitment

F. Regulation Approval

G. Working Documents
    16. Working Drawings
    17. Specifications
    18. Contract Documents
    19. Bids and Contracts

H. Construction by Contractor

I. Marketing

J. Evaluation

Given a land unit that is being planned for new development, the planner must consider not only the needs of a projected but unknown population, but also the whole range of land uses within the limits imposed by the capability, suitability, and feasibility of the land itself. One way to project the needs of the unknown population is to make assumptions about who the population will be; describe that population in terms of age, class, etc.; try to determine their most critical needs in terms of activities; and translate these activitiy needs into a program.

STEP BY STEP INPUT OF USER NEEDS INFORMATION INTO THE DESIGN PROCESS GIVEN
AN UNDEVELOPED LAND UNIT

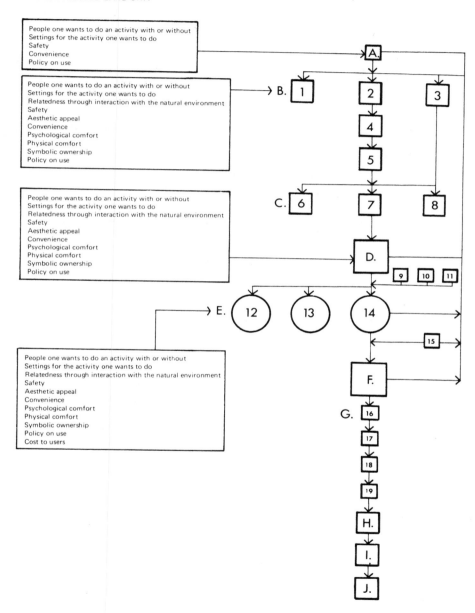

GIVEN A LAND UNIT . . .

ANALYSIS STEPS	LAND USE	Transportation	Housing	Neighborhood Open Space	Commercial Facilities	Other Neighborhood Services
Land Use Capability						
Land Use Suitability						
Land Use Feasibility						

LAND UNIT POTENTIAL

USER NEEDS	CHARACTERISTICS OF FUTURE POPULATION	Life Cycle Stage	Class	Life Style	Sex	Region	Ethnicity
People I want to do an activity with or without							
Settings for the activities I want to do							
Relatedness through interaction with the natural environment							
Safety							
Aesthetic Appeal							
Convenience							
Psychological comfort							
Physical comfort							
Ownership							
Policy on use							
Cost							

ACTIVITY SETS BASED ON USER NEEDS
PROJECTED FOR FUTURE POPULATION

When the designer plans a neighborhood for an undeveloped land unit, he is faced with the problem of projecting who the users will be and what their needs will be.

Automobile use tends to orient to the front of the house while pedestrian and bicycle use orients to the back. But orientation is not fixed as a result of the design, which allows for changing user needs based on changes in the residents' life-cycle stage, class, and so on. Such flexibility emphasizes social suitability in the design of new neighborhoods.

IDENTIFICATION OF USER-NEEDS PERFORMANCE STANDARDS

If user needs are to be applied to the design of neighborhood space, they must be translated into a form that allows the designer to focus on the essential information that can be gathered and measured.

To determine what essential recreation-needs information could be gathered and measured, Richard S. Wurman outlined a series of performance standards for recreation. These standards—a projected measure of how well an environment will respond to the needs of the users—are in the form of checklists of the user-needs factors that a designer should consider before creating a recreation facility. Wurman suggests that activities be looked at in terms of the following performance standards:

Is the activity active or inactive?

Is the activity for an individual or a group?

Is the activity for the young or the old?

Does the activity require a specific space and equipment?

Does the activity require a linear or non-linear space?

Does the activity require a flat or sloped terrain?

How frequently does the activity need to be provided for?

Does the activity require specific movement and service systems?

Does the activity require special safety and comfort facilities?

Is the activity strongly affected by time, weather, and temperature?

Does the activity need a natural setting?

Does the activity require special maintenance?[37]

Instead of considering design as a function of everything, Wurman focuses on the most important user-needs information that the designer needs to know. If the designer lacks an answer, he must gather that information directly from the potential users. For example, if the designer is considering boccie as a major activity but does not know what age groups will use the facility, he must get that information from the residents. If he finds that teenagers, young adults, and the elderly play boccie, he must discover how frequently people play and how many boccie areas are needed to prevent conflicts over their use. He must determine what special movement and sitting patterns are associated with the game. The designer then hypothesizes that boccie is played in a certain pattern and requires certain special provisions. These hypotheses are actually performance standards, a projected measure of how well an environment will respond to the needs of the users.[38]

By using a checklist of performance standards, the designer can define activity settings in terms of the essential user-needs components and evaluate various design alternatives before they are built. Wurman states that, by concentrating on the essential needs, designers can avoid creating an inappropriate product such as providing "beautiful light poles, when the issue is lighting," concerning ourselves with "building playgrounds, when our real need is for recreational opportunities,"[39] or providing a boccie area with no seating nearby, when the need is for the game around which elderly men can gather and talk.

Wurman's approach suggests that user needs can be translated into performance standards that are useful in planning and designing recreational facilities, but these standards do not represent a user-needs framework for nonrecreational activities. The performance standards must be expanded to include all the potential neighborhood-space activities: work, political, educational, and circulation activities as

Design = f(everything)

By expanding Wurman's performance standards to include descriptions of work, political, educational, and circulation activities as well as recreational activities, the designer might list all the activities

ACTIVITY	USER NEEDS PERFORMANCE STANDARDS	PEOPLE ONE WANTS TO DO AN ACTIVITY WITH/WITHOUT	*This activity is for:*	Preschool children	Elementary children	Adolescents	College Students	Unmarried adults	Young married adults	Married adults with elementary and younger children	Married adults with adolescents	Middle aged adults	Elderly	*Conflicts are likely to occur between:*	Preschool children	Elementary children	Adolescents	College Students	Unmarried adults	Young married adults	Married adults with elementary and younger children	Married adults with adolescents	Middle aged adults	Elderly	*The conflicts make this activity:*	Compatible with no other activities	Compatible with activities for the same age group	Compatible with some activities	*This activity is:*	Sex specific	Not sex specific	Ethnicity specific	Not ethnicity specific	Class specific
Sitting on a park bench																																		
Having a picnic																																		
Playing football																																		
Playing basketball																																		
Swinging in a swing																																		
Fantasy play																																		
Running track																																		
Playing volleyball																																		
Building a secret tree house																																		
Hanging out on a corner																																		
Walking to work																																		
Waiting for a bus																																		
Making a political speech																																		
Playing in a water fountain																																		
Studying nature																																		
Doing an outdoor theatre																																		
Dancing in the street																																		
Having a craft fair																																		
Doing yard work																																		
Watching birds																																		
Working on a car																																		
Talking to your lover																																		
Riding a bike																																		
Walking in the woods alone																																		

the users have said they expect a space to provide and describe each activity in terms of the user needs. This should give a complete picture of each activity and prevent the omission of any one important user need.

Not class specific	*This activity is:*	Likely to be peer specific	Not likely to be peer specific	Likely to be teacher specific	Not likely to be teacher specific	Strongly influenced by the peoplescape	Not influenced by the peoplescape	Enhanced by an audience	Not enhanced by an audience	*This activity requires:*	Privacy	No privacy	Vis-a-vis interactions	Inclusiveness	Exclusiveness	Congruent interactions	Incongruent interactions	Parallel interactions	*This activity encourages:*	Overcrowding	Little crowding	Territorial behavior	Dominant behavior	*This activity is for:*	One person (1)	Several people (2)	A small group of people (3–25)	A large group of people (25–50)	A crowd of people (more than 50)	*This activity requires interaction at:*	Intimate distance	Personal distance	Social distance	Public distance	SETTINGS FOR THE ACTIVITY ONE WANTS TO DO	*This activity requires:*	A small space	A medium sized space	A large space	An enclosed space	A partially enclosed space	An open space

USER NEEDS PERFORMANCE STANDARDS

Column headings:
- A flat space
- A sloped space
- A steep sloped space
- A linear space
- A nodal space
- A simple space
- An intricate space
- Props
- No props
- A fixed space
- An adaptable space
- *This activity is:*
- Compatible with a variety of other activities
- Compatible with no other activities
- Unaffected by microclimate
- Dominated by microclimate
- RELATEDNESS THROUGH INTERACTION W/NATURAL ENV.
- *This activity requires:*
- A natural environment
- A man-made environment
- *This activity fosters:*
- Relatedness through interaction with the natural environment
- No relatedness
- SAFETY
- *This activity requires:*
- A special location to be safe
- Any location to be safe
- Special facilities to be safe
- No special facilities to be safe
- Normal maintenance to be safe
- Special maintenance to be safe
- Resident supervision to be safe
- Special supervision to be safe

ACTIVITY

Activity
Sitting on a park bench
Having a picnic
Playing football
Playing basketball
Swinging in a swing
Fantasy play
Running track
Playing volleyball
Building a secret tree house
Hanging out on a corner
Walking to work
Waiting for a bus
Making a political speech
Playing in a water fountain
Studying nature
Doing an outdoor theatre
Dancing in the street
Having a craft fair
Doing yard work
Watching birds
Working on a car
Talking to your lover
Riding a bike
Walking in the woods alone

| Special programs to be safe |
| *This activity:* |
| Encourages user conflicts |
| Discourages user conflicts |
| Encourages vandalism |
| Discourages vandalism |
| **AESTHETIC APPEAL** |
| *This activity:* |
| Dictates its own aesthetic style |
| Can incorporate the style desired by the users |
| Can incorporate the taste of the users |
| Can not incorporate the taste of the users |
| Contributes to a sense of visual unity |
| Takes away from a sense of visual unity |
| **CONVENIENCE** |
| *This activity should be located:* |
| Within a block of home |
| Within walking distance of home |
| Near school |
| Near other functional focal points |
| Within the paths of neighboring patterns |
| Anywhere in the city |
| Elsewhere |
| *This activity requires:* |
| A specific circulation system |
| No specific circulation system |
| **PSYCHOLOGICAL COMFORT** |
| *This activity:* |
| Allows emotional release |
| Does not allow emotional release |
| Encourages social reinforcement |
| Discourages social reinforcement |
| Offers security |
| Offers new experience |
| **PHYSICAL COMFORT** |
| *This activity requires:* |
| A noise pollution free environment |
| An air pollution free environment |
| A water pollution free environment |
| A surface pollution free environment |
| No pollution free environment |
| Special control of the site microclimate |
| No special control of the site microclimate |

ACTIVITY	USER NEEDS PERFORMANCE STANDARDS	Special facilities for physical comfort	No special facilities for physical comfort	SYMBOLIC OWNERSHIP	*This activity encourages symbolic ownership:*	Through use	Through involvement	Through the provision of status objects	By being in public ownership	By having ambiguous ownership	By being easy to personalize	By being close to home	*This activity discourages symbolic ownership:*	Through use	Through involvement	Through the provision of status objects	By being in public ownership	By having ambiguous ownership	By being easy to personalize	By being close to home	POLICY ON USE	*This activity requires:*	Enabling policies to maximize use	Restrictive policies to maximize use	No policies to maximize use	COST	*This activity requires:*	An admission cost	No admission cost
Sitting on a park bench																													
Having a picnic																													
Playing football																													
Playing basketball																													
Swinging in a swing																													
Fantasy play																													
Running track																													
Playing volleyball																													
Building a secret tree house																													
Hanging out on a corner																													
Walking to work																													
Waiting for a bus																													
Making a political speech																													
Playing in a water fountain																													
Studying nature																													
Doing an outdoor theatre																													
Dancing in the street																													
Having a craft fair																													
Doing yard work																													
Watching birds																													
Working on a car																													
Talking to your lover																													
Riding a bike																													
Walking in the woods alone																													

well as recreational activities. Other questions must be answered to establish a complete set of performance standards:

> Who will participate in the activity? What conflicts are likely to occur and between whom?
>
> Is the activity sex, age, ethnicity, class, peer or teacher specific?
>
> Is the activity strongly influenced by the peoplescape or enhanced by an audience? Does it require privacy? Does it contribute to overcrowding? Is the activity for one person or a crowd or people? Does the activity require interaction at an intimate distance or public distance?
>
> Is the activity compatible with other activities? Does it contribute to relatedness?
>
> Does the activity require special facilities, maintenance, supervision, or programs to be safe? Is it supervised by residents?
>
> Does the activity dictate its own aesthetic style and taste? Does it contribute to a sense of unity?
>
> Should the activity be located in a functional focal point or in the path of a neighboring pattern?
>
> Does the activity allow for emotional release, social reinforcement, security, or new experience?
>
> Does the activity require a pollution-free environment? Does it necessitate special facilities for physical comfort?
>
> Does the activity encourage symbolic ownership through use, involvement, status objects, or ease of personalization? Will its symbolic ownership by one group discourage other people from participating?
>
> Does the activity require changes in the policy on the use of a place?
>
> Does the activity cost money for admission?

The answers to each of these questions must be included to have a complete checklist of user needs and to establish a complete set of performance standards. Although it is unlikely that all these performance standards would provide important design insights in any one situation, the omission of any one user-needs component could be a serious oversight.

Few applications of user-needs performance standards have been recorded, but the design process used for the Fred Olds School Playground in Raleigh illustrates the value of considering user needs in terms of performance standards. After doing extensive studies to determine what activity settings were appropriate (appropriate activity settings had to be established by the users before the performance standards were applied), the designers described the attributes of each activity setting by eleven performance components: physical, human, social, interaction, circulation, convenience, security, comfort, ownership, policy, and developmental. These performance components not only provided a focus for determining what information had to be gathered about various user needs, but also aided the designers directly in locating and designing activity settings.

When the designers first attempted to describe the activities by performance components, it became obvious that they needed more information on the size of space necessary for various child games, on how children interacted in various sized spaces, and on what activities needed to be supervised. The performance standards provided the focus for the additional data that had to be gathered.

The performance standards also provided insights that were directly applicable to the design of the playground. Because one major goal of the project was to allow the children to feel that the playground was their own, the designers explored symbolic ownership in detail. They found that five activities had the greatest potential for symbolic ownership: water play, outdoor theater, construction-component play, basketball, and tennis. Tennis was eliminated because it scored low in terms of user preferences, but the other four activities were designed as major activity focal points that the children could help construct. These activities were included in the first phase of construction.

Another insight gained through the performance standards related to the developmental attributes that

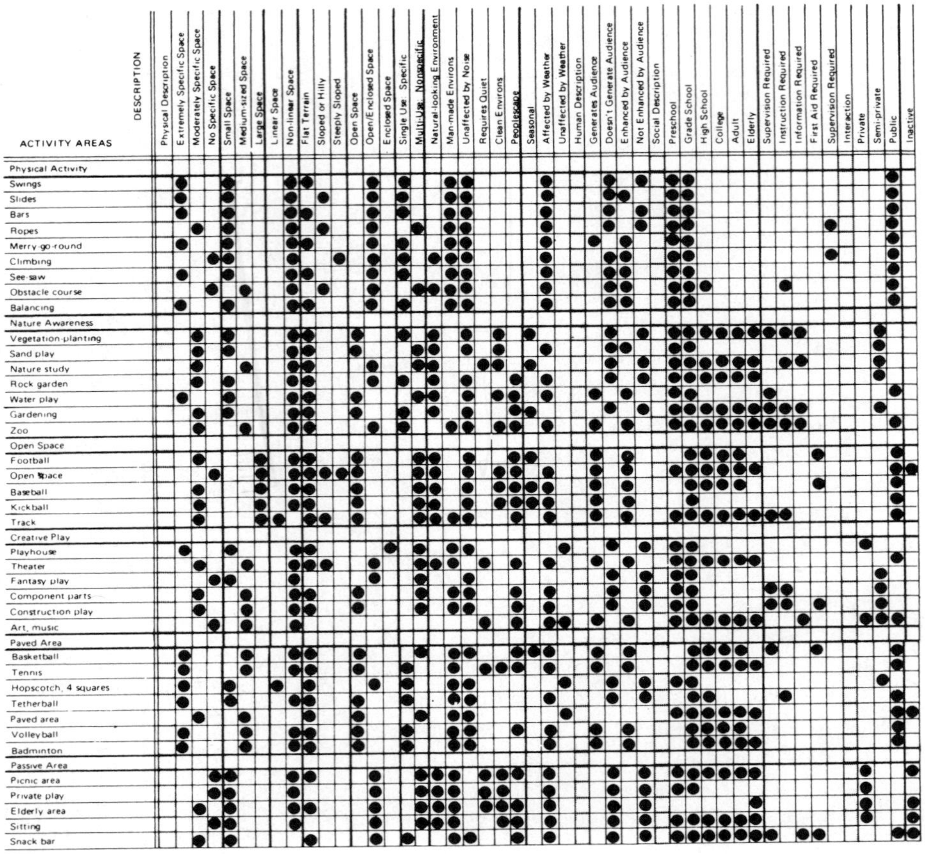
DESCRIPTION
ACTIVITY AREAS
Physical Description
Extremely Specific Space
Moderately Specific Space
No Specific Space
Small Space
Medium-sized Space
Large Space
Linear Space
Non-linear Space
Flat Terrain
Sloped or Hilly
Steeply Sloped
Open Space
Open/Enclosed Space
Enclosed Space
Single Use: Specific
Multi-Use: Nonspecific
Natural-looking Environment
Man-made Environs
Unaffected by Noise
Requires Quiet
Clean Environs
Peoplescape
Seasonal
Affected by Weather
Unaffected by Weather
Human Description
Generates Audience
Doesn't Generate Audience
Enhanced by Audience
Not Enhanced by Audience
Social Description
Preschool
Grade School
High School
College
Adult
Elderly
Supervision Required
Instruction Required
Information Required
First Aid Required
Supervision Required
Interaction
Private
Semi-private
Public
Inactive
Physical Activity
Swings
Slides
Bars
Ropes
Merry-go-round
Climbing
See-saw
Obstacle course
Balancing
Nature Awareness
Vegetation planting
Sand play
Nature study
Rock garden
Water play
Gardening
Zoo
Open Space
Football
Open space
Baseball
Kickball
Track
Creative Play
Playhouse
Theater
Fantasy play
Component parts
Construction play
Art, music
Paved Area
Basketball
Tennis
Hopscotch, 4 squares
Tetherball
Paved area
Volleyball
Badminton
Passive Area
Picnic area
Private play
Elderly area
Sitting
Snack bar

In one application of performance standards, the designers of the Fred Olds School Yard described each desired activity in terms of eleven user needs. This approach not only provided a focus for

the teachers felt were important. Although the children thought that physical activities like swings, slides, monkey bars, and seesaws should be the top priority, the performance standards projected that these activities would have less value for child development than a paved area, a nature study area, or a creative-play area. Therefore, the activities that the children wanted most were designed into the creative-play area, which made it not only the most popular area but also a supplement to the indoor classroom.

The performance standards further showed that a number of significantly different activities, including a picnic area, a private play area, an elderly activity area, and a sitting area, were observed to have surprisingly similar projected characteristics: similar spatial requirements, social and human descriptions, interaction patterns, and developmental attributes. Also, a complementary relationship was observed between this set of passive activities and physical activities, nature-awareness activities, and open-space

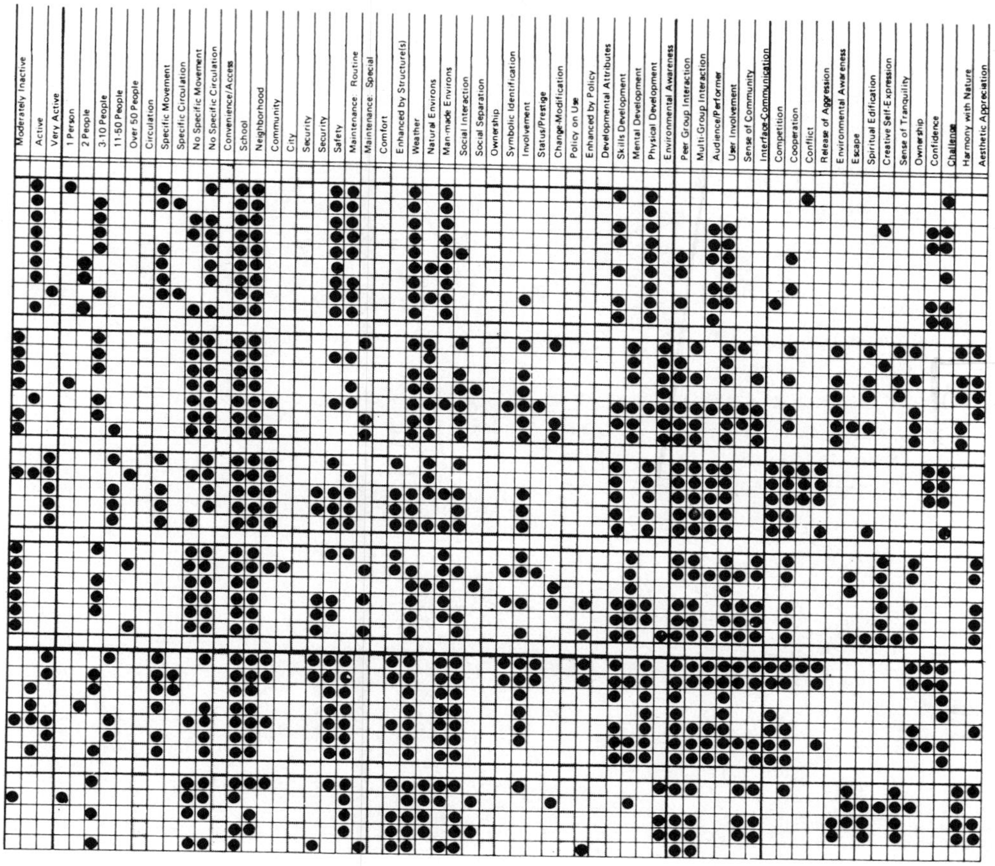

Column headings (left to right):

Moderately Inactive · Active · Very Active · 1 Person · 2 People · 3-10 People · 11-50 People · Over 50 People · Circulation · Specific Movement · Specific Circulation · No Specific Movement · No Specific Circulation · Convenience/Access · School · Neighborhood · Community · City · Security · Safety · Maintenance Routine · Maintenance Special · Comfort · Enhanced by Structure(s) · Weather · Natural Environs · Man-made Environs · Social Interaction · Social Separation · Ownership · Symbolic Identification · Involvement · Status/Prestige · Change-Modification · Policy on Use · Enhanced by Policy · Developmental Attributes · Skills Development · Mental Development · Physical Development · Environmental Awareness · Peer Group Interaction · Multi-Group Interaction · Audience/Performer · User Involvement · Sense of Community · Interface-Communication · Competition · Cooperation · Conflict · Release of Aggression · Environmental Awareness · Escape · Spiritual Edification · Creative Self-Expression · Sense of Tranquility · Ownership · Confidence · Challenge · Harmony with Nature · Aesthetic Appreciation

determining what information had to be gathered, but also aided the designers directly in locating and designing activity settings.

activities. The passive activities, although neither generating an audience nor being enhanced by an audience, could provide the audience and supervision required for the other activities. As a result of this finding, the designers carefully analyzed the other projected uses. They discovered that there existed a similar relationship between sitting and observing and basketball.

These findings were corroborated by a compatibility analysis, a summary of the performance standards in which similar activities are grouped. This analysis indicated that there were (1) distinct activities compatible only with each other, (2) transition activities, (3) activities that could provide linear links, and (4) totally incompatible activities. Although passive activities like sitting and supervising seemed incompatible with active games like basketball and open-field sports, the compatibility analysis verified the complementary relationship. As a result, one passive area was located adjacent to the active areas on the conceptual plan. From the performance standards, the design team projected that the passive area would serve as a private play area for children, as a sitting area, as a place for elderly activities, and as a picnic area for families. In addition, the passive area needed to provide a space suitable for basketball observation for all ages, basketball playing and hanging out for teenagers, teacher supervision of play, and play by children.

Four specific locations were found for such a passive area. Each was evaluated in terms of how well it would respond to the needs of the users, and the best location, that is, the location best satisfying the projected user needs, was chosen. The designers predicted from the performance standards that the passive area chosen would satisfy all the desired activities except those of the elderly.

These examples from the Fred Olds School Playground design process demonstrate how user-needs concepts can be translated into performance standards that can be used to project the social suitability of a given design. Such performance standards can be derived for the design of any neighborhood space. Although specific criteria would vary for a neighborhood shopping center, a teen hangout, or a senior citizens' center, the process of establishing performance standards to evaluate various plans before they are built would be the same. Performance standards, even if derived from a simple checklist to remind the planner of the needs of the users, can be a significant aid in designing neighborhood spaces that respond to the special wants and needs of the users.

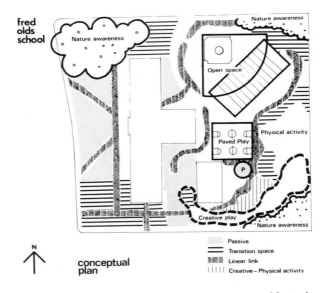

The performance-standard descriptions were compared for each activity to determine which activities were compatible with each other. This indicated that there were (1) distinct activities compatible only with each other, (2) transition activities, (3) activities that could provide linear links, and (4) totally incompatible activities based not only on physical criteria but on user-needs criteria as well. The findings of the compatibility analysis were translated into a conceptual plan.

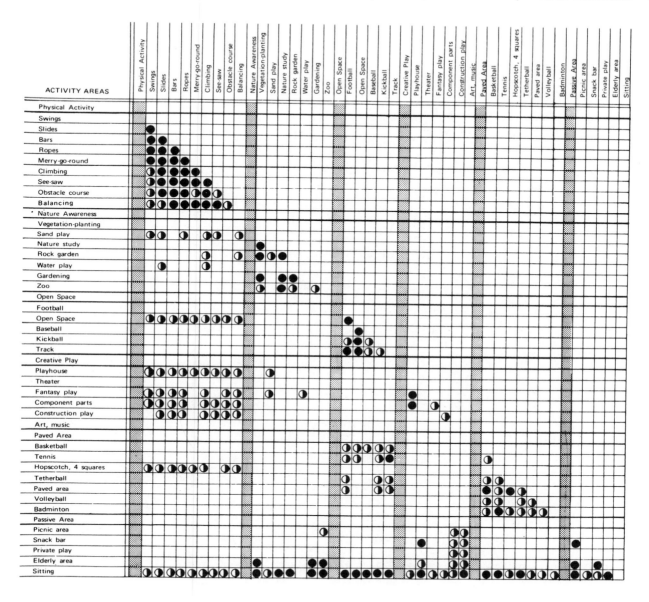

compatibility analysis

● Compatible
◑ Somewhat compatible
Incompatible

fred
olds
school

N

Key

This location satisfies:

1	2	3	4
picnic	viewing	teachers	private
private	picnic	viewing	
elderly	teens	picnic	
	basketball	teens	
	private	basketball	
		private	

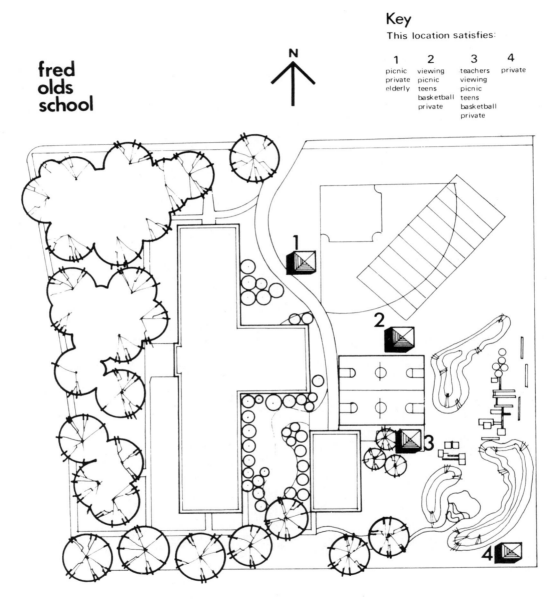

When the designers tried to decide where to locate a passive area that would be used by all age groups, they used the performance standards to predict which location would best satisfy the most users' needs. Location 3 was chosen, and postconstruction evaluations indicate that it does work as the designers predicted from the performance standards, although children use the space more frequently than others.

THINGS FOR YOU TO DO

The following exercises will clarify the issues raised in this chapter. Some will check your understanding of the material; others will help you articulate your own values or give you insights into neighborhood-design issues. You may do these exercises alone, but I would suggest sharing them with others.

1. What user need is consistently the most important in determining the use of neighborhood space?
2. How would you describe to users the impact of changing the interior roof height of a picnic shelter from 8 feet to 12 feet?
3. Draw your ideal neighborhood open space.
   a. What other kinds of people are there with you?
   b. What activities do you do there?
   c. What else is important to you about the space?
4. Diagram your process in carrying out a design project. At what steps do you think user input is valuable? Why?
5. Draw a series of diagrams illustrating settings that might contribute to a sense of privacy in a large neighborhood park.
   a. Do any of your settings create a situation so private as to be isolated?
   b. Who might use such spaces?
6. For a design project you are doing, draw a compatibility matrix for the different activity settings. Are there any new patterns or information that become obvious to you through this process?
7. Imagine yourself as the designer of a neighborhood park for which the residents have requested as flexible and adaptable a space as possible. You are trying to advise them on the merits of different types of furniture. When would it be appropriate to use movable furniture or walls, fixed tables and benches, to provide only grass, or to rent chairs?

NOTES AND REFERENCES

1. Abraham H. Maslow, *New Knowledge in Human Values*, Harper & Row, New York, 1959, p. 122.
2. Undertaken for Community Development Section Evaluation, Cambridge, Mass., 1969-1972.
3. Undertaken for North Carolina State University Research Project 00510, Raleigh, N.C., 1973.
4. The search consisted of a review of the neighborhood space design considerations presented in *Progressive Architecture and Landscape Architecture* from 1969-1973.
5. Undertaken in Psychology 691B Systems Modeling, North Carolina State University, Raleigh, N.C., 1974, under the direction of Dr. Frank J. Smith.
6. Undertaken in DN 212 and LAR 211, North Carolina State University, Raleigh, N.C., and in a seminar at the Department of Landscape Architecture, University of Illinois, Urbana, Ill.
7. Site capability refers to the carrying capacity of the site in its ecological context: for example, how many people can use a site before their use prevents a forest from regenerating itself? This is normally outside the realm of the user's awareness and concern.
8. Albert J. Rutledge, *Anatomy of a Park*, McGraw-Hill, New York, 1971, pp. 54-57.
9. Richard Saul Wurman, Alan Levy, and Joel Katz, with Jean McClintock and Howard Brunner, *The Nature of Recreation; a Handbook in Honor of Frederick Law Olmsted, Using Examples from His Work*, MIT Press, Cambridge, Mass., pp. 32-33.
10. Rutledge, *Anatomy of a Park*, pp. 57-58.
11. Wurman, *Nature of Recreation*, pp. 30-31.
12. Kevin Lynch, *Site Planning*, 2nd ed., MIT Press, Cambridge, Mass., 1971, p. 353.
13. John O. Simonds, *Landscape Architecture*, McGraw-Hill, New York, 1961, pp. 10-14, 75. The theory of landscape architecture presents a concept of man and nature as one, similar to Eastern thought and contrary to the Western attitude of man over nature.
14. Harold F. Searles, *The Non Human Environment in Normal Development and in Schizophrenia*, International Universities Press, New York, 1960, p. 25.
15. Searles, *Non Human Environment*. Searles discussed these ideas in the context of the entire nonhuman environment. I have deleted such considerations as inanimate objects and pets since the idea here appears to be more natural environment oriented. However, I agree with his thesis that the entire nonhuman environment be included.
16. Searles, *Non Human Environment.*, pp. 78-89.
17. This is especially true of dense urban neighborhoods in which little natural environment is available but in which some of the relatedness factors can be accomodated by inanimate environments.

18. Garrett Eckbo, *Urban Landscape Design*, McGraw-Hill, New York, 1964, pp. 231-239.

19. Oscar Newman, *Defensible Space: Crime Prevention Through Urban Design*, Macmillan, New York, 1972.

20. Jane Jacobs, *Death and Life of Great American Cities*, Random House, New York, 1969, pp. 55-73.

21. Robert Ardrey, *The Territorial Imperative*, Atheneum, New York, 1966, p. 335.

22. Paul Friedberg notes the use of the enclosed and unsupervised 'elderly garden of Riis Plaza by teenagers as a prime example of this phenomenon.

23. Rutledge, *Anatomy of a Park*, p. 35.

24. Norma Skurka, "Housing out of Tune with the Times," *New York Times Magazine*, Feb. 24, 1974, p. 75.

25. Simpson F. Lawson, ed., *Workshop on Urban Open Space* U.S. Department of Housing and Urban Development, ASLA 1, Washington, D.C., p. 18

26. Christopher Alexander, *Notes on the Synthesis of Form*, Harvard University Press, Cambridge, Mass., 1964; Rudolf Arnheim, *Art and Visual Perception* University of California Press, Berkeley, Calif., 1954; Stephen Carr, "Some Psychological Functions of Environmental Form," *Course* 11.35, Department of City and Regional Planning, Massachusetts Institute of Technology, Cambridge, Mass., Fall, 1967.

27. Randolph T. Hester, Jr., "Visual Pleasure," *Course Landscape Architecture 56*, Pennsylvania State University, University Park, Pa., Fall, 1969.

28. Peter L. Hornbeck, *Highway Esthetics*, Landscape Architecture Research Office, Graduate School of Design, Harvard University, Cambridge, Mass., 1968.

29. Werner Nohl, "Man's Need for Variation Stimulation," *Course 299*, Department of Landscape Architecture, University of California at Berkeley, Berkeley, Calif., Spring, 1968; Werner Nohl, "Motion: Its Nature and Application in Planning and Designing Open Space," *Course 299*, Department of Landscape Architecture, University of California at Berkeley, Berkeley, Calif., Summer, 1968; Randolph T. Hester, Jr., "A Visual Pleasure Model," unpublished masters thesis, Department of Landscape Architecture, Graduate School of Design, Harvard University, Cambridge, Mass., 1969.

30. Arthur D. Little, Inc., *A Study of Human Response to Visual Environments in Urban Areas*, Cambridge, Mass., May, 1967.

31. Robert Gutman, "Site Planning and Social Behavior," *The Journal of Social Issues*, **22**(4): 103-115. (1966).

32. Lynch, *Site Planning*, p. 17.

33. In addition, the user-needs concepts appear to be more internally consistent and parallel than the social factors, the assumptions underlying the concepts have been made more explicit, and the concepts have been decomposed into the appropriate variables for data collection.

34. North Caroline State University Study.

35. From a study under the direction of Randolph T. Hester, Jr., by Tom Ridgeway and Carol Anne Wilson, North Carolina State University, Raleigh, N.C., Spring, 1974. This study indicates that people do not identify the concept of psychological comfort as being important in itself, but consider the specific components of the concept as being major factors in their use of neighborhood open space.

36. North Carolina State University Study.

37. Wurman, *Nature of Recreation*, pp. 46-47.

38. Wurman, *Nature of Recreation*, p. 19.

39. Wurman, *Nature of Recreation*, p. 18.

4

User-Needs Techniques

To determine which of the various user needs described in Chapter 3 are salient in the design of a particular outdoor space, designers need to involve the potential users in the design process either directly or indirectly. As an example Bill Taylor of Carol R. Johnson and Associates in Cambridge, Massachusetts, used yellow tape to mark the alternative routes for Pedestrian Path East, then sent community members reminders to walk the paths and decide which routes were most suitable.[1]

J. Edward Washington uses another approach in designing neighborhood spaces with first through sixth graders. He has the children make drawings, lists, and models. This is usually done in their neighborhoods since he insists that it is in the streets where you get the childrens' interest.[2]

In this chapter, we shall outline and discuss various specific techniques that designers employ to assess what a space must provide to ensure its social suitability. These techniques offer other tangential rewards as well. In particular, direct participation in the design of neighborhood space can promote a stronger sense of community through the mobilization of energies around a common problem. This mobilization in turn can promote a stronger community-organization structure to achieve other neighborhood goals. The benefit has been well expressed by a participant in the Workshop on Urban Open Space:

There should be a feeling . . . that it is the community that is important. That's what we are all talking about. The point is, all of these different things that an architect does, that a planner does, that any kind of technician does, should be the product of organization. . . . You see, it's not the park that's important, it's the way the park is built. It's the way the community is organized. . . . The users of neighborhood open space must be involved in the whole cycle of development.[3]

Architect Sam Sloan summarized a host of other tangible benefits at an Environmental Design Research Association conference:

User participation (1) relieves the anxiety of the unknown; (2) aids in self-actualization; (3) produces a design more related to the balance of the user's values; (4) allows a setting in which a range of values and preferences can be uncovered; (5) provides a democratic climate and individual responsibility; (6) creates an awareness of the design process which the participant can use elsewhere; (7) dispels the idea that nobody cares; (8) builds a better relationship between artifacts and the individual human being; (9) deals realistically and openly with conflicts and resolves them through positive complementarity; (10) provides a logical framework for interdisciplinary action to complement each other rather than contend for dominance.[4]

Whether the designer's primary concern is the social suitability of a neighborhood space, the promotion of community organization, or other benefits of user participation, he will need to develop skills unknown to designers who deal only with city mayors, land developers, or directors of parks and recreation departments. No longer can he arrive at program-design alternatives and a final plan through personal discussions and salesmanship with a single client. A public neighborhood client, consisting of large numbers of people who display a variety of life-styles, requires a whole range of techniques aimed at measuring a complex pattern of user needs, which will be different in different neighborhoods. User-needs techniques are methods by which information is gathered firsthand on the activities, interactions, and feelings of the potential users of a neighborhood space. The techniques may be used to acquire information at any stage in the design process prior to construction: problem definition, analysis of existing situations, program development, site location, synthesis of alternative plans, and so on. The techniques include neighborhood forums, brainstorming, synectics, role playing, interviews, questionnaires, observations for activity mapping and social-ecology mapping, activity logs, and semantic differentials.

Many of these techniques are borrowed from social survey research; but it should be made clear that user-needs techniques do not pretend to provide findings based on pure research methodology. Their aim is not to prove or disprove any theory, nor to discover truths that can be generally applied. Rather, findings based on user-needs techniques are intended to provide information that can be directly applied to a particular neighborhood space. Pamela Dinkel explains how the whole matter of facilitating open-space use is unique to each situation, because "all the variables operating in any given situation represent one case study essentially unreplicable" and that they therefore "require specific study, not a precast solution."[5]

BASIS FOR CHOOSING AMONG USER-NEEDS TECHNIQUES

Before describing the various user-needs techniques, the basis for choosing among such techniques needs to be outlined. The choice of any technique will be based on a number of standard considerations. First, *the kind of information sought must be specified.* We must decide whether the crucial question is what people will do in a space, how they will feel about the space, or how they will interact in a space. Then we need to consider *the phase of the design process at which the technique will be employed.* Does the designer want to analyze an existing situation, define a problem, generate ideas, set goals, evaluate alternative courses, or resolve user conflicts?

Another consideration, of course, is *the cost of a given technique.* Cost is a function of the level of professional input necessary to use a technique, the speed with which the instrument can be developed and administered, the number of times the technique has to be repeated to get reliable information, the extent to which it can be used with any size group, the degree to which it can be self-administered, the extent to which it has to be done on the site, and the ease of interpreting the results. Another cost-related factor is the accuracy required by a given technique. The validity of the sample in predicting real needs is critical, but the users of neighborhood space often represent such a diversity of economic classes, age groups, and life-styles that it is difficult to obtain a valid cross section of user needs. Moreover, the cost of a technique often increases with the validity coefficient.

Two other cost-related factors are flexibility and

versatility. Flexibility refers to the ease with which a technique can be duplicated in another setting; this is important because, if flexible, the technique has only to be learned once. Versatility refers to the ease with which a technique can be applied to a variety of situations, which is important because the technique can be applied again and again, without the elaborate training required for learning a new one.

A final basis for choosing among user-needs techniques is *a technique's compatibility with other neighborhood goals.* The technique may not only be used by designers, but also by community leaders to provide a stimulus for educating the residents of the neighborhood. A major consideration before choosing a user-needs technique is its compatibility with the development of neighborhood power through grass-roots organization, local control of various facilities and services, and the corroboration of neighborhood leadership.

DESCRIPTION OF USER-NEEDS TECHNIQUES

Before the importance of directly obtaining user-needs information was recognized, a number of indirect methods were employed. Although these methods may overlook unique and idiosyncratic neighborhood needs, they can still be used to project general use patterns. National recreation standards that describe the facilities needed in regional, city, and neighborhood parks offer general parameters for an area's needs based on needs determined in other areas. Demographic information concerning age, occupation, income, sex, housing conditions, and property values is readily available in census data and can be analyzed to gain insights into the most general needs of a particular neighborhood. Then, within the given neighborhood, contact with "gatekeepers"—people who control the exchange of information such as mailmen, storekeepers, firemen, and community leaders—can provide valuable data for the design of neighborhood space.

Another traditional method of indirectly assessing user needs is the designer's intuitive process of sorting through past experiences with different neighborhoods and different designs as he examines a problem by creating simulations—models, drawings, perspectives, movies, or plans. For example, recalling the pattern of use in a shopping area where benches outside the drugstore were always overcrowded, a designer may include in his plans for a similar store a larger sitting garden in the expectation that people want such a space. Designers are often correct in such judgments; but when the designer's simulations are shown to the potential users, their direct feedback can further improve upon the initial evaluations.

Town Meeting

"Town meeting" is a name given to a group of techniques that involve participatory decision making. It is much like the New England town meeting in which all participants have a voice and issues are discussed, alternatives given, and decisions made in a truly democratic fashion.

Neighborhood Forum

Probably the best example of a town meeting is the neighborhood forum, which is a public meeting open to any neighborhood resident. Ideas and problems are discussed by all members of the group, and there is no distinction between audience and performer. The drawback to the neighborhood forum as a user-needs technique is that it obtains information only from the people who attend the forum. For this reason, it is not an accurate measure of the needs of the total neighborhood. It is biased toward people who are likely to attend meetings—young adults, concerned citizens, and aspiring leaders—and excludes children, teenagers, the elderly, the unconcerned, social deviants, and other social isolates. Because of the difficulty in overcoming this bias, the

Adults' Priorities

1. Basketball with lighting and one court for small children
2. Tot lot
3. Shelter with restroom, drinking fountain, and bar-b-que grill.
4. Benches throughout the park.
5. General lighting throughout the park.
6. Maintain natural beauty of the site
7. Utilize swamp area for nature study.

Teenagers' Priorities

1. Shelter with dance space, tables and benches, and electricity
2. Four basketball goals with lighting
3. Tot area with "far out" equipment
4. Bike trail and pathway
5. Bigger grass area for open space activities.
6. Drinking fountain
7. Delete tennis courts.

The designer used a series of eight neighborhood forums to develop a plan for the Kingwood Forest Park. At the final meeting, the neighborhood teenagers presented their list of priorities and the plan that best satisfied their needs. Although there were a few differences in the teenagers' and the adults' priorities, both groups agreed that plan number 1, which the city had developed, was unsuitable. The neighborhood finally agreed on plan number 2, which best satisfied the teenagers' priorities. Before the park was constructed, the residents who had attended the neighborhood forums organized to picket city hall in an effort to speed up the process. The special benefit of the neighborhood forum is that it allows face-to-face decision making, which can lead to group political activity.

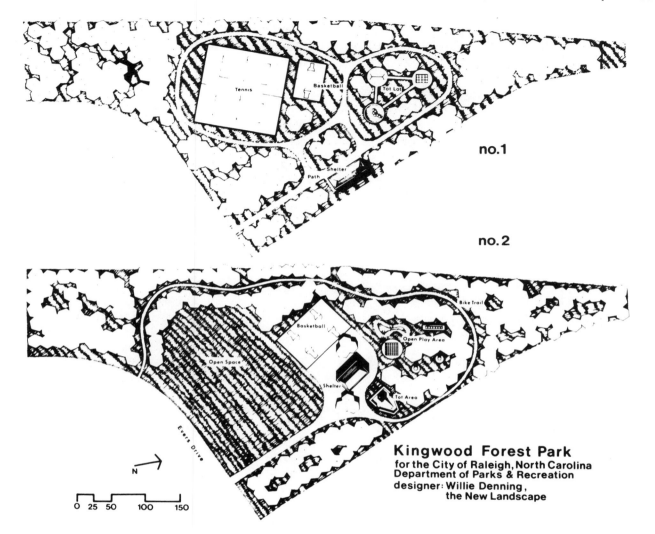

no.1

no.2

Kingwood Forest Park
for the City of Raleigh, North Carolina
Department of Parks & Recreation
designer: Willie Denning,
**   the New Landscape**

repeated several times, the neighborhood forum requires relatively little time. A possible problem lies in both recording and interpreting the data. Accurate notes must be kept by someone other than the chairperson who is sensitive to the kinds of social factors that can be translated into design criteria. It is impossible for the person who is chairing the meeting to remember the critical comments. A recorder is particularly needed when the designer is presenting a simulation for discussion. Because the designer usually records the feedback directly on the plans, he often misses comments that do not relate directly to the plans. Also, to make interpretation of the data easier, the designer needs to make clear what information he needs and in what form.[6] As an example, if the designer tells the recorder that he needs information related only to how people think they will use the spaces in a number of alternative plans, the interpretation of the feedback from that meeting will be facilitated because the recorder can focus on that data.

The neighborhood forum technique rates well as a low-cost technique for a number of other reasons: (1) it can be used with large groups—up to several hundred people can participate, although effective personal participation is limited by such large numbers; (2) it requires no professional for administration; (3) it does not have to be done on the design site; (4) it can be easily duplicated; and (5) its versatility allows its application to a wide range of design process situations. Another advantage of the neighborhood forum technique is that it can be used to accomplish other neighborhood goals at the same time that user-needs information is being gathered. It is useful in developing neighborhood power as well as in promoting neighborhood education and communication.

Kingwood Forest Park in Raleigh, North Carolina, provides an illustration of how the neighborhood forum can be used in the design process. From the following notes on the process, it is easy to see the value of the neighborhood forum both as a user-preference technique and as a decision-making mechanism.

neighborhood forum has limited use in the analysis of existing situations, problem definition, and idea generation. But in the subsequent stages of the design process—setting goals, projecting futures, giving, evaluating, and making choices, and resolving conflicts—the neighborhood forum ranks as one of the most effective techniques for determining user preferences. These stages require the type of deliberation that the neighborhood forum allows.

In terms of cost, the neighborhood forum is also an excellent technique. Although it may have to be

The New Landscape was asked by the Neighborhood Association to work on the project in September, 1971. The designer used information compiled by the Association leaders to draw five alternative plans.[7] These were used as the basis for discussion at a series of eight neighborhood meetings. During the first five meetings, it became apparent that the plan the City Recreation Department had drawn was not consistent with the priorities of the neighborhood; the most obvious difference being the inclusion of a tennis court.

Advertising on WLLE radio, in local stores, and through flyers got the attention of adults who attended regularly and agreed on what were the important design considerations. However, the teens were not involved. Since they would be a major user, the Neighborhood Association scheduled a neighborhood social forum for them. At the social forum, the designer met with 75 teens and got their input without adult intrusion. A month later the teens held another forum and agreed on their priorities. In February, 1972 two priority lists existed—the teens' and the adults', and a neighborhood forum was held to resolve the conflicts. About 100 residents of various ages debated the priorities for several hours although there were only minor conflicts in the priorities. Finally, an elderly gentleman suggested that since the teens were the primary users, only the teens should decide on the design program. The teenagers voted overwhelmingly in favor of their priorities and their design plan.[8]

This case study illustrates many of the positive factors of the neighborhood forum as a technique for determining user preferences. Most notable are the versatility of this technique in its use throughout the design process from problem definition to conflict resolution, the use of the technique to stimulate further political activity, and the ease with which new techniques can be incorporated into the method for the purpose of receiving user feedback. In recent years the neighborhood forum has been the setting for numerous experimental participatory techniques. The use of guided fantasy, hypnosis, group graphics, and modified nominal group techniques were tested in neighborhood forums before they received more widespread application.

Panel Discussion

Another technique in the town-meeting category is the panel discussion. The panel usually consists of residents who, confronted with several alternatives, must choose a plan of action to solve a neighborhood problem. But because the panel discussion can be used throughout the design process, the audience may simultaneously be tackling other problems. They may be defining a problem, setting goals, generating ideas, solving a problem, projecting what each idea would mean for their neighborhood, or resolving conflicts among residents about what should be done. Although the panel discussion exposes the preferences of only the panel members, it provides the residents with information on which they can base further decisions. Thus, it accommodates the goal of fostering neighborhood education. Also, this technique is relatively low cost because it can be used with large groups and can be arranged by neighborhood residents without any professional skill.

To illustrate the use of the panel discussion, consider the case study of the Dennis Chávez Park, in Albuquerque, New Mexico. After Model Cities approved the general plans for park improvements, the designers presented a scale model to various neighborhood groups, and a panel discussion followed each presentation. The panels included an architect, an artist, a sculptor, a parks and recreation staff member, a cultural coordinator for Model Cities, a representative of the Office on Aging, and knowledgeable neighborhood residents. Each presented his views on the proposed plan. Because the plan included a series of unusual play towers and an amphitheater, it was necessary for the panel members to explain to the community the underlying concepts. Also, each panel member discussed the advantages and disadvantages of the project and raised questions. Was it safe? How would it be maintained? Was there enough lighting? What activities would there be for the elderly? Who would be in charge of the performances?

After each discussion the audience gave feedback and the plans were modified accordingly. Provision was made for special activities for the elderly—a place for craft fairs and get-togethers in the shade of portable tents. The towers were carefully redesigned

Panel discussions were used to explain the design of the Dennis Chávez Park to receive suggestions for changing the plans to better suit the needs of the users. (Photograph courtesy of Julie Graham)

to be as safe as possible, while still allowing the freedom to explore. After twenty panel discussions with various groups, the plans responded to the questions raised by the panel members and the concerns of the residents.[9] Citizen support for the project increased as the plans increasingly reflected their needs, and the project was passed by the city commission with only one dissenting vote.[10]

Since some of the panel members were not neighborhood residents, the panel discussions themselves could not be used as a measure of the needs of the neighborhood; however, the feedback afterwards could be used. In general, it is better for the panel mem-

bers to be neighborhood residents. Their comments not only reflect firsthand user needs, but residents can better communicate ideas to their neighbors than a panel of outside experts who speak in professional jargon.

Brainstorming

The use of the brainstorming technique is more limited than either the neighborhood forum or the panel discussion. Brainstorming is confined to generating ideas and giving alternative choices, and the technique is usually applied to design by groups of between five and ten people who try to generate as many alternatives as possible to solve a stated problem. If the brainstorming session creates enthusiasm and spontaneous responses, it can be useful in determining what people would like to do in a space. However, it is not an accurate measure of the user needs of an entire neighborhood since the effective group size is quite small, usually less than ten people. If large groups can be subdivided into small brainstorming sessions and the results later combined, the validity of the technique increases slightly as a measure of total neighborhood preference.

The following example shows the utility of brainstorming as a method of idea generation. In Cambridge, Massachusetts, a few parents, concerned about the lack of playgrounds, met with a city planner to consider alternatives. After much heated debate about who was to blame for the paucity of playgrounds, the group was ready to abandon its effort—until the suggestion was made that they try brainstorming. Everyone agreed to think of as many alternatives for play spaces as he could, and these rules were established:

1. Negative criticism is suspended.
2. The sky is the limit.
3. The more ideas the better.
4. Group improvement on ideas is desirable.[11]

One person was informally designated the leader, one the recorder, and one the sheriff to guarantee that the rules were being followed. After a few minutes of uncertainty, the group began to rapidly produce uninhibited suggestions, building on each other's ideas and discovering creative suggestions beyond the grasp of any person by himself. For example, where can the kids play?

the vacant lot on the corner
the library
the schoolyard
the tot lot
the back alley
the tot lot for kids and the vacant lot for basketball

And, what could be included?

a sandbox
swings
a wall mural
a cave with rope swings
a slide from the cave
a tower on top of the cave
the swings could be attached to the cave
a doll house
a tower with caves in it
a fort
sand under the tower
a tower with colored panels the kids could move around
a construction area
an adventure playground
a floor mural
different textures
rocks
stones
sand
water
a water cave[12]

The group discovered five places where the small children could play and found a place where teenagers could play basketball. They then concentrated on the tot lot and considered what might be included. Although several traditional items were mentioned, most of the alternatives brainstormed were creative, like a cave with rope swings, a tower with caves in it, and a floor mural. The recorder, in this case the city planner, not only recorded but also sketched each idea so everyone would have a visual image of the possibilities. After the session, he categorized the ideas, evaluated them, and worked out the details of construction. At the next meeting he presented plans based on the brainstormed ideas. The technique had cost little, had taken little time, and the results were easily interpreted and translated into a design plan. Although the technique requires little training, to effectively employ brainstorming the leader must be sensitive to the ideas of each person. Each person's enthusiastic participation is necessary for ideas to be spontaneously generated. Especially with people who are "uptight" or shy, the leader must be capable of involving everyone in a positive and rewarding manner. The leader must also be able to clearly define the goal and to keep the group focused on the goal.

Buzz Session

The buzz session is similar to brainstorming in that it involves a few people, usually less than five, who informally generate ideas. The distinction between the two techniques is that the buzz session is less goal directed, and the problem is less clearly defined.

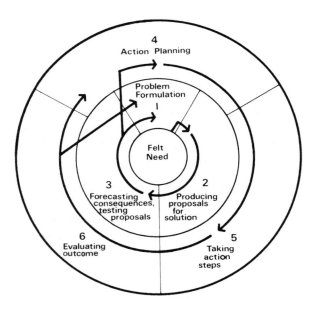

Buzz sessions frequently expose a felt need in a neighborhood, which leads to action to solve a problem.

A buzz session can be nothing more than an informal sidewalk chat during which a common neighborhood problem is discussed, or it can be a meeting called to discuss the solution to a problem. The buzz session frequently exposes user preferences, but because there are better techniques to systematically gather preferences, it is most often used to generate ideas and provide alternative choices. The following excerpt from the notes of a meeting of neighborhood leaders shows how a buzz session, although informal and undirected, may lead to a new idea:

The group discussed the general problems of the neighborhood and why people were not interested in the Community Action Group. Mr. Joyce mentioned that the neighborhood was apathetic because it has a false sense of security in the everlasting stability of the community. Mrs. Green pointed out that the neighborhood was presently threatened by a number of highway construction projects of which the residents were unaware. Mrs. Baker suggested delivering flyers door to door prior to the next meeting, warning people of the threat the highway posed to their neighborhood. Mr. Joyce, wondering out loud why they hadn't thought of that before, agreed to be in charge of distributing the flyers.[13]

Although the need for an issue to mobilize the residents may seem perfectly obvious in retrospect, the leaders realized the need only after a lengthy buzz session. In their case, the leaders had discovered the key issue and the neighborhood rallied around it. Several hundred people began participating in the effort to stop the highway projects. The buzz sessions had provided the idea of the critical need of a process to begin action that ultimately led to the redesign of the comprehensive plan for the neighborhood.

Synectics

Another excellent technique for generating ideas and for stating and solving problems is synectics, a process through which individuals with different backgrounds can maximize their group creativity by consciously using the awareness of each person's emotional and irrational functioning.[14] A general problem is presented to the group. As an example, one neighborhood group was given the problem of how to move people and goods throughout the neighborhood in a way that was not disruptive. The group had to clearly state the problem. In this case, they decided to focus on alternatives to the continual expansion of the street system. Then the group concentrated on making the strange familiar and familiar strange through personal, direct, symbolic, or fantasy analogy. One analogy pursued was to move people "by mail." The idea was originated by a retired mailman who suggested that a truck that made deliveries in the neighborhood could be used to pick up and disperse people as well. The mail analogy was finally developed into a concrete solution. Pavilions would be constructed at 2 block intervals throughout the neighborhood. The pavilions would include a post office, grocery, and other delivery stations as appropriate for the neighborhood. People could walk to the pavilion to pick up groceries or packages that had been delivered by the "mail" truck. This same mail truck would run to the central city every half hour to pick up other goods. People could ride either way for free, thereby significantly reducing the number of automobile trips in a day. Through the use of an analogy with the familiar mailman, the group had explored the movement of goods and services and discovered a creative way to reduce the use of the automobile.

Because the synectics process requires considerable professional training and has been used mainly for the invention of products, it has not enjoyed widespread use by neighborhood residents. But the principles are familiar to designers,[15] and neighborhoods supply a ready resource of diverse backgrounds. Therefore, this technique has promise beyond its rather limited use to date.[16]

Role Playing

Another town-meeting technique is role playing. Role playing is used in a small group to discover how people feel about and interact in a space as well as what they do in the space. The role allows people to project real feelings, which they otherwise might be reluctant to express, in an uninhibited manner. When people play either their own roles or the roles of others in a space, the use of that space becomes clearly articulated, an understanding of the needs that different groups have for the space is possible, and alternatives that satisfy the conflicting needs may be explored. Therefore, it is useful in analyzing an existing environment, in projecting future uses for that environment, and in resolving conflicts over the use of the environment. In addition, role playing has the asset of being one of the few user-needs techniques that can further neighborhood education. Another advantage is that the basic guidelines for a role-playing situation can be established and repeated throughout the neighborhood. But role playing ranks low in versatility, and it costs more than other techniques because professional aid is necessary to set the guidelines and monitor the role playing. Also, professionals are needed to interpret the results.

To illustrate, consider the value of role playing in the following neighborhood park-planning process, in which the existing park was virtually a battleground for teen and elderly conflicts.

The setting was a meeting of the Senior Citizens Organization to review plans for a neighborhood park to which the teen gang had come uninvited. After a few minutes of disruptive and hostile shouting, it was suggested that the group try role playing. After considerable prompting and a rather unfruitful warm-up to the roles, the following dialogue took place between the leader of the teen group playing the role of an elderly woman and the president of the Senior Citizens Organization playing the role of a teenager. (Teenager playing the role of an elderly woman = TE. Elderly man playing the role of a member of the teen gang = ET.)

TE: You don't have any right to be playing in the park. It's for old people.
ET: Hell if I don't. I live here same as you.
TE: Don't you have any respect for us old people?
ET: Respect? This is the only place we have to go to hang out.
TE: Why don't you go down by the river?
ET: Why don't you? We like it here.
TE: So do we. And besides, it's too far for us to walk.

ET: It's too far for *us* to walk, and you are always in our way.

TE: And you are always making noise and drinking and busting the benches and playing cards and breaking bottles and sexing around and causing trouble. Why can't you sit in the park and enjoy it like the rest of us normal people?

At this point the teenagers broke into laughter at the admission by their leader of the whole array of their "evils," many previously unknown to the elderly. But the session had served its purpose by bringing out a number of user needs. First, the teens viewed the space as their own and perceived the elderly as not respecting their need to have a place of their own. Second, the elderly man realized the need the teens had for a "hanging" space and that the teens considered the elderly as being in the way. Finally, the teen leader realized the need the elderly had for a place to sit closer to home than the river. Through role playing, the two groups had come to recognize their mutual needs for the park

and the conflicts caused by their shared use. This information was utilized by the designer to revise the plans and resolve the conflicts between the teen and elderly users in the park.[17]

Role playing can be used to get the users to project real feelings in an uninhibited manner that they might otherwise be reluctant to express. (Photograph by Marge Hackmann)

Our Playground

We like the monkey bars, the the climbing poles, four square, and hop scotch. We like to play ball.

If we could have what we wanted on our playground, we would choose lots of things:

1. swing set
2. basketball court
3. sliding board
4. trampoline
5. merry go-round
6. teter totter
7. football field
8. tennis court
9. tree house
10. swimming pool
11. train
12. roller coaster
13. hobby horse
14. tire swing
15. play house
16. chinning bar
17. bicycles and rack
18. markings for track
19. pipes
20. balance beam
21. play car
22. cubes
23. funny mirrors
24. skating rink

We enjoy playing at the beach, the Y. the mountains and at home.

By having school children pretend they could change their playground, the designers for this schoolyard were able to incorporate many of the things the school children wanted. This resulted in a much more exciting environment, filled with swings, tree houses, bars, cubes, play cars, and junk where previously there had only been barren ground.[18] (Photographs by Marge Hackmann)

One problem with role playing is apparent in this example. Because it can only be used in small groups, it is difficult to achieve an accurate measure of the entire neighborhood's needs.

There are, however, role-playing techniques that can be employed with larger groups. These are based on having the people pretend or wish something such as "pretend you are a kid and describe the kind of place where you would like to be; make believe you are an old man and draw the kind of park you would like to have; write a wish poem for your neighborhood; write a story about a little girl in this space." With this technique, descriptions can be collected from several hundred people at a time and tabulated to give total group preferences that more accurately represent the needs of the entire neighborhood than a single role-playing situation.

Gaming

A game is a model of reality,[19] a simulation in which the users are players who express their preferences by making choices cooperatively or competitively with each other to arrive at some outcome. The outcome or solution in this case would be the design of a neighborhood space. The player may be a single person or a group of persons with similar needs. The choices a player makes during the game are determined by his personal preferences, group pressure, and his power as defined by the rules of the game. The rules generally define the extent to which players can communicate with each other—whether or not the players can enter into binding agreements; whether or not the rewards of the game may be shared with other players; what the formal, causal relation is between the player's actions and the outcome of the game; and what information is made available to the players.[20]

There is a wide range of applications for neighborhood-design games. Gaming techniques such as Planning Outdoor Play (POP)[21] and Selection of

In the redevelopment of the Jaycee Community Center, the Minipug game was used, which allowed the residents of the neighborhood to actually design their own park. By using abstract game pieces and an actual budget, and by following a set of rules that fostered cooperation and compromise, the residents developed an abstract plan that was used by the designer to draw a final plan.

Sites (SOS)[22] are applied to determine what people want to do in a space. These techniques are most useful in analyzing existing environments and in setting goals because they focus on the theoretical decisions that influence user needs. As an example, in POP the users choose the kinds of activities they want to do but do not choose the type of equipment or the specific settings for the activities. Other games, however, are not only useful in analyzing existing environments and setting goals, but can also be used to compress all phases of the design process into a few sessions. Games like Urban Design Investment Game (U-Dig),[23] Developing Recreational Resources (DDR),[24] Community Land Use Game (CLUG),[25] and Mini-Park User's Game (Minipug)[26]

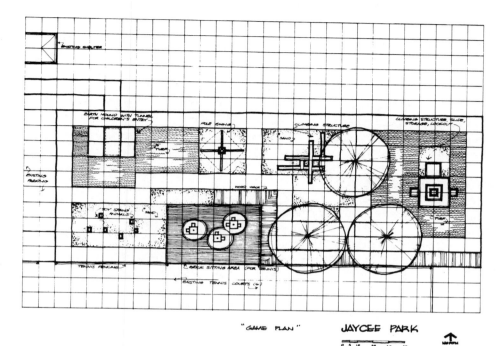

"GAME PLAN"   JAYCEE PARK

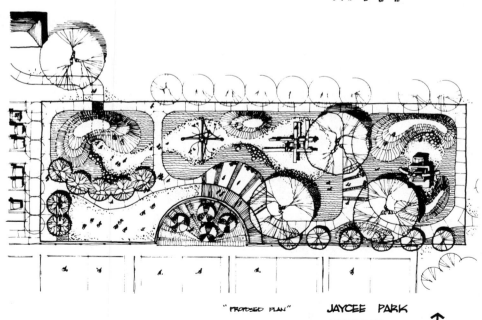

"PROPOSED PLAN"   JAYCEE PARK

can be used in charrettes when complex decisions must be made in a short period of time. These techniques can be used to project and evaluate futures and to resolve conflicts among users in order to produce a final design. For these methods to be successful, the problem must be clearly defined and the relevant information about the alternative choices must be obtained before playing the game.

Gaming can be an extremely beneficial technique for self-education by the neighborhood residents, the only drawback being the cost. In terms of cost, gaming ranks only moderately well because professional aid is necessary to develop and administer games. Also, the participants must be trained before using the game.[27] Frequently, it appears that games are more educational for the users than the results are for the designers. Since the game is often an abstraction of reality and does not accurately describe the actual process for which it is a model, the results may be suspect. And since most games cannot accommodate more than a dozen players, it is difficult to be sure that the information resulting from even the most accurate games provides a reliable measure of total neighborhood preference. Nonetheless, gaming produces a finite result that is easily interpreted, it does not have to be done on site, and it is easily duplicated and moderately versatile.

In the redevelopment of a Jaycee community center in Raleigh, gaming was used to assess user needs. The user-input process consisted of two town meetings, the first to prepare the participants for the game, and the second to play Minipug with resident representatives. At the first meeting, the players were briefed on the budget for the project, and slides were shown to stimulate creative thinking. At the second meeting, the designer gave a brief introduction to the design game, explaining the various pieces, the price list, how much each player could spend, the layout dimensions of the board, and the general rules.

There seemed to be confusion as to the rules of the game and playing procedure; the participants needed a practice round to get the feel of the gaming procedures. After the practice round, participants were instructed to list a set of five personal priorities in terms of general activities—like swinging instead of a swing set, climbing instead of monkey bars, sliding instead of a sliding board. Satisfying these priorities became the goal of each person throughout the process of the game.

After the priorities were listed, play began with each player taking his turn in order. Each player kept an account of the money spent so that the total budget would not exceed $8,000.

During the course of the game, numerous trade-offs and compromises were reached concerning equipment, surfaces, and location. Design criteria were discussed, and decisions concerning play concepts were reached as the game progressed. Continual information was fed into the group by Frank Evans, director of the City Parks and Recreation Department, concerning maintenance, cost, practicality, and the special concerns of his department.

The game lasted approximately an hour, at the end of which time an abstract model was completed for the play area.[28]

In this instance, gaming proved to be quite effective. By focusing attention immediately, it eliminated the time lag that is usually necessary in neighborhood forums to establish priorities. The discussion was directed at moving abstract game pieces to form a real plan—a plan acceptable to all the factions represented. Using all the information gathered, with primary emphasis on the decisions made during the Minipug game, a final design was reached and accepted by the city. Detailed drawings were then prepared for the actual construction of the facility.

The main difficulty with town-meeting techniques is that the accuracy of the information is questionable since it is difficult to get a representative cross section of the neighborhood to attend; consequently, the results may not adequately reflect the user needs for the entire neighborhood. Therefore, other user-needs techniques are potentially more accurate.

Interviews

The interview is a technique whereby a trained field worker obtains information from the people of a neighborhood, one by one, through the use of a set of questions to determine specific patterns of activ-

The interview is often used to determine user activities, feelings, desires, or values. It is particularly useful in analyzing existing environments and in defining problems because it can potentially provide an accurate assessment of user attitudes.

ity, feelings, desires, or values in regard to neighborhood space. Its major applications in the design process are for the analysis of existing environments and for the definition of problems. In other phases of design—setting goals, generating ideas, evaluating and making choices, projecting futures, and resolving conflicts—the use of interviewing is more limited. Furthermore, interviewing is costly. There is also a need for professional aid with this technique— professionals must define the problem, study other research, formulate hypotheses, draw a sample, define variables, draft questions, design the questionnaire, pretest the instrument, prepare for, do, and verify the field work, and analyze the data. Before using interviews, a number of questions must always be answered. Exactly what is the neighborhood problem? What must be determined? What studies have been done that relate to this problem? What were the results? Can the findings be applied to this neighborhood? What does the designer expect to be the outcome of the study? What are the variables? How should the question be asked: formally or informally, open-ended or closed-ended, first or last? All these questions must be answered by someone skilled in the technique.

There are a number of resources for learning the basics of these methods: *Methods in Social Research* by William J. Goode, and Paul K. Hatt, *Survey Research* by Charles H. Backstrom and Gerald D. Hursh, *Research Methods in the Behavioral Sciences,* edited by Leon Festinger and Daniel Katz, and *Empirical Foundations of Educational Research* by Gilbert Sax.[29] These resources can help the designer communicate with persons skilled in interview techniques when he obtains their professional assistance throughout the process of developing an interview. It takes skill and time to develop an interview, and a designer should not think he can "whip one out" in a day or so. In most cases, the interview should be developed by someone professionally trained in research methods.

The interview is not only difficult to develop, it is difficult to administer. Each interview must be done separately by a trained interviewer. Interviewers must be carefully chosen, taught the techniques of interviewing and the specifics of the interview schedule, and then organized into groups with explicit interviewing assignments. But although the interview is costly and difficult to develop and administer, it is valuable as a user-needs technique because it gives extremely reliable and valid information when done with precision and focus. If the technique is used well, the sample chosen and interviewed is both representative of the potential users and is large enough to make precise predictions about the needs of the population; little bias is introduced into either the sample or interview results.

The ease with which the results can be interpreted is also important. If the interview is developed by skilled professionals, the results should be easy to analyze because the appropriate questions will have been asked. If one asks, "Would you rather play basketball or football?" when what one really wants to know is, "What do you do in your leisure time?", the results would be difficult to analyze. Equally difficult would be the analysis of "What do you do in your leisure time?" if one really wants to know "What do you do most often when you visit your neighborhood park?" Also ease of interpretation is a function of how readily the results can be categorized according to age, sex, income, and the like. Another difficulty can be avoided through careful coding of responses. In general, multiple-choice questions and questions requiring specific answers are easier to code and interpret that open-ended questions.

The Roberts Park planning process in Raleigh, North Carolina, shows the value of the interview technique. The city had given the design team a list of improvements based on standard park facilities, but the designers were not convinced that these improvements met the needs of black residents. Since there was no visible neighborhood organization, and the design team wanted to check the user needs in an accurate manner in order to show the city the results, they turned to the interview technique. They wanted information on the backgrounds of the residents—their age, their class, their neighborliness. They also wanted to know what park-related activities the residents participated in, how frequently, and where these activities occurred, because they felt that each of these factors contributed to the needs of the users. The designers described how the interviewing was done:

The population interviewed in Roberts Park neighborhood was determined by a random-sampling method whereby we personally talked with the head of household or spouse of every fourth house in our predetermined block. Whenever a case arose whereby no one was at home or would not respond to the questionnaire at each fourth house, we immediately went to the fifth house. If there was still no response, we returned to the third house. Generally, we were received by one of the three households. If not, we returned another time. The total number of interviews administered in Roberts Park was 96, or approximately 25 percent of the households in the neighborhood.

For purposes of compiling the information into a form whereby interpretations could be accurately made, we utilized computer services. The Statistical Analysis System (SAS) Chi Square and frequency program was selected in order to obtain frequency percentages of response distributions for each respective subneighborhood. Each question on the interview was coded and results tabulated individually so that accurate representations could be made and evaluated. Correlations of variables were made primarily of percentage distribution.[30]

From the interviews, the design team was able to establish socioeconomic information on the Roberts Park neighborhood such as education, income, employment, needs related to park facilities in terms of age, and homogeneity of the neighborhood. They found that in Roberts Park, 58 percent of the people interviewed had a high-school education or less but 43 percent had attended college or post-graduate school:

The socioeconomic data compiled from our survey information indicated that the highest percentage of income level for the park neighborhood was the $3,000 to $6,999 range which included 34 percent of the people interviewed. Also of interest was the percentage of families in the Roberts neighborhood with incomes of less than $3,000 per year. Twenty-nine percent of the families surveyed fell into this category. It was interesting to note the correlation between these percentages in comparison with age. Thirty-three percent of the people interviewed in Roberts were 51 or older, which may account for the low income level.

Of the families interviewed, 45 percent were blue-collar workers, while only 26 percent were white-collar workers. In the nonworkers classification, 29 percent resided in the Roberts community. It should be noted, however, that 26 percent of those residents in the nonworkers classification were retired or disabled. The high percentage of retired or disabled people closely correlated to the age-income breakdown mentioned earlier. All of these factors indicated low mobility and a high dependence on the neighborhood park for leisure-time activities.[31]

To determine the homogeneity of the Roberts Park neighborhood, questions were included that would give an indication of the neighborliness exhibited in this neighborhood. By using neighborliness in conjunction with mobility, social interaction, and stability of the neighborhood residents, the design team arrived at a generalization in regard to homogeneity. First, they had to determine the degree of neighborliness in the neighborhood. A high ranking using a modified Guttman scale was found for neighborliness:

In addition, by examining the socioeconomic data, we found that the Roberts Park neighborhood is a relatively stable neighborhood. The large number of elderly residents indicate a permanence of individuals in the neighborhood, and a high percentage of home ownership gives an added indication of the residents' longevity. Considering these factors, we concluded that the Roberts Park neighborhood exhibits a high degree of homogeneity and has a high potential for compatible shared park use.

In order to determine the needs of the neighborhood as they relate to park facilities, we used question number 20 of the interview schedule.

Of the 96 people interviewed in the neighborhood, 88 percent of the subjects were dissatisfied with the park and facilities and

had some recommendations as to how their park needs could be met. Of the recommendations listed, some were completely out of range of our limited budget. For example, 36 people indicated a need for a swimming pool. Below is the total breakdown in numbers of responses of recommendations requested by the neighborhood residents.

Requested park recommendations	*Number of responses*
Tot lot	56
Picnic facilities	36
Swimming pool	36
Basketball court	30
Benches	29
Tennis court	26
Landscaping	20
Lights	10
Bleachers	8
Water fountains	4
Toilet-facility improvements	2

This can be compared to what people presently do in the park.

	Frequency of Open-Space Usage		
Activity	*Once a week*	*Once a week– once a month*	*A few times a month*
Sitting	103	9	7
Walking	93	19	7
Running	51	4	3
Basketball	38	3	3
Football	33	2	1
Baseball	24	8	8
Swimming	23	12	22
Jumping rope	21	2	4
Picnicking	21	33	53
Tennis	18	10	9
Walking dog	9	1	3

Since the need for play equipment for small children appeared to be outstanding, we began to correlate user needs in terms of age breakdown. For example, no facilities were available for small children. By the same token, no facilities were available for the elderly who comprise a large percentage of the neighborhood population. Both of these groups are neighborhood bound; therefore, the need for a tot lot, benches, and picnic facilities ranked high on the list of design priorities.[32]

After the preliminary neighborhood investigation was completed, a plan for the park was prepared using the recommendations of the people surveyed

ROBERTS PARK INTERVIEW SCHEDULE

Interview Number _____

Cod 1

Introduce yourself. Explain that the city has a certain amount of money to do improvements in the Park, supposedly for a tot-lot. Explain that you are working with the City/University Program to develop plans for the Park, and that you need their ideas so the park will be what they need. Ask to speak to the head of household or the spouse.

1. What is your present address? _____

Cod 2

2. What was your reason for selecting this house?
    A. Park related reason
    B. Non-park related

Cod 3

3. How long have you lived at this address?
    A. Less than 6 months   C. 1 to 3 years
    B. 6 months to 1 year   D. Over 3 years

Cod 4

4. Age:
    A. Less than 30
    B. 31-50
    C. 51 and above

Cod 5

5. Sex:
    A. Male
    B. Female

Cod 6

6. Including yourself, how many members of your family are living in your household at the present time? _____

Cod 7   Cod 8

7. What are the ages and sexes of any children living in your home?
    Age   Sex

Cod 9   Cod 10

Cod 11

Cod 12

8. Where do the people live that you visit with most?
    (House and street number--BE SPECIFIC) How often? At least once a week, less than once a week to once a month, few times per year

Cod 13

    A.

Cod 14

    B.

Cod 15

    C.

Cod 16

9. Do you and your neighbors exchange or borrow things from one another such as food, tools, dishes?
    _____ Yes
    _____ No

Cod 17

10. How many of the adults in this neighborhood do you know on a first-name basis?
     A. 4 or less
     B. 5 to 10
     C. 10+

Cod 18

11. Would you say that real friends are hard to find in this neighborhood?
     _____ Yes
     _____ No

Cod 19

12. I do not want names, but I want you to think about the people who live in this same area that you like. Would you say you like:
     A. Few
     B. Half
     C. Almost all

     Why do you like them?

Now I would like for you to think of the members of your own household and their use of the outdoors for recreation.

Cod 20   Cod 21

13. Which of the following activities have the adults in your home done in the past year? What others?
     A. Basketball   F. Walking
     B. Baseball   G. Picnicing
     C. Football   H. Sitting
     D. Tennis   I. Walking dog
     E. Running   J. Swimming
                             K. List others

Cod 22   Cod 23

Cod 24   Cod 25

Cod 26   Cod 27

Cod 28   Cod 29

Cod 30

From the interviews conducted in the Roberts Park Neighborhood, the designers established the needs related to park facilities in terms of age and homogeneity, present activities, and requested activities.

Cod 31   Cod 32

Cod 33   Cod 34

Cod 35   Cod 36

Cod 37   Cod 38

Cod 39   Cod 40

Cod 41

Cod 42   Cod 43

Cod 44   Cod 45

Cod 46   Cod 47

Cod 48   Cod 49

Cod 50   Cod 51

Cod 52

Cod 53   Cod 54

Cod 55   Cod 56

Cod 57   Cod 58

Cod 59   Cod 60

Cod 61   Cod 62

Cod 63

Cod 64   Cod 65

Cod 66   Cod 67

Cod 68   Cod 69

Cod 70   Cod 71

Cod 72   Cod 73

Cod 74

Cod 75   Cod 76

Cod 77   Cod 78

Cod 79   Cod 80

Cod 81   Cod 82

Cod 83   Cod 84

Cod 85

Cod 86

Cod 87

Cod 88

Cod 89

Cod 90

14. Where do the adults participate in the above listed activities? (List to correspond with preceding letters)
A.   F.
B.   G.
C.   H.
D.   I.
E.   J.
                     K.

15. How often do the adults in your home participate in the above listed activities?

1 - at least once a week
2 - less than once a week to once a month
3 - few times per year

A.   F.
B.   G.
C.   H.
D.   I.
E.   J.
                     K.

16. Which of the following outdoor activities have the children in your home done in the past year? What others?

A. Basketball   F. Jumprope
B. Baseball   G. Running
C. Football   H. Walking
D. Swimming   I. Picnicing
E. Tennis   J. Sitting
                     K. List other outside games

17. Where do the children participate in the above listed activities? (List to correspond with above letter)
A.   F.
B.   G.
C.   H.
D.   I.
E.   J.
                     K.

18. How often do the children in your home participate in the above listed activities?

1 - at lease once a week
2 - less than once a week to once a month
3 - few times per year

A.   F.
B.   G.
C.   H.
D.   I.
E.   J.
                     K.

19. If there were a large field behind your home, but you did not like the other neighbors whose homes surrounded it, would you use it for outdoor activities? Yes, No - Why or why not?

20. Are you satisfied with the park as it is now, or would you like to see anything else there that is not now? And what do you think the children would like to have there? _____

These last questions are only used to divide the interviews into groups.

21. What was the last grade of school completed by the chief breadwinner for your home?
A. attended grade school   D. attended college
B. attended high school   E. graduated from college
C. technical/business school   F. Post-graduate work

22. What type of work does the chief breadwinner for the household do? _____

23. Is the total yearly family income over or under $_____? Is that over or under $_____?
A. less than $3,000   C. $7,000 to $9,999
B. $3,000 to $6,999   D. over $10,000

to determine a priority list. Within the framework of the budget, the design team tried to incorporate as many recommendations as possible. The initial design scheme included, in order of priority, a tot lot, picnic facilities, basketball courts, benches, tennis courts, landscaping, lights, bleachers, and a drinking fountain, all arranged in an informal way to accommodate the interaction of the residents.

The initial design scheme based on information from the interviews apparently was accurate enough that only two neighborhood meetings were required to reach an approved plan. This plan, which differed greatly from the one originally proposed by the city, was accepted by the Parks and Recreation Department. Of the priorities stated in the interviews, only the swimming pool and basketball court were omitted in the final plan. The swimming pool was simply too costly, and the neighborhood decided to press for an indoor gymnasium instead of outdoor basketball courts.[33]

In the case of Roberts Park, the interview provided information detailed enough to proceed from a specific definition of the problem to an actual form design. The interview data not only described the general patterns of neighborhood-space use but also the specific priorities of the residents for neighborhood improvements. In many cases, the interview would be used only to define general problems, to determine the relative importance of various problems to the neighborhood, or to get specific design priorities that might influence the use of certain neighborhood spaces.

Questionnaires

Another user-needs technique, the questionnaire, resembles the interview because it can accurately discover users' activities and interaction patterns in and feelings about a neighborhood space. The questionnaire is particularly valuable in problem definition. The difference between the two techniques is that the questionnaire requires the respondent to fill out the form himself.[34]

The questionnaire has uses similar to the interview. In addition, it has the advantage of being self-administered, which can, in certain situations, save the designer time.

By eliminating the cost of trained interviewers, the questionnaire becomes a less-expensive technique; but it can also be less accurate because it loses the random sample that is possible with an interview. If the questionnaire is either mailed or passed out by hand to be picked up later, the return response is usually less accurate a measure of user needs than an equal number of interviews, because the sample is biased to respondents who are motivated to return the questionnaires. In one community, questionnaires were delivered door-to-door, in an effort to determine the need for a neighborhood facility. Even though the questionnaires were left with explicit instructions and were picked up the following day, the responses were not representative of the total community. Of the small percentage retreived, there was a bias toward residents who had lived in the area a long time.

It appeared the newer the resident was in the community, the less likely he was to return the questionnaire because he felt less concern about acquiring a park. In contrast, the older, more settled members of the neighborhood saw a great need for a park and returned a high percentage of the questionnaires.[35]

This is a common problem in using the questionnaire. But in spite of this shortcoming, the questionnaire can be effectively used when potential users can be identified as groups to whom the questionnaire can readily be given. If the users are the students and staff at Public School 23, the Underwood PTA, Boy Scout Troop 49, or the Longwood Neighborhood Association, questionnaires can be handed out and collected during a meeting or class with a high rate of return. But to get a reliable and valid sample, one must be able to identify representative groups and to administer the questionnaires when the groups have a high turnout of members.

In the case of the redevelopment of an elementary schoolyard in Raleigh, the use of questionnaires was advisable. Since the teachers, staff, and students were readily available and interested, 97 percent of the questionnaires distributed were returned. The principal suggested that a similar questionnaire be given to the parents at the first PTA meeting (he suggested the first meeting of the year because he knew from past experience there would be a high turnout). Over 100 parents were present, and all but three returned the questionnaire. The parents answered questions such as:

1. How often do you go to the schoolyard?
2. If you do use the schoolyard, what do you do most when you are there?
3. What things does the schoolyard have now of which you approve? Disapprove?

4. What things would you like to see added to the schoolyard for your children's benefit?
5. How can the yard be redesigned to serve the whole community, adults as well as children?
6. Would you use the yard if there were things for adults to do? If so, what facilities or activities would you want?
7. Where did you play most often when you were young? Describe the place.

The results indicated that the parents almost never went to the schoolyard but would like to if there were more attractions, places to sit and talk while supervising the kids, more variety of kids' things, a nature-study area, more green living things, basketball courts, a garden, a theater, and water. Some of these ideas— places to sit and talk while supervising the kids and more living things—had been mentioned beforehand. There is no doubt that the final design more accurately reflected the parents' preferences because of their input through the questionnaire. . . . A secondary effect of the questionnaire was that the parents were pleased that their ideas were important enough for the designer to ask for them. As a result they were willing to help during the construction of the yard.[36]

Observation

Observation techniques provide another method for assessing user needs. They have long been the basis of site analysis for designers who make mental notes of what they see and then transfer them into a design form. What landscape architect has not made these notations: "Save grove of mature oaks," "topo and vegetation give a sense of enclosure," or "good point of entry." Whereas a casual visit to a natural site gives the designer a "feel" for the place, a vegetation or soil analysis requires more systematic, precise, and long-term observation. The same is true for meaningful analyses of residents' use of neighborhood space. The art of looking must be systematic and precise.

Such observation is the single best technique for discovering what people do and how people interact with other people in neighborhood space. However, it has limited value in measuring how people feel

Activity recording can often be done with a camera or tracers. By recording where paths are made, where garbage is left, or where plants are broken, one can determine how spaces are used without interrupting the normal patterns of the residents. In this space, an analysis of the condition of plant materials suggested that several areas (indicated by arrows) were used as a bicycle service area and a major circulation path. This indicated the need for paved surfaces rather than plants in these areas. (Photograph by Susan Foster)

about the space. In the overall design process, observations are most useful in the analysis of existing situations and in the definition of problems. They can also be helpful in projecting future patterns of use but have almost no value in generating ideas, setting goals, giving alternative choices, evaluating and making choices, and resolving conflicts. Observation is a rather costly technique because professional input is necessary to develop and administer a good instrument. The same process outlined for developing an interview must be followed in developing observation techniques: define the problem, study the research, state expected observations, choose sample times, design specific methods to observe the critical variables, and pretest the instrument. Also, the administration of the technique is costly—the observations must be done on site in an unobtrusive manner by a trained observer, and they must be repeated to give valid and reliable results. Observations should be done at different hours of the day, different days of the week, and if possible, different seasons of the year. When the results are interpreted, it is difficult to predict "what could be" because the data give only a description of "what is." Any projection must be done with caution.

Although observation methods are not versatile and are costly, they are flexible. They can be easily duplicated from one neighborhood to another after the techniques have been developed and tested. Earlier in this discussion, it was noted that observations can also provide accurate descriptions of what people do in a neighborhood space and how they interact with others. For each of these descriptions there are different things to look for and different types of observation techniques to direct the looking. These techniques can be classified as activity observation, interaction observation, and ecology observation and mapping.

Activity Observation

Activity observation is a straightforward recording of what people do in a space. The important factors to record are the various kinds of activities and the different people according to age, sex, and race who are doing these activities. Activities are frequently categorized as active or passive or as to whether they are supported by a particular environment or a general environment. For example, the observer may record activities that occur in all types of settings, like walking or stopping to talk, in one category, or he may record activities that occur only in special settings, like waiting for a bus or working on a car. Robin Moore categorizes activities by whether they involve primarily psychomotor, muscular, perceptual, or cognitive skills because they are most relevant to the environments he plans and builds for child development.[37] Other categories are useful for observing infants, elderly people, working people, or handicapped people or for observing particular set-

tings like schoolyards, business areas, transportation stops, playgrounds, front steps, or parks. In a study of a neighborhood with a high percentage of elderly people, observers discovered that a significant pattern of open-space use was being omitted because they could not categorize whether people were actively participating or watching. The observation categories were altered to include headings for "participants" and "audience."

A good rule is to do some informal observing before developing a specific technique or instrument for activity recording. While making informal observations, one might discover the appropriate categories, or one might realize that it is better to do the activity recording mechanically—with a camera or tracers. Or it might be necessary to record only at peak-use times, or to have the recording done by a participant observer. To illustrate, informal visits to a neighborhood business area that was being redesigned indicated that the use of the shopfronts would be interrupted by the observer and that a camera should be installed in a second-floor window to do the recording. Photographs were taken every 15 minutes throughout the day without interfering with normal patterns of stopping to chat and sitting down to rest.

By imaginatively using tracers to record where paths are made, where garbage is left, or where plants are broken, one can also determine how spaces are used without interrupting the normal patterns of the residents. Although choosing the appropriate categories for observation and the appropriate times and ways to observe can be difficult, activity observation can be extremely useful in the design process, as in the following site analysis of a school-ground project:

Our first inclination was to remove the rusted swing set which really was an eyesore and start all over, creating a playground which would stir the imagination. But our observations told us differently. After a week of seven hourly observations daily, the activity totals indicated that the swings, even though quite ugly, were the most popular piece of equipment. They remained.

In another case, the residents indicated that they wanted to remove the basketball court from the neighborhood park. Activity observations indicated why: the most frequently observed activity was basketball; the predominant age, teens; the predominant race, black. The neighborhood was all white and lower-middle class. The teenage boys played unaware that their racially mixed basketball games threatened the adults. The activity observations provided the key to the problem with the neighborhood space.

In a final example, the observation technique was used to check what people said they did most often in a neighborhood space. People mentioned child-related activities when asked "what do you do most often when you are here?" But upon observation, the space was found to be most used for walking and waiting for transportation, although the space was not designed for these activities. These had not been mentioned by anyone who had been interviewed. As a result of these observations, a path system and a bus-stop shelter were incorporated into the design.[38]

Interaction Observation

The interaction-observation technique is most frequently employed in conjunction with activity observation to provide a more complete picture of how certain activities occur in a social context. Interaction observation provides answers to questions such as: Is the person alone, in a small group, or in a large group? Is the interaction impersonal, cooperative, competitive, conflictive or accommodative? Such information can be valuable in learning how to maximize the use of small neighborhood spaces by reducing conflicts among neighborhood users. For example, in one neighborhood, a playground was used almost exclusively by preschool children and their mothers. The mothers frequently gathered in groups of three or four, standing and talking uncomfortably in the corners of the playground where the children played. This suggested that several separate sitting areas for small groups should be incorporated into the plan to redevelop the playground. Frequently, mothers are now observed in groups of four playing bridge while the children play; three or four games often are going on at the same time. Although one big sitting area would have been adequate, the recognition of the separate, small-group interaction pattern provided a more suitable design.

In another neighborhood, the opposite interaction pattern was observed. It was noted that large numbers of elderly residents gathered at the local drugstore daily. The small, separate booths were constantly rearranged to allow for larger group chats. It was proposed that an adjoining garage be demolished and replaced with an outdoor sitting area where the elderly residents could meet in groups of twenty or more with no barriers to their group discussions. In still another case, interaction observations made over a period of a month indicated that the residents of one particular neighborhood frequented a local shopping center. They usually walked, but they often had uncomfortable and hazardous encounters with automobiles driven by people from other neighborhoods who came to shop there. A proposal was made to reduce conflict between pedestrians and automobiles by closing the street to automobiles, turning the street into a pedestrian mall, and providing parking in the rear alleys.

Ecology Observation and Mapping

The third and most useful observation technique is ecology observation and mapping, which combines the above techniques by considering activities, interactions, actual settings, and their influence on each other. Ecology observation records how the activity relates to the place or niche in which it occurs. Frequently, the recording is done directly on maps or plans that are called ecology maps. Since this technique gives information concerning both behavior and interaction and then relates these to the setting, it is most applicable to the design of neighborhood space. As an example, the design team used ecology observations extensively to answer a number of complex questions in redesigning the Fred Olds School Yard in Raleigh:

First, we needed to know what activities were done most frequently so we could incorporate those into the plans for renovation. Second, we wanted to know in which activity settings what

FRED OLDS SCHOOL OBSERVATION SHEET _____

| Date | Hour | Weather | | Observer | | | | | | | | | | | |

	Pre-School		1-8 Grade		9-12 Grade		College		Adult		Elderly		Social Activity*	Setting for Interaction**
	F	M	F	M	F	M	F	M	F	M	F	M		
a. Walking														
b. Sitting														
c. Working														
d. Stop to talk														
e. Neighborhood meeting														
f. Active recreation														
g.														
h.														
i.														
j.														
k.														
l.														
m.														
n.														
o.														
p.														
q.														
r. Commercial														
s. Waiting for transportation														
t. Art														
u. Fantasy play														
v. Construction														
w. Role play														
x.														
y.														
z.														

*Record the Interaction Process associated with each activity and the number of people interacting in that manner. Use the key: P = Private, I = Impersonal, C1 = Cooperation, C2 = Competition, C3 = Conflict, A = Accommodation.
**Indicate the setting in which each activity takes place and the numbers of people, particularly in that setting.

The interaction-observation technique is most frequently employed in conjunction with activity observation to provide a more complete picture of how certain activities occur in a social context.

interactions took place because a number of teachers thought that conflicts occurred most often around the monkey bars and field. If so, they wanted these settings altered. Third, we needed to know what spaces were most intensively used in order to disturb these "identity areas" as little as possible.[39]

The design team decided to do ecology observations and mapping seven times daily for 2 weeks. An instrument was developed that would allow activities to be recorded by age and sex as well as by the interaction process observed. These data were expected to answer the questions about what activities were done most frequently and what interaction processes occurred in which settings. The raw data were tabulated to give the frequency of observed activities as follows:

Frequency of Observed Activities[40]

Activity	Number of times observed
Walking through or around	197
Playing on monkey bars	181
Waiting for transportation	159
Jumping rope on paved area	116
Stopping to talk on edges	85
Running in field	83
Racing in field	80
Exercising in field	76
Sitting on edges in shade	74
Four square on paved area	56
Football in small space	49
Red rover in field	45
Walking across field (adults)	44
Standing on edges of field	39
Kickball in field	36
Role playing: monster all over	32
Hunting insects in grass	29
Fighting in field	28
Flying paper airplanes in field	28
1-2-3 red light on edges	25
Bicycling	24
Wrestling	23
Fantasy play	23
Tug-of-war	22
Turning flips	20
Dodge ball in field	18
Role playing: Wizard of Oz	13
Sitting on edge of field (adults)	13
Pulling up grass	10
Basketball	10
Working (adults)	9
Squat thrust in field	9
Softball in field	8
Throwing rocks from field	8
Ball	8
Walking dog	6
Frisbee in field	6
Playing in box	6
Role playing: horse	6
Hopscotch on paved area	5
Tag	5
Cub Scouts	5
Twirling around in grass	5
Hunting snakes in grass	4
Climbing fence	4
Playing on fire escape	4
Raising flag	4
Throwing pennies	2
Broad jumping	2
Nature study	2
Jogging (adults)	2
Role playing: pulling down trees	2
Role playing: fantasy football	1
Role playing: scarecrows	1
Playing with plastic bag	1
Riding motorcycle	1
Bicycling (adults)	1
Driving	1

The design team was surprised by some of the information, especially the fact that walking and waiting for transportation were among the most frequent activities:

We concluded that the frequency of walking was due to a combination of factors. Adults used the schoolyard for walking around the block, school children walked from activity to activity, and walking represented a lack of other things to do. The design implications were these: a clearly defined pathway both through and among the activity settings would be desirable to provide clear connections for the children and safe passageways for the neighborhood residents and teachers. The monkey bars were popular partly from the lack of diversity, we concluded. The design implications were these: leave the monkey bars, add more climbing apparatus, and diversify the activity settings generally.[41]

The design team suggested that waiting for transportation ranked high because half the students were bused from other neighborhoods. The new plans included several informal waiting places that allowed for small-group play. Continuing down the list of most frequently observed activities, the design team attempted to explain why the activity occurred and to draw conclusions about how to accommodate these activities in the new plans for the school.

The design team had less success in answering the teachers' questions about conflicts occurring most often around the monkey bars and open field. Although fights were frequently observed in the field, and pushing was often observed as a part of playing on the monkey bars, the design team was not able to explain conflicts in terms of activity settings:

As far as the most frequent interactions were concerned, it was impossible to validate that different interactions were related to different activity settings. There were many more instances of cooperating in all activity settings, followed by privacy, competition, and accommodation. Almost all of the adult interactions were private. We drew no conclusions from these data that we could apply to the design process.[42]

Although no conclusions were drawn, the school principal thought that the fights were due to the competition to play on the monkey bars, which were the only equipment in the yard. A design-team member offered the hypothesis that the fights on the field were due to conflicts between the people playing competitive sports and the people racing, exercising, flying airplanes, or playing games like softball, dodgeball, or kickball, all of which frequently occurred in the same space at the same time. Fewer conflicts after construction of a set of towers suggest that the principal was correct in his assessment.

A second part of the Fred Olds observation technique was designed to answer the question, "What areas have the most intense use?" By marking where the most activity occurred and leaving blank the areas of least activity, the observers developed maps that indicated the intensity of use of each area of the yard for each hour of the day. The design team itself was surprised by the insights that the maps allowed:

The activity-intensity maps provided enlightening results. There was no activity during the weekend observation periods. The design implication: Fred Olds School needed to provide settings for community activities to encourage weekend use. Therefore, such things as picnic facilities, a shelter, basketball, nature study, more shade, an amphitheater, and special events were considered in the planning process.

The activity-intensity maps for each hour provided only supporting information to what we already had discovered; the kids milled around the entrances before and after school since there was so little to do in the playground. Play was concentrated during morning recess play; dispersed during lunch and afternoon recess. The schoolyard was virtually unused after the children left the school in the afternoon.[43]

The most valuable information was the composite maps that indicated the areas that were most intensely used. The designers concluded that these areas should remain in their present locations because the children probably had symbolized these spaces as the settings for certain activities and would be dissatisfied with changes in them:

The most intensely used outdoor areas were the area around the monkey bars and the areas used for basketball, kickball, and other organized games. We decided to leave these undisturbed. The second most intensely used areas around the bus stop and entrances corroborated the need for places to wait for the bus. The least intensely used areas seemed the most suitable for quiet activities. We suggested that nature study, an outdoor classroom, a garden, the shelter, and private sitting and play spaces be located in these areas.[44]

The ecology observations and mapping technique were beneficial to the process of redesigning the Fred Olds School Yard, but the technique employed had one drawback. Because the researchers could only map a few factors at a time, only intensity of use was mapped, not the acutal activities.

In another example, the redevelopment of the Jefferson Park Housing Project in Cambridge used an ecology-mapping technique that mapped both the intensity of activity and the activities themselves. As each activity was observed, it was given a letter as a key, and each time the activity occurred the letter was marked on the plan at the approximate location

FRED OLDS SCHOOL
INTENSITY OF ACTIVITY

Key to Intensity of Activity

Most
Intense

Least
Intense

TYPICAL WEEKDAY

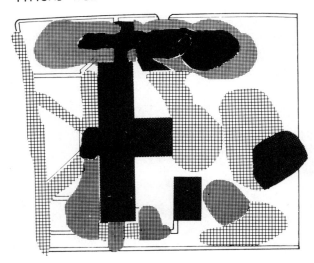

7:30 to 8:30 am

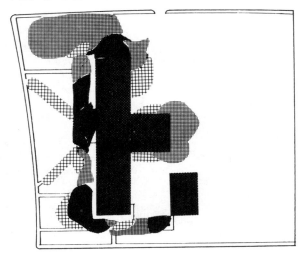

9:30 to 10:30 am

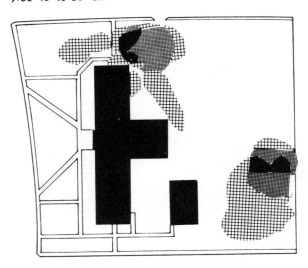

12 to 1 pm

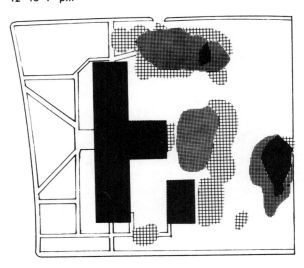

At the Fred Olds School, ecology mapping provided a means to determine what areas of the schoolyard were most intensely used. The "Typical Weekday" map, a composite of the hourly observations, was used to define areas in which activities already occurred that should not be disturbed.[45]

2 to 3 pm

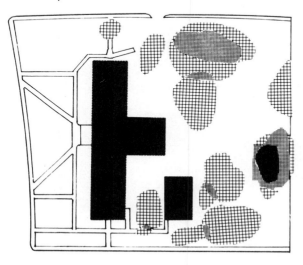

3 to 4 pm

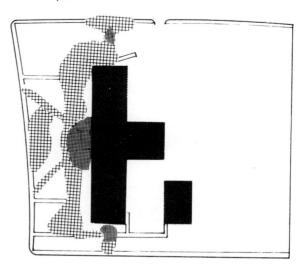

7 to 8 pm

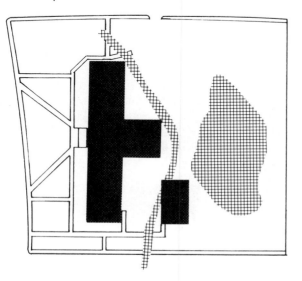

9 to 10 pm

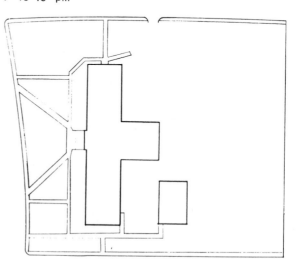

FRED OLDS SCHOOL: Characteristics of Observed Activity Settings

ACTIVITIES BY PREDOMINANT SETTING TYPE	FLAT OPEN SPACE	Racing	Football	Red Rover	Kickball	1-2-3 Redlight	Tug-of-War	Turn Flips	Dodge Ball	Basketball	Ball	Softball	Fantasy Horse	Frizbee	Twirl Around	Broad Jump	Fantasy Football	NATURAL SPACE	Hunting Insects	Pulling up Grass	Hunting Snakes	Nature Study	LINEAR ROUTES	Walking	Running	Tag	Jogging	Bicycle	Driving	Motorcycles
Number of Observations		80	49	45	36	25	22	20	18	10	8	8	6	6	5	2	1		29	10	4	2		197	83	5	2	1	1	1
SETTING CHARACTERISTICS																														
Large Flat Open Space	●	●	●	●	●	●	●	●	●	●	●	●	●	●	●	●	●							●	●	●	●			
Special Setting									●										●	●	●	●								
Linear Route																								●	●	●	●	●	●	●
Nodes																														
Small Enclosed Space																														
Any Space			●							●																				
Needs Props			●	●			●	●	●	●	●	●							●	●	●	●						●	●	●
Large Group Space				●	●		●		●	●	●																			
Small Group Space																			●	●	●	●		●	●	●	●	●		
Private Space																								●	●	●	●	●		
Enhanced by Audience Space	●	●	●		●		●	●		●						●														

KEY: ● Indicates secondary setting characteristics

where the activity was observed. This provided a significant aid to the designer who was accustomed to making form decisions in plan view. He was able to look at the composite map and judge what activities would be affected by a change in the layout. For instance, he knew that the proposed basketball courts and the hockey rink would eliminate the baseball games because the courts would subdivide the baseball area. The designer could also visualize what activities would be increased and where they would occur by comparing the proposed plan with the ecology map. He assumed that there would be an increase in people stopping to talk because he provided niches along the edges of the walkways. He assumed that street hockey would increase during the fall in the ice-hockey rink and that teenagers would hang out in the private shelter, although on the ecology map few teenagers were recorded as hanging out. Generally, the designer was able to consider user needs that he normally would have ignored because the information could not be transferred into plan view.

In the case of the redesign of the Jefferson Park Housing Project, ecology mapping was done before and after the renovations, thus providing an excellent technique to evaluate the social suitability of the new plan. From a comparison of the "before" and "after" maps, the plan could be ranked high in satisfaction of user needs. Stopping to talk greatly increased, as did playing street hockey and hanging

One problem in the Fred Olds School mapping arose because the activities and the intensity of the activities were recorded separately. Some techniques use a sophisticated coding system to allow age, sex, activity, interaction, and intensity to be recorded on the base map.

ACTIVITIES BY PREDOMINANT SETTING TYPE	NODES	Waiting for Transportation	Stopping to Talk	Sitting	Standing	SMALL ENCLOSED SPACE	Jump Rope	Fighting	Flying Paper Airplanes	Fantasy Play	Wrestling	Throwing Pennies	Playing with Plastic Bag	NEEDS PROPS	Monkey Bars	Four Square	Playing in Box	Hopscotch	Climbing on Fence	Playing on Fire Escape	Raising Flag	ANY SPACE	Exercises	Monster	Wizard of Oz	Throwing Rocks	Cub Scouts	Role: Pulling down Trees	Scarecrow
Number of Observations	159	85	74	39		116	28	28	23	23	2	1		181	56	6	5	4	4	4		76	32	13	8	5	2	1
SETTING CHARACTERISTICS																													
Large Flat Open Space							●		●	●			●										●						
Special Setting			●																					●	●				●
Linear Route							●																						
Nodes		●	●	●	●																								
Small Enclosed Space			●	●			●	●	●	●	●	●	●																
Any Space			●	●			●																●	●	●	●	●	●	●
Needs Props							●						●		●	●	●	●	●		●				●				
Large Group Space															●								●						
Small Group Space		●	●	●	●		●	●							●	●	●	●								●			
Private Space		●		●							●									●									●
Enhanced by Audience Space							●	●		●	●				●	●													

KEY: ● Indicates secondary setting characteristics

out.[46] Thus, if user-needs information can be transferred into plan view, it is more likely to be applied to the design of neighborhood space, which is precisely the value of ecology mapping.

Observation techniques are clearly applicable in determining neighborhood residents' needs, just as they have been, traditionally, in determining natural-site factors. Activity observation, interaction observation, and ecology observation and mapping provide different insights into user preferences; each uses the designer's highly developed skill of seeing precisely both the usual and the unusual, both what is and what could be. These techniques can be applied in the analysis of existing situations and in problem definition. Of the observation techniques, ecology observation and mapping offers the greatest amount of information about people's activities and their interaction in space. Therefore, this technique should be the focus of greater refinement and increased application.

Other Techniques

Activity logs and semantic differentials were mentioned previously as methods useful for determining user needs, although to a lesser extent than the previous techniques. These techniques are unquestionably useful in postconstruction evaluation, and they can be useful in determining user needs before the design synthesis process.

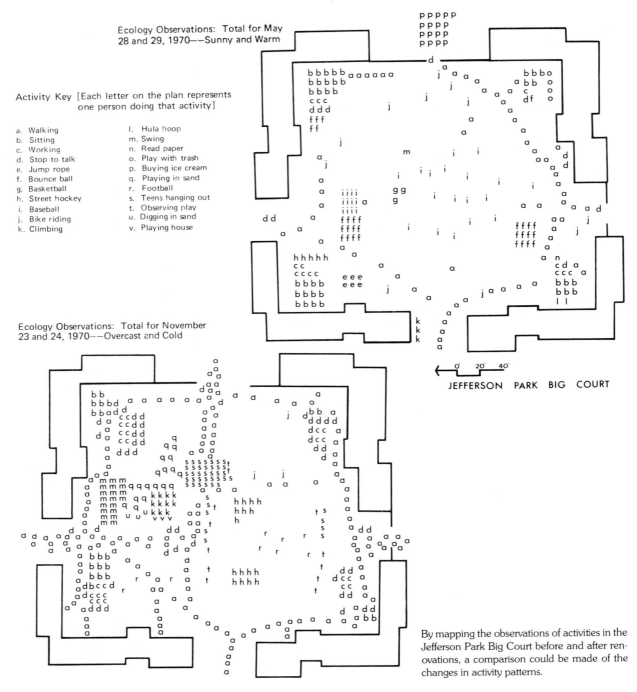

Ecology Observations: Total for May
28 and 29, 1970——Sunny and Warm

Activity Key [Each letter on the plan represents
one person doing that activity]

a. Walking
b. Sitting
c. Working
d. Stop to talk
e. Jump rope
f. Bounce ball
g. Basketball
h. Street hockey
i. Baseball
j. Bike riding
k. Climbing

l. Hula hoop
m. Swing
n. Read paper
o. Play with trash
p. Buying ice cream
q. Playing in sand
r. Football
s. Teens hanging out
t. Observing play
u. Digging in sand
v. Playing house

JEFFERSON PARK BIG COURT

Ecology Observations: Total for November
23 and 24, 1970——Overcast and Cold

By mapping the observations of activities in the
Jefferson Park Big Court before and after renovations, a comparison could be made of the
changes in activity patterns.

Activity Logs

The activity log, a diary-like recording of self-observations, is useful in determining what people do in a neighborhood space. When using this technique, a person records what activity he is doing, how much time he spends doing it, where he is doing that activity, and what that place is like. The results often elucidate what changes are needed in the neighborhood to facilitate people's activities. To illustrate, the results of the compiled activity logs for a 2-week period for a group of elderly people indicated that the average older person spent approximately 2 hours waiting for the bus in areas that had no benches, shelters, or landscaping. Although these were common problems shared by the group, they never discussed the problem until the activity logs disclosed the extent of their plight. They proposed that the city improve the bus-stop facilities.

The activity log is a low-cost technique since it is self-administered; its only major costs lie in developing the instrument and in analyzing the data. Psychogeographer Roger Hart has used this technique to record children's activity patterns in their leisure time. Children's activity logs indicate that they spend very little time in actual playgrounds and that their play occurs throughout the neighborhood. Such insights obtained from activity logs can be readily used in evaluating designed environments. The diaries of children or other residents can simply be tabulated to see if the environment is used as the designer expected and how it "performs."

Semantic Differentials

Semantic differentials have also been widely used as an evaluation technique. Charles E. Osgood developed this technique and readers should refer to *The Measurement of Meaning*[47] for a detailed explanation of its use. Semantic rating can be used to describe how people feel about a neighborhood when one is analyzing existing environments or defin-

Friendly   Unfriendly

By studying the data from semantic differentials, the designer can assess how strongly the residents feel about what they want changed or preserved in their neighborhood.

ing community problems. By offering neighborhood residents a choice of various descriptive adjectives such as "friendly," "unfriendly," "clean," "dirty," "pleasant," "unpleasant," "colorful," or "drab," the designer can discover the residents' collective feelings about the neighborhood. By studying the data from such semantic differentials, the designer can assess how strongly the residents feel about what they want changed or preserved in their neighborhood. This technique requires highly skilled professional assistance in its development and administration, but because of its accuracy, a whole series of sematic-differential techniques have been developed, including activity checklists, mood checklists, numeral ratings, ladder ratings, and step ratings that are often incorporated into questionnaires and interviews.

Summary

In this discussion, both direct and indirect methods of assessing user needs have been considered. Recreation standards, census data, gatekeepers, and the process of making simulations have long provided indirect glimpses at user needs. But these techniques provide only the grossest data; as a result, primary user-preference techniques have become necessary in designing socially suitable neighborhood space. Primary techniques are town meetings, interviews, questionnaires, observations, activity logs, and semantic differentials. Each has been discussed in terms of its suitability for use in the neighborhood design process. Primary attention has been given to what the technique can be used to determine, but each method has been viewed in terms of its appli-

KEY:

- ● Positive Value in that consideration
- ◐ Neutral Value in that consideration
- ○ Negative Value in that consideration

TECHNIQUES (columns, left to right):

Semantic Differential · Activity Log · Ecology Observation and Mapping · Interaction Observation · Activity Observation · Questionnaire · Interview · Gaming · Role Playing · Synectics · Buzz Session · Brain Storming · Panel Discussion · Neighborhood Forum

CONSIDERATIONS

1. WHAT THE TECHNIQUE DETERMINES:
   A. What people do in the space
   B. How people feel about the space
   C. How people interact in the space

2. DESIGN PROCESS APPLICABILITY:
   A. Analyzing existing situation
   B. Defining a problem
   C. Generating ideas
   D. Setting goals
   E. Projecting a future
   F. Giving alternative choices
   G. Evaluating and making choices
   H. Resolving conflicts
   I. Evaluating post construction

3. COST
   A. Overall cost (need for professional input)
   B. Speed developing technique
   C. Technique administration
   D. Necessity of repeating
   E. Ease of interpretation (recording and analyzing data)
   F. Accuracy, reliability and validity of sample in predicting real want-needs of total group
   G. Ease of carrying out technique—Can be administered by any size group
   H. Ease of self administration
   I. Feasibility of off site administration Does not have to be done on site
   J. Flexibility (can be easily duplicated)
   K. Versatility (can be applied to a variety of situations)

4. ACCOMODATION OF OTHER GOALS:
   A. Neighborhood education
   B. Neighborhood power (organization Leadership, and control)
   C. Neighborhood communication

130

cability to various stages in the design process, its cost, and its compatibility with other neighborhood goals. The illustrations indicate some of the possible uses of these techniques. There are many other techniques that have been used and that can be derived from combining techniques to solve a particular problem. The designer must continually focus on the most important social factors and choose a technique appropriate to the situation. There has been no discussion of the actual development of the techniques or the analysis of the data. The designer must consult the other sources listed for detailed discussions of some of the techniques. Nonetheless, this discussion of user-needs techniques can serve as an introduction for design students who are just being exposed to user needs, and it can assist professionals who must select an applicable technique for a certain situation.

ROLE OF THE DESIGNER IN POSTCONSTRUCTION EVALUATION

Thus far, we have focused on the techniques that, if properly employed, can increase the designer's awareness of the social variables that are influencing the use of a neighborhood space before the construction of that space. These techniques are important when designers are called on to produce better space design. But equally important is the designer's responsibility to evaluate what he has designed after it is constructed and to determine if indeed it is socially suitable. Amazingly little is known about how designs perform, how people behave in them, and how people feel about and interact in them. Postconstruction evaluation is just as vital a part of the design process as is a preconstruction site visit, because through postconstruction evaluation new knowledge can be gained that can in turn be applied to subsequent designs.

As Paul Friedberg has said, designers were "flying by the seat of their pants"[48] in this regard because evaluation has not been considered a part of the

design process. Because of the lack of meaningful postconstruction evaluation done in the past, the professional organizations made efforts to facilitate such evaluations. The American Society of Landscape Architects established a task force in 1974 to propose systematic and comprehensive techniques for evaluating the performance of designed landscapes. Although the work of the task force did not lead to wholesale changes in the professions, postconstruction evaluation became much more widely practiced afterwards. The work of Clare Cooper-Marcus, Mark Francis, David Stea, Henry Sanoff, and Donald Appleyard, among others, has made postconstruction evaluation of neighborhood projects more practical and cost effective.

Mayer Spivack has suggested a simple technique for evaluating neighborhood space designs. He maintains that the proper role for designers is to begin at the beginning:

If you are interested in the evaluation of projects you design, you must know what the assumptions are. There are four easy rules. First, write down your assumptions about how the space will be used as you go through the design process. Second, design those assumptions. Third, change the assumptions or predictions or design decisions into working hypotheses. Statements such as "I expect this space to be used thus and so by this group and that group at such and such times" should suffice. Fourth, after construction, observe to see if the hypotheses are validated. This does not require sophisticated, quantitative techniques but, rather, qualitative, precise, unbiased looking.[49]

This is a good starting point. But the need for designers to play a more active role in every aspect of postconstruction evaluations of neighborhood space designs is clear and will increase their ability to provide suitable neighborhood environments.

THINGS FOR YOU TO DO

The following exercises will clarify the issues raised in this chapter. Some will check your understanding of the material; others will help you articulate your own values or give you insights into neighborhood-design issues. You may do these exercises alone, but I would suggest sharing them with others.

1. At a neighborhood meeting, there is conflict over which is the better of two design alternatives that you have proposed. Discuss the ways in which you might attempt to resolve this user conflict.

2. In the design for a park in an ethnically diverse neighborhood, how might you determine the following:
   a. The activities that are desirable?
   b. Their arrangement on the site?
   c. The costs and benefits of the plan?

3. What do you think are your best skills as a trained designer? Which of your present skills would be most useful in working with a neighborhood group? List additional skills you would like to have in designing with user-participants.

4. Within your class or a small group, try out some of the techniques mentioned in Chapter 4. Use synectics to solve a specific problem in your group. Or use role playing to simulate neighborhood open space conflicts between rich and poor users (then, use consensus decision making to resolve the conflicts). Or use a guided fantasy to have your group members recall their favorite play spaces as children. Or use a group graphic to outline your team's goals and implementation strategies. Afterwards, try these out in real design problems.

5. Keep an activity log for a week by recording what you are doing every hour, where you are doing it, and how you feel about the space. You might draw the spaces and just put notes on the drawing—that is more fun for designers.

NOTES AND REFERENCES

1. Bill Taylor, from a newsletter concerning the Pedestrian Path East for Lowell, Mass., produced by Carol R. Johnson & Associates, Cambridge, Mass., May 11, 1973, p. 1.
2. Simpson F. Lawson, ed., *Workshop on Urban Open Space,* U.S. Department of Housing and Urban Development, ASLA 1, Washington, D.C., p. 20.
3. Lawson, *Workshop,* pp. 14, 17.
4. From a lecture by Sam Sloan, Environmental Design Research Association Conference, 1973, Blacksburg, Va.
5. Pamela Y. Dinkel, "Two Neighborhood Case Studies in Neighboring and Open Space," p. 4. Unpublished paper prepared at North Carolina State University, Raleigh, N.C., 1972.
6. In this sense, the recording, interpreting, and analyzing of the meeting notes requires some professional skill, but since this skill relies most heavily on practice, it can be assumed that the people learn how to work together and that this is more important than formal, professional input.
7. Plan simulations were used throughout the process to get direct feedback from the users. Although the use of specific simulations early in the process limits the users' choices, this technique works well if the simulations offer a wide range of alternatives as was the case in the Kingwood Forest Park process.
8. From a summary of meeting notes on Kingwood Forest Park, from the New Landscape, North Carolina State University, Raleigh, N.C., 1972.
9. From an interview with Julie Graham in Albuquerque, N.M., May 13, 1973.
10. From a report on F-20 Total Environmental Play Area, City of Albuquerque, N.M., 1971, p. 1.
11. Arthur M. Coon, "Brainstorming—A Creative Problem-Solving Technique," *Journal of Communication* **7**(3): 111-118 (1957).
12. From meeting notes of the Urban Beautification Program, City of Cambridge, Mass., 1969.
13. From R. Hester's notes of the Five Points Process, Goals for Raleigh, N.C., 1973. The names of the participants have been changed.
14. William J. J. Gordon, *Synectics,* Harper & Row, New York, 1961.
15. Christopher Jones, *Design Methods: Seeds of Human Futures,* John Wiley & Sons, New York, 1971, pp. 48-49.
16. Gordon, *Synectics.* See this book for a review of the application of the synectics process to specific design problems.
17. Based on a planning process of the Community Development Section, Cambridge, Mass., 1969-1970.
18. Courtesy of the Fred Olds School, Raleigh, N.C., Pat Gryder, principal.
19. Morton D. Davis, *Game Theory: A Nontechnical Introduction,* Basic Books, New York, 1970, p. viii.
20. Davis, *Game Theory,* pp. ix-x.
21. Henry Sanoff, *POP (Planning Outdoor Play),* Community Development Group, Raleigh, N.C., 1973.
22. *SOS (Selection of Sites),* The New Landscape, North Carolina State University, Raleigh, N.C., 1972.
23. Ervin J. Bell, *U-Dig (Urban Design Investment Game),* University of Colorado, Boulder, Colo. Developed in the 1968-1969 academic year.

24. Richard Saul Wurman, Alan Levy, and Joel Katz, with Jean McClintock and Harold Brunner, "Developing Recreational Resources," *The Nature of Recreation: a Handbook in Honor of Frederick Law Olmsted, Using Examples form His Work,* MIT Press, Cambridge, Mass., 1972, pp. 60-64.

25. Allan G. Felt, *CLUG (Community Land Use Game),* Cornell University, Ithaca, N.Y., 1966. See Allan G. Felt, *CLUG: The Community Land Use Game,* Systems Gaming Associates, Ithaca, N.Y., 1966.

26. Wayne Maynard and Guy L. Angster, *Minipug (Mini-Park Users Game),* North Carolina State University, Raleigh, N.C., 1972. See Wayne Maynard, "Game Simulation and Community Advocacy," *Landscape Architecture* **62**(4): 335-338.

27. For applications of gaming, See Richard D. Duke, *Gaming Simulation in Urban Research,* Michigan State University, East Lansing, Mich., 1964.

28. C. Long and A. McBride, *A Comparative Analysis of Research Methods for Determining User Want-Needs in Urban Neighborhood Park Decisions,* The New Landscape, Raleigh N.C., 1972, pp. 10-11.

29. William J. Goode and Paul K. Hatt, *Methods in Social Research,* McGraw-Hill, New York, 1952, 386p.; Charles H. Backstrom and Gerald D. Hursh, *Survey Research,* Northwestern University Press, Chicago, 1963, 192p.; Leon Festinger and Daniel Katz, eds., *Research Methods in the Behavioral Sciences,* Dryden Press, New York, 1953, 660p.; Gilbert Sax, *Empirical Foundations of Educational Research,* Prentice-Hall, Englewood Cliffs, N.J., 1968, 443p.

30. From meeting notes, The New Landscape, 1972.

31. From meeting notes, The New Landscape, 1972.

32. Long and McBride, *A Comparative Analysis,* pp. 12-22.

33. From meeting notes, The New Landscape, 1972.

34. Goode and Hatt, *Methods,* p. 133.

35. Long and McBride, *A Comparative Analysis,* p. 27.

36. From notes on the Fred Olds Bozo, The Community Development Group, North Carolina State University, Raleigh, N.C., 1973.

37. From a letter from Robin Moore, Jan. 1974.

38. From meeting notes, The New Landscape, North Carolina State University, Fall, 1971, Spring, 1972, Fall, 1973, Raleigh, N.C.

39. From notes on the Fred Olds Bozo, The Community Development Group, North Carolina State University, Raleigh, N.C., 1973.

40. From notes on the Fred Olds Bozo, The Community Development Group, North Carolina State University, Raleigh, N.C., 1973.

41. From notes on the Fred Olds Bozo, The Community Development Group, North Carolina State University, Raleigh, N.C., 1973.

42. From notes on the Fred Olds Bozo, The Community Development Group, North Carolina State University, Raleigh, N.C., 1973.

43. From notes on the Fred Olds Bozo, The Community Development Group, North Carolina State University, Raleigh, N.C., 1973.

44. From notes on the Fred Olds Bozo, The Community Development Group, North Carolina State University, Raleigh, N.C., 1973.

45. This was expanded to include an entire range of user performance standards that were used as a design-evaluation tool in the master-planning process.

46. From evaluation notes, The Community Development Section, Cambridge, Mass., 1971.

47. Charles E. Osgood, George J. Suci, and Percy Tannenbaum, *The Measurement of Meaning,* University of Illinois Press, Urbana, 1957, 352p.

48. From a telephone conversation with M. Paul Friedberg, Oct. 24, 1973. Friedberg made this statement in regard to user input into the design process of Jacob Riis. There was little citizen input in the early 1960s, but Friedberg used the results of careful evaluation of Carver house to design Riis, which became the model for urban neighborhood space design in the 1960s.

49. From a discussion with Mayer Spivack at the 4th Annual Environmental Design Research Association Conference in Blacksburg, Va., April 1973.

5

Site Planning by Archetypes and Idiosyncrasies

Armed with a checklist of the needs of users, the major socio-spatial concepts, and user-needs techniques, the designer must develop a site-planning process that is personally effective and efficient within the limits of available time, energy, and money. In addition to translating and giving form to technical information, the designer's process must include developing and testing his social assumptions, uncovering the variations arising from these assumptions, and organizing both into coherent themes. The designer must then provide the residents with choices and produce a *socially responsive solution* to the community problem.

In this chapter, such a process is described. Although the process fits within the community-development framework established in Chapter 3, this discussion excludes neighborhood organizing and related activities that provide the political context for design. The topic here is neighborhood site planning, and the focus is how to design small spaces close to home with the people who live there.

The process has evolved from my work with neighborhood groups over the past fifteen years. It incorporates the social patterns and user needs described in the previous chapters but simplifies them for ease of use into *archetypes*, expected socio-spatial patterns based on the literature and expertise and experience, and *idiosyncrasies*, variations from what is expected given the specific neighborhood. Throughout the site-planning process, the designer is developing and testing archetypes and discovering the social idiosyncrasies or nuances of the neighborhood. These are combined with site factors into a *gestalt* that expresses the essence of the changing neighborhood as a whole. Within the framework of the gestalt, a range of choices and evaluative criteria or a *spectrum* is presented to the residents who, in turn, can determine the most desirable tradeoffs of *costs and benefits*.

The process that is described is iterative. The steps are basically the same whether one is doing neighborhood-wide land-use planning, locating an industrial or community center within a neighbor- *135*

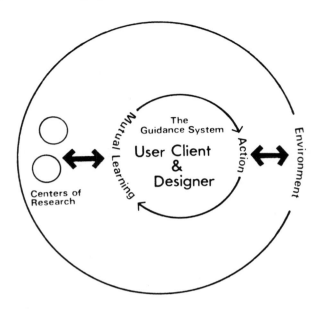

Designers Contribute

--Concepts
--Theory
--Analysis
--Processed knowledge
--New perspectives
--Systematic search procedures
--Creative ways of looking at things

User Clients Contribute

--Intimate knowledge of context
--Realistic alternatives
--Norms
--Priorities
--Feasibility judgments
--Operational details
--Details about behavior
--Idiosyncrasies of neighborhood

John Friedmann describes the transactive planning process as one in which both the planners and users participate in face-to-face decision making.

hood, or designing a park or a bench at a bus stop. The social patterns relevant to the site-planning problem simply shrink as the scale of the project is narrowed.

This process of site planning by archetypes and idiosyncrasies is provided as a model. It should be useful for students to see a step-by-step application of user needs as the basis of neighborhood planning, but two cautionary notes are in order. First, although each step is important and the procedure follows a logical order, some of the steps are frequently reversed or go on at the same time, and the

process is never as pure as it is presented. Second, each designer has to develop a process that suits his own problem-solving style and unique neighborhood situation.

For each of the twelve steps in the process, there is a description of the procedure and an illustrated example from the redevelopment of an old neighborhood in Manteo, North Carolina where the community is economically depressed and hopes to share its neighborhood business district with tourists as an economic recovery strategy. In addition, there is a summary of what the designer should learn from that step, what the users' role might be, and what techniques might be useful.

STEP ONE: LISTENING

Begin the neighborhood site-planning process by listening to residents for several weeks. Get a list of opinion leaders and interview them informally about their neighborhood and potential problems, or simply let them talk. Write or draw notes on a big map of the neighborhood. You and the opinion leader can use the map for reference, and you can have a spontaneous record of the conversations. Be sure you make your notes so the person can see what you are putting down, thus creating the atmosphere of honesty that you need. Also, it is less intimidating if your note taking is public. Mark important places. Get people to define the neighborhood boundaries, and describe their patterns, but do not try to direct the conversation. This is your opportunity to get their opinions about the problem instead of you introducing an outside bias. Usually, you are hired by elected officals or an agency to solve a specific problem. Use this opportunity to see if other people perceive the problem as real or as just a symptom.

When I was hired by the town board in Manteo to develop the site plan for a waterfront park, I was eager to begin designing; but my partner insisted on talking to neighborhood residents first. After two days of these discussions, I was overwhelmed by the

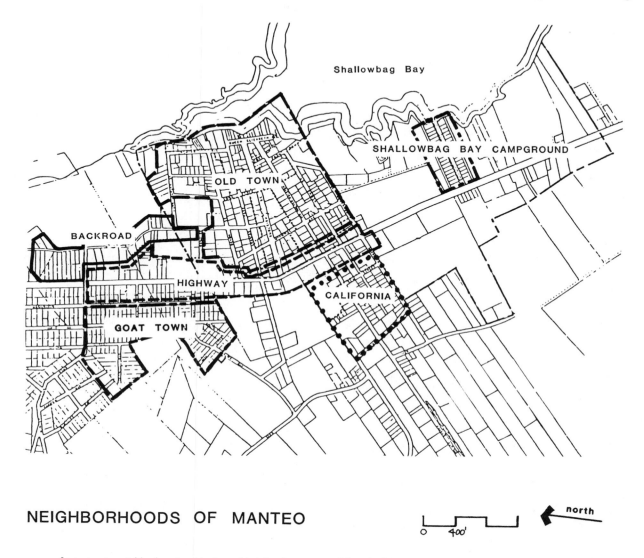

Shallowbag Bay

SHALLOWBAG BAY CAMPGROUND

OLD TOWN

BACKROAD

HIGHWAY

CALIFORNIA

GOAT TOWN

NEIGHBORHOODS OF MANTEO

0   400'   north

Listening to neighborhood residents enabled the designers to define the boundaries of the neighborhoods of Manteo.

emotion conveyed in residents' personal stories but realized I was seeing the neighborhood from the inside out. After a week, the problem was redefined as a result of residents telling us over and over about the community's economic troubles and the need to attract more tourist dollars. The town board agreed that the waterfromt park needed to be designed later and in the context of an overall plan, so we renegotiated a contract to develop an economic recovery plan for the community.

What the designer should gain from step one:

Clarification of the problem from the users' perspective

An emotional involvement with the residents

A sense of value conflicts among residents

A definition of the neighborhood boundaries

Enough information to write questions for the goals survey

An idea of what needs to be inventoried

An awareness of how committed the residents are to neighborhood improvements

The role of the users in this step:

To provide first-hand insights on community values, problems, and potential

Useful technique:

Informal interview

STEP TWO: SETTING NEIGHBORHOOD GOALS

Goals are the foundation of design. Community-wide goal setting is essential to determine neighborhood needs and priorities. Whereas listening focused on opinion leaders, the goals survey must be representative of the whole community. The designer will need (1) a goals survey instrument, (2) a scientific sample of the neighborhood, (3) people to do the surveying, and (4) someone to analyze the results. To develop a survey, start with an existing format similar to the one included here for the goals for Manteo interview schedule and modify it to suit your needs.

When doing the survey, you should generally have open-ended questions first and detailed, multiple-choice questions later. (The detailed questions will come from the knowledge gained from the opinion leaders.) Ask specific questions about design-related issues like daily patterns, activity preferences, and user conflicts. These results will be used later, but you can save money by including them in the survey.

In choosing a sample for survey purposes, it is easiest to select dwelling units on a random geographic basis. Mark the ones to be surveyed on a map, but be sure to include alternative rules in case no one is at home. The interviewers can later take the maps with them to find the right dwellings. If your survey is administered carefully, a sample of about 100 carefully chosen residents will give reliable results about neighborhood goals.

Personal interviews are preferred because they reach a broader range of people than telephone surveys or questionnaires. Usually, civic groups will volunteer to do the interviewing, but they must be trained in survey techniques. The training usually can be done in a day by a professional survey methodologist.

After the interviews are completed, the designer can tally the responses by hand. There is seldom reason to do more complicated analysis of goal-setting data for design decision making. Simple, ranked lists will be helpful for the neighborhood. For example, in response to an open-ended question about what residents liked best in their Manteo neighborhood, 44 percent of the respondents listed "quiet and peaceful." Although this is a typical response, we didn't expect nearly half the people to have the same response (usually 15 percent is significant agreement to open-ended questions). From that overwhelming response, it was clear that the most important asset of the neighborhood was its quiet and peaceful character. We could also assume that the preservation of that character would be essential in any changes made to the community.

By similarly tallying the responses to each question, the designer can provide a ranking of neighborhood assets and problems. This raw information should be published and circulated among residents—local newspapers are usually eager to assist. This informs and further involves residents as well as providing them a means of evaluating design plans later in the process. Residents can compare the

Goals for Manteo Interview Schedule

Number _____

Visit _____

Type of Housing Unit:
_____ Single-family dwelling   _____ Mobile home
_____ Duplex   _____ Other
_____ Townhouse or apartment

1. SEX: _____ Female _____ Male
2. RACE: _____ Black _____ White _____ Other

Hello, my name is _____ . I'm working on the Goals for Manteo Project. You may have heard about it. We are taking a survey of the whole community and your household has been chosen. We'd like your opinions on the questions I have here. (Ask to speak to the head of household.)

3. How Long Have You Lived in Manteo?

_____ Less than 6 months
_____ 6 months-1 year
_____ 1 year-2 years
_____ 2 years-5 years
_____ 5 years-10 years
_____ Over 10 years

4. Why did you move here? (For those who have moved here within the last 10 years)

5. Do you intend to live here (in the Manteo area) for the foreseeable future?

_____ Yes
_____ No
Why? Why not?

6. How many generations has your family lived in the Manteo area?

_____ 1 generation
_____ 2 generations
_____ 3 generations
_____ 4 generations
_____ 5 or more

7. Do you rent or own this home?

_____ Rent
_____ Own
_____ Neither

8. What things do you like most about your neighborhood?

9. Most neighborhoods have some problems or needs. What do you consider to be the most serious problems or needs of your neighborhood?

10. What things do you like most about Manteo?

11. What problems or needs in the town of Manteo do you consider to be the most serious?

12. Where do you do most of your shopping?

    _____ Downtown Manteo
    _____ Stores on Highway 64
    _____ Stores on the beach
    _____ Other cities

13. How often do you use the stores downtown?

    _____ Daily
    _____ Weekly
    _____ Monthly
    _____ Yearly

14. How often do you use the stores on Highway 64?

    _____ Daily
    _____ Weekly
    _____ Monthly
    _____ Yearly

15. What kinds of new stores would you like to see in Manteo?

16. What improvements are needed in the town launch and dock facilities?

17. If it were possible, would you like to see a beach or other water-related recreation facilities located in Manteo?

    _____ Yes
    _____ No

_____ No response
_____ Where?

18. Is there a need for a teen center in Manteo?

_____ Yes
_____ No
_____ Don't know
_____ No response
Where should it be located?

19. Would you like to see the island across dough's creek developed?

20. What type of tourist attractions would you like to see in downtown Manteo?

21. Would you like to see the 400th anniversary of the first English settlement in America celebrated in Manteo? (You may have to preface this with an explanation.)

_____ Yes
_____ No
_____ Don't know
How?

22. Would you like an Elizabethan ship docked in Manteo?

_____ Yes
_____ No
_____ No response

23. We have listed some problems and needs as being important to the community at this time. This may or may not be the case. You may consider some problems to be more serious than others. Now we would like your opinion on how serious the problems in the following list are in Manteo. Choose either:

4. Very serious
3. Serious
2. Somewhat serious
1. Not so serious
0. No problem's (Don't know, won't answer)

(These last responses were weighted, giving four points for each "very serious" response, three for each "serious" response, two for each "somewhat serious" response, and one for each "not so serious" response. This gave us a total weighted score for each problem that indicated its relative seriousness to the people in Manteo.)

_____ lack of health-care facilities
_____ lack of doctors and dentists
_____ need for picnic and sitting places
_____ need for a boardwalk on the waterfront
_____ need for town planning
_____ local taxes too high
_____ repairing present housing
_____ rundown waterfront
_____ preserving neighborhoods from commercial development
_____ property taxes too high
_____ need for downtown redevelopment
_____ visual clutter and congestion on Highway 64
_____ water pollution
_____ too many power lines above ground
_____ quality of your water supply
_____ cultural opportunities
_____ not enough choice in entertainment
_____ development on Highway 64
_____ lack of a Manteo Merchant's Association
_____ quality of the town boat launch and docks
_____ unemployment
_____ zoning
_____ lack of tourist attractions in Manteo
_____ emergency medical services
_____ annexation
_____ lack of trees downtown
_____ need to recycle waste materials
_____ building on lowlands that may be flooded
_____ need for new streets
_____ dirtiness and litter
_____ lack of sidewalks downtown
_____ way the city looks
_____ development of marshland
_____ natural parks
_____ lack of town bus service
_____ lack of sidewalks in your neighborhood
_____ population growth at Nags Head
_____ crime
_____ sewage disposal
_____ destruction of trees
_____ political disagreements
_____ poor education for children
_____ street lighting
_____ lack of a beach in Manteo
_____ not enough tourists
_____ noise pollution
_____ preservation of historic buildings and sites
_____ police protection

_____ school construction in residential areas
_____ garbage disposal
_____ need for another restaurant downtown
_____ family disagreements over town business
_____ racial discrimination
_____ too many tourists
_____ not enough welfare programs
_____ fire protection
_____ other (please list)

(These last few questions were used only for statistical purposes to see if we had a cross section of the population in Manteo.)

24. What was the last grade of school that you completed?

25. Which of the following would you choose to describe yourself?

    _____ Conservative
    _____ Moderate
    _____ Liberal
    _____ No response

26. Into which of the following categories does your age fall?

    _____ Under 21
    _____ 21-30
    _____ 31-50
    _____ 51-60
    _____ Over 61
    _____ No response

27. What is your occupation?

28. Where do you work?

29. Do you have a car?

    _____ Yes
    _____ No
    _____ No response

30. Do you own a boat?

    _____ Yes

_____ No
_____ No response

31. Where do you put your boat in?

32. Are there any children living here?

_____ Yes
_____ No

What are their ages? (Just check the category of the children's ages—it is not necessary to indicate the number of children in each.)

_____ less than 1 year old
_____ 1-3 years old
_____ 4-5 years old
_____ 6-10 years old
_____ 11-15 years old
_____ 16-21 years old
_____ over 21 years old

33. What is your approximate yearly family income?

_____ less than $3,000
_____ $3,000-6,000
_____ $6,000-9,000
_____ $9,000-12,000
_____ $12,000-15,000
_____ over $15,000
_____ No response

34. Would you like to be more involved in planning Manteo's future?

_____ Yes
_____ No
_____ No response

Thank you for your time. The results of the survey will be in the newspaper in about three weeks.

plans to the survey results to see if, for example, the peace and quiet has been maintained.

At the same time, the tallied responses must be analyzed to determine patterns that can form the framework for the goals. This should be done by the designer and a community group like a goal setting committee or a planning board. The designer should content analyze the responses and develop a tentative set of goals by listing five to ten statements that seem to incorporate the most representative responses, include minority concerns, and express the unique concerns of the neighborhood.

After the community group has agreed on the primary goals statements, the designer can incorporate the objectives under the appropriate heading. In Manteo, the framework statements consisted of developing a new purpose for the village downtown, preserving the existing character of the community, improving services to residents, celebrating the quadricentennial of the first Roanoke Colonies in Manteo, developing a more economically viable community, and providing recreational opportunities for all Manteo residents. After these were adopted by the planning board, goals for Manteo were completed by listing other responses as objectives. For example, the recreational goal was broad enough to include objectives of providing a teen center, parks for residents of all ages, and a beach and improved marina.

Additionally, the Manteo goals survey produced explicit and implicit information that alerted us to issues that would influence the neighborhood design. First, the residents had potentially conflicting goals: one was to develop tourism, and the other was to preserve the village character of the neighborhood. This indicated that we needed to know more about the details of the village character before proceeding and had to be careful not to sacrifice that character to tourism. Second, residents listed street paving, sidewalks, recreation places for children and teenagers, low-income housing, and jobs as the most critical needs of their community. They were able to use this explicit list of needs later to determine which plans met their goals.

What the designer should gain from step two:

Further clarification of the neighborhood problem

A reliable list of the best and worst things about the community

A priority list of resident needs

A set of goals to direct the planning process and evaluate proposed plans

A sense of what overall strategy to pursue (social changes, conservation, or economic redevelopment)

A list of design considerations to be used later

A clearer list of what needs to be inventoried

Information to use in "introducing" the community to itself

The role of the users in this step:

To provide information through survey

To interview the sample

To set the goals

Useful techniques:

Interview

Questionnaire

Neighborhood forum

STEP THREE: MAPPING AND INVENTORY

From *listening* and *setting goals,* the planner should have a good idea of what information is needed. You always need a base map (an air photograph is excellent) and most city governments have topographical maps, census data, and information on land values, building conditions, utilities, zoning, traffic, historic places, neighborhood resources, and ownership available for the public. It is likely that you will also need an inventory of the neighborhood's economic potential (a market analysis is excellent if one has been done) and environmental constraints and potentials (sometimes available from local governments). Get whatever inventories and maps that

Manteo Residents

Take A Minute!

Manteo will face many changes in the next ten years. Its population will grow, new businesses will be established, tourism will increase and the 400th anniversary will be celebrated. Residents have continually pointed out that changes in the town should not disrupt the quality of living that makes Manteo so important. One way to help insure the protection of that quality is by identifying the objects and places in town that help form Manteo's special qualities. By identifying special places and measuring their importance in relation to future changes, the lifestyle and qualities that are unique to Manteo can be preserved.

We on the NCSU planning team would like to locate all the features in Manteo that are especially meaningful to the town. Please help us identify them by answering the following questions. All responses will be kept confidential. The results of this questionnaire will be published for your information.

1. There are certain features in town that are part of Manteo's special atmosphere. List the three places in order of their importance that contribute most to the image of Manteo.
   1.
   2.
   3.

List the three places in Manteo that detract from the town's image.
   1.
   2.
   3.

2. Certain features in Manteo will need protection as tourism increases in the town. We would like to know what would be worth giving up for increased tourism, and what aspects of the town should remain as they are now.

A. It is more important to keep the Sir Walter Raleigh Statue in Bicentennial Park than to increase tourist visitation by moving the statue to a more visible place in town.
   1. agree
   2. disagree

B. It is more important to build and improve parking lots than to have parallel street parking closer to the stores.
   1. agree
   2. disagree

C. It is more important to leave the memorial cross where it now stands in Bicentennial Park than to move it to accomodate the construction of a gazebo, picnic shelter or children's play equipment.
   1. agree
   2. disagree

D. It is more important to leave the downtown gravel lot as a town parking lot than to convert it to a recreational park.
   1. agree
   2. disagree

E. It is more important to keep the post lamps in Bicentennial Park than to replace them with another type of lighting system.
   1. agree
   2. disagree

F. It is more important to see new development and commercial businesses in Manteo than to see marsh and wildlife close by the town.
   1. agree
   2. disagree

G. It is more important for the Post Office to remain located downtown than to locate on Highway 64/264.
   1. agree
   2. disagree

H. It is more important to leave the Christmas Tree in the gravel lot downtown than to use that space for parking.
   1. agree
   2. disagree

I. It is more important for the town to improve docking facilities for tourist boat traffic than to improve boat ramp and docking facilities for residents.
   1. agree
   2. disagree

J. It is more important to keep a general goods store like the Ben Franklin in downtown Manteo than to encourage the development of speciality shops in its place.
   1. agree
   2. disagree

We have listed below twenty features in and around Manteo that townspeople have described to us in interviews and discussions. Please rank them in order of their importance, number one being the most important and number twenty being the least important. There are spaces at the bottom of the list to add additional features important to you that have been left out of this list. Please rank your additions with the rest of the list.

Bicentennial Park
Town Cemetery
The Christmas Shop
   The Christmas Tree in the

downtown gravel lot
The Court House
The Duchess Restaurant
Fearings Drugstore
Front Porches
Andy Griffith's House
Town Launch Area
The Lost Colony Site
Marshes close to town
Manteo High School
New stores on Highway 64/264
Post Lamps in Bicentennial Park
The Post Office
Sir Walter Raleigh Statue
Town Hall
Town Street Signs

Next, there are questions that are more personal but equally important to our study. This information too will be kept confidential.

1. AGE:
   1. under 25
   2. 25 to 35
   3. 35 to 45
   4. 45 to 60
   5. over 60

2. SEX: 1. Female   2. Male
3. RACE: 1. Black   2. White
             3. Other

4. How long have you lived in Manteo?
   1. less than 6 months
   2. 6 months to one year
   3. over one year to 5 years
   4. over 5 years to 10 years
   5. over 10 years

5. Do you intend to live in Manteo for the forseeable future?
   1. Yes   2. No
6. Do you work in Manteo?
   1. Yes   2. No

7. What is your occupation?
   1. service   2. governmental
   3. manager/professional/teacher
   4. Sales   5. domestic
   6. craftsman/tradesman
   7. disabled   8. retired
   9. unemployed   10. other

8. Is your occupation tourist related?
   1. Yes   2. No

Thank you for your help. There will be a box placed in Town Hall for your responses. They can be mailed to: Planning Team, Manteo Town Hall, Manteo, NC 27954. The deadline for sending responses is March 27, 1981.

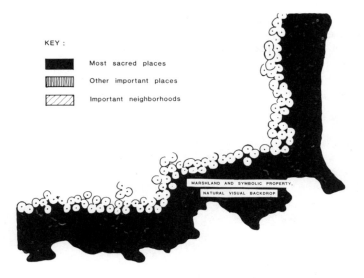

KEY :

- **Most sacred places**
- Other important places
- Important neighborhoods

MARSHLAND AND SYMBOLIC PROPERTY.
NATURAL VISUAL BACKDROP

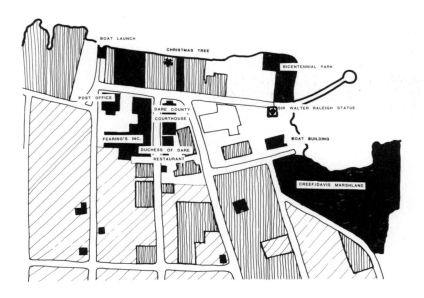

BOAT LAUNCH

CHRISTMAS TREE

BICENTENNIAL PARK

POST OFFICE

DARE COUNTY
COURTHOUSE

SIR WALTER RALEIGH STATUE

BOAT BUILDING

FEARING'S INC.

DUCHESS OF DARE
RESTAURANT

CREEF/DAVIS MARSHLAND

The sacred-structure survey allowed the designers to map the most important places in the community to the residents. This later dictated where development could be located in order not to disturb the sacred places.

THE SACRED STRUCTURE

0   100'

exist; the cost is nominal. Also be sure to search the literature for information particularly relevant to the neighborhood. (In Manteo, this included research on village character and the impact of tourism on the social structure.)

Some information will have to be gathered first-hand and should involve users because they are aware of the subtleties of the information that might escape the designer. This information usually includes maps of what the users consider attractive in the environment (visual-inventory maps), maps showing where inequities exist in the neighborhood (environmental-injustices maps), maps showing what places are particularly meaningful to local residents (sacred-structure maps), and maps of existing activity patterns (get the residents to do as much of this mapping as possible). This last map will be the first test of the expected activity patterns (archetype) the designer expects based on the literature and experience. This kind of firsthand mapping is costly, therefore you never want to map anything you will not need.

In response to the information from the Manteo goals survey about neighborhood priorities, we did a special inventory of street and sidewalk conditions, recreational patterns of children and teens, availability of jobs and low-income housing, the components of the village character, and activity-pattern conflicts of tourists and residents. From ecology mapping we found that most local teenagers worked or went to nearby beaches in the summer and did not conflict with tourists at the watefront nearly as much as was expected (an archetype dispelled by an idiosyncrasy). However, a few older teens did dominate one area of the docks, precluding other users. The teens complained that there was nothing for them to do in the winter and that a teen center was needed in the neighborhood (corroborating the survey).

The residents' concern about maintaining their unique village character (clearly stated in the goals survey) led to a newspaper survey in which residents were asked to make trade-offs to determine what local institutions they were unwilling to sacrifice to attract tourists. Marshes that defined the neighbor-

hood, two historic sites, a park, a drugstore hangout, a cafe, and the post office all were ranked more sacred than the local churches (another archetype dispelled by an idiosyncrasy). This provided us with an important map of the neighborhood sacred structure.

What the designer should gain from step three:

Necessary base maps
Technical information about environmental, social, economic, and political factors bearing on the neighborhood
A review of the literature related to areas of particular concern in planning the neighborhood
First-hand data about the sacred structure of the neighborhood, environmental injustices, and existing activity patterns with subtleties only residents can provide
Tests of archetypes against idiosyncrasies in map form
Special maps of factors of concern to residents like sidewalk conditions in Manteo

The role of the users in this step:

To assist in gathering the necessary firsthand data

Useful techniques:

Questionnaires
Ecology observation and mapping

STEP FOUR: INTRODUCING THE NEIGHBORHOOD TO ITSELF

After gathering, analyzing, and mapping the inventory, the designer has a unique perspective on the neighborhood: the objectivity of an outsider, insights into the emotional intimacy of residents, and an awareness of daily patterns and spatial nuances. When shared with residents, this information serves to introduce the neighborhood to itself, making people aware of their community as never before.

Although various techniques such as newspaper

stories and workshops in which residents take part in collectively discovering their environment are used to introduce a neighborhood to itself, the most effective method I have observed was a slide show using children's responses to the goals survey for their community. The responses shocked the adults because they were so candid. The elementary and high-school respondents pointed out environmental injustices, conflicts in the neighborhood, values and activity patterns the adults would never discuss. Although some adults were offended, the presentation opened a much-needed dialogue. This also gives the designer an opportunity to present to users the data on which his assumptions will be based, to have them respond to the data, and then to modify it if inaccurate.

A neighborhood forum was used to introduce the Manteo community to itself. A map of each inventory was discussed and resident corrections were made directly on the drawings. This let the users know their comments were taken seriously and encouraged less-vocal residents to give the designer feedback.

What the designer should gain from step four:

Detailed corrections to the base data
Additional neighborhood interest
Greater sensitivity to the users
An understanding of the salient issues

The role of the users in this step:

To correct mistakes in the inventory
To redirect the designer if incompatible values or interpretations of patterns are exposed

Useful technique:

Neighborhood forum (using a slide show)

STEP FIVE: GETTING A GESTALT

The next task for the designer is to extract from the various inventories the salient issues that describe the neighborhood situation simply yet completely, give form to the heart of the matter, and express its essence.

In Manteo, for example, it became clear that the salient issues were economic recovery, the sacred life patterns, the old neighborhood waterfront character, and the upcoming quadricentennial anniversary of Sir Walter Raleigh's Roanoke Colonies that had been established in the vicinity and remained a major tourist attraction. These four forces had to be combined, however, to provide a unifying theme to guide the neighborhood change.

This process relies on the designer seeing the soul of the neighborhood and thinking of the problems as a whole, comprehending the archetypes and idiosyncrasies, and combining all these into a gestalt. Whereas most of the steps thus far have been orderly and disciplined, getting a gestalt is not. It may require a brainstorming session, synectics, daydreaming, self-hypnosis, meditation, or a day off. In Manteo the gestalt was discovered in a phone conversation between the mayor and me after weeks of searching individually and in community groups. I went over with him the words and phrases we kept repeating—economic recovery, history, tourism, Elizabethan-village character, porches, rural homeyness, the lost colony, dreams of freedom—all important parts of our earlier inventory. Suddenly, he responded, "Come sit on our front porch, let us tell you of the dreams we keep." It expressed the essence of what the community was trying to achieve and it became the theme that guided the rest of our planning process.

What the designer should gain from step five:

A gestalt that expresses the totality and soul of the neighborhood situation
Resident agreement with that theme or another

The role of the users in this step:

To participate in uncovering the gestalt
To decide if the gestalt is appropriate

Useful techniques:

Brainstorming
Synectics
Buzz sessions

STEP SIX: DRAWING ANTICIPATED ACTIVITY SETTINGS

At this point, the designer begins to give form to the socio-spatial archetypes and idiosyncrasies important in the neighborhood. First, he should list all of the major activities anticipated. These come from three sources: the existing uses (take this information directly from the existing activity-patterns map and the sacred-structures map), desired uses (these may be taken from the results of the goals survey), and uses necessary to meet desired goals (these are implied by the goals survey, but the designer must interpret what activities to include).

In Manteo, the existing uses included such idiosyncratic activities as sitting on front porches, going to the diner, "newsing" at the post office, hanging out at the docks, and "marsh meditating." Desired activities from the goals survey included walking around the neighborhood (indicating the need for sidewalks), creating places to work (indicating the need for more jobs) and live (indicating the need for low-income housing), and making places for children and teens to play (indicating the need for parks and recreation). Implied in the goals survey were low-key, history-based activities for tourists that would not disrupt the neighborhood. We listed the possible tourist activities like driving, parking, getting information, boating, docking, shopping and learning-by-doing (this included detailed projections of the number of tourists and cars per day, length of visits, and services required).

Thumbnail sketches of each activity and its associated setting should then be drawn to show the nuances of the activity setting and the interaction pattern. Include spatial factors like props, essential separations, and scale, as well as social factors like territoriality, symbolic ownership, class, and life-cycle subtleties that seem important. If you do not remember how an existing setting is used, go back and observe it again. Look for details. Write down design implications on the drawings.

In Manteo, the drawing of hanging out at the docks described these nuances: racially mixed older teens establishing territorial control over the piers, using the pilings as diving boards, controlling all of the picnic tables, and parking their cars and four wheelers next to the docks but with a view of the main streets. Younger teens were shown claiming other piers for swimming and tag—their activities sometimes conflicting with crabbers—and docked boats were shown preventing any other activity. The design implications included needs for numerous pier territories: separate but connected spaces for picnicking, crabbing, swimming, hanging out, viewing and docking, and some spaces amidst the docks where no docking is allowed to provide nonboaters access to the water.

What the designer should gain from step six:

A list of all the important activities desired or needed to meet residents' goals
Drawings of each activity setting with spatial and interaction nuances noted
An increased sensitivity to the subtleties of the neighborhood
Potential design implications of each activity setting
An awareness of how user patterns can inspire the form of design

Useful techniques:

Ecology observations

STEP SEVEN: LETTING ARCHETYPES AND IDIOSYNCRASIES INSPIRE FORM

The designer now transforms the information gained from the activity-setting drawings into performance

The designer should draw thumbnail sketches of each activity setting making detailed notes about how the space is used and drawing conclusions that may direct design decisions.

D!

We Also Off
• Deep Scr
(for heavily so
DuPont T
Pet Odor/
Flood Dan
24 Hrs.
xpert Upho
riental Rug
ea Treatmen
ergy Relief

%

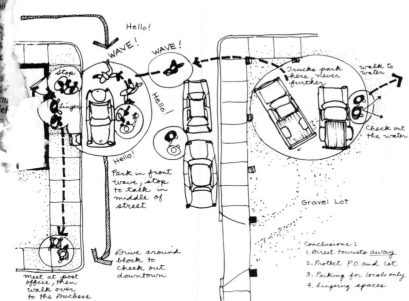

Hello!

WAVE!

WAVE!

Hello!

stop

Lingers

Hello!

Trucks park here, never further

walk to water

Check out the water

Park in front wave; stop to talk in middle of street

Gravel Lot

Drive around block to check out downtown

meet at post office, then walk over to the Duchess

Conclusions:
1. Direct tourists away
2. Protect P.O. and lot
3. Parking for locals only
4. Lingering spaces

NEWSING AT THE POST OFFICE

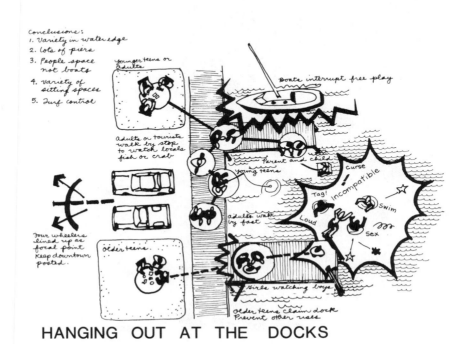

Conclusions:
1. Variety in water edge
2. Lots of piers
3. People space not boats
4. Variety of sitting spaces
5. Surf control

younger teens or adults

Boats interrupt free play

adults or tourists walk by stop to watch locals fish or crab

Parent and child

young teens

Curse

Incompatible

Tag!

Swim

Loud

Sex

Four wheelers lined up as focal point keep downtown posted.

older teens.

adults walk by fast

Girls watching boys

older teens claim dock Prevent other uses

HANGING OUT AT THE DOCKS

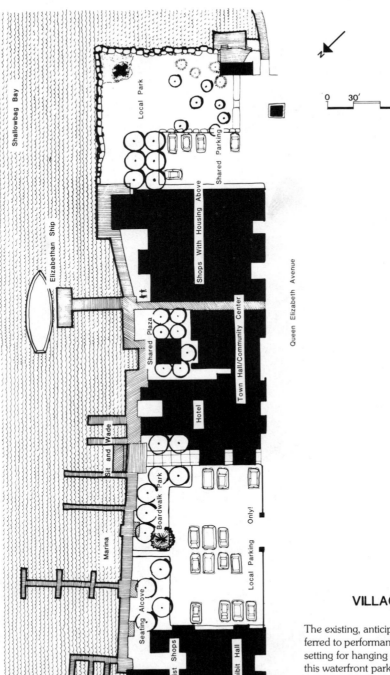

Shallowbag Bay

Local Park

Shared Parking

Elizabethan Ship

Shops With Housing Above

Queen Elizabeth Avenue

Shared Plaza

Town Hall/Community Center

Sit and Wade

Hotel

Boardwalk Park

Marina

Local Parking Only!

Seating Alcove.

Tourist Shops

Exhibit Hall

0   30'

VILLAGE WATERFRONT PARK

The existing, anticipated, and required activity patterns can be transferred to performance criteria that can later direct design. The activity setting for hanging out at the docks along with other patterns led to this waterfront park plan. Note the numerous piers, nearby parking, the sit-and-wade space without boats, and the separate sitting areas all inspired by the performance standards.

standards (see Chapter 3) or statements about *what* and *whom* each activity setting needs to function well and *how, where* and *when* it is expected to function given the patterns and nuances of the particular neighborhood. These performance standards can then be used to generate designs and as hypotheses to evaluate designs before construction and test them after construction.

Begin with the list of activity settings. Beside each, write sentences that describe in detail the what, where, when, how and whom for that activity setting. To avoid missing an important factor, you might refer to the checklist of performance standards in Chapter 3. Using the example of teenagers hanging out on the docks, we listed performance standards like these:

1. No more than a dozen teenagers use the docks at any given time during the summer since most are working.
2. The activity is age but not race segregated; spatial but not visual separation is required.
3. The activity requires at least two easily territorialized spaces about 100 square feet each extending into a swimming area.
4. Hanging out is combined with socializing, swimming, diving, showing off, and watching for friends, precluding docked boats.
5. There needs to be sitting and parking for several cars within 20 feet of the pier. The parking needs to be at the apex of the site lines from Budleigh and Sir Walter Raleigh Streets.
6. The piers and picnic areas being used by teenagers are not likely to be used by others, necessitating somewhat separate but not isolated facilities.

These performance criteria were specific enough for us to generate and evaluate designs from them later in the process. Do not worry about conflicts between activity settings at this step. Allow yourself to miss the big picture, and concentrate on developing performance criteria that maximize each activity set-

ting separately. In the next step, compromises will be made to put all of the activity settings together.

What the designer should gain from step seven:

Explicit performance criteria that can be used to generate detailed design alternatives

A set of hypotheses that can be used for evaluating the design before and after construction

Performance criteria for each activity setting that can be used to determine which settings are compatible so they can be fit into an overall conceptual plan

The role of the users in this step:

To check the performance criteria for accuracy

STEP EIGHT: MAKING A CONCEPTUAL YARDSTICK

At this point, the designer has a gestalt and activity settings, but the gestalt has no substance and the activity settings have no context. For either to be useful the planner must combine the two to produce a *conceptual yardstick* to evaluate plans drawn later. Start by comparing the performance standards of each activity setting to those of *every* other one to determine compatibility between the activity settings within the context of the gestalt and goals previously set. (The goals and gestalt may conflict with some activity settings. Mark those conflicts first. For example, we expected tourists to want to spend the night in the neighborhood center, but Manteo residents had set a goal to encourage only people taking day trips. We later reduced the number of overnight tourists to those who could stay in a fifty-room inn.)

If there are a lot of activity settings, you may need a matrix to display the compatibilities. If so, cut out paper shapes for the activity settings and arrange them to maximize the adjacency requirements for the whole set of activities. (Note: in the example we

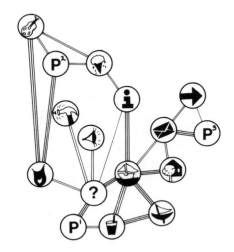

Key :

- ● uses require adjacency
- ◑ uses reinforced by adjacency
- ◕ uses enhanced by adjacency
- ⊕ whole experience reinforced by separateness
- ○ uses are incompatible
- ☐ uses have a neutral relationship

RELATIONSHIPS BETWEEN ACTIVITY SETTINGS

To develop a conceptual yardstick, the designer may need to display the major activity settings in a matrix in order to see the relationships. These can be summarized by using paper cutouts arranged to maximize the desired adjacencies and then fitting the cutouts onto the site by adjusting the activities to match the places with development potential.

SUMMARY OF RELATIONSHIPS BETWEEN ACTIVITY SETTINGS

DEVELOPMENT POTENTIAL MAP

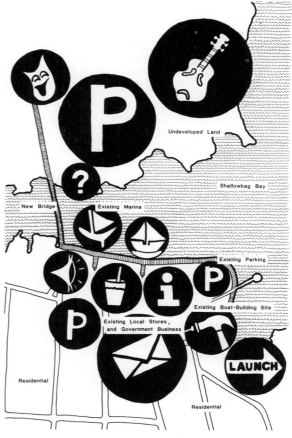

FITTING THE ACTIVITY SETTINGS ONTO THE SITE

have excluded overnight-tourist accommodations.) This summary gives the overall picture of how the activities fit together. You now have your best arrangement based on the gestalt, the goals, and the performance standards. Be sure to add the specific dimensional requirements for each activity setting.

Now try to fit this to the site, compromising your activity settings as little as possible. This is where the details of the inventory will be most useful. Such things as ownership, building condition, existing infrastructure, fragile environmental areas, and legal constraints will modify the location of the activity settings. The result of this procedure is a conceptual plan that maximizes the desired activity patterns of the residents within the constraints of that community.

To accommodate tourists, Manteo residents had to incorporate parking for 250 additional cars near the community center. When we added that dimensional requirement to the activity settings, it indicated that certain existing activity patterns would have to be replaced to accommodate parking. It seemed more socially responsive to move tourist parking to a nearby undeveloped island, thereby keeping the local sacred structure and desired activity patterns of residents intact. We continued to modify the idealized activity-setting relationships until we had a conceptual plan that could serve as a practical yardstick to measure the alternative design plans that were then to be developed.

What the designer should gain from step eight:

A summary of relationships between the activity settings that has been modified in accordance with neighborhood goals, the gestalt, dimensional requirements, and site factors

A conceptual plan by which to measure detailed design plans

A further narrowing of acceptable alternatives

The role of the users in this step:

To check the conceptual plan to see if important, detailed social patterns have been unacceptably compromised

STEP NINE: DEVELOPING A SPECTRUM OF DESIGN PLANS

Now the task is to generate alternative design plans generally being guided by the conceptual plan. But be free. Seek the problem instead of solving it. Although the conceptual plan is in the back of your mind, pursue new ideas. Go back to the gestalt, choose key points, try to see these points in a new, detailed light, and generate sketch plans that symbolically address one or more of the points.

In Manteo we assumed that attracting more tourists meant sacrificing some existing life patterns and that residents needed to see a range of choices. With that in mind, we drew up detailed sketch plans. One plan turned the neighborhood into an Elizabethan-theme village; another played on the village's past as a boating and mercantile center; one stressed a living-learning waterfront where locals shared their history with visitors; one foresaw the neighborhood's continued economic decline. Then we arranged the plans along a continuum with preserving the sacred structure at one pole and attracting tourist dollars at the other. The design team discussed the important ideas contained in each plan, rendered all the plans in the same style to show their relative strengths and weaknesses, and estimated the development cost of each plan.

What the designer should gain from step nine:

New ideas about how to solve neighborhood problems

Insights into how activity settings might be arranged creatively to solve specific problems

Specific ways the site can contribute to the solution

A spectrum of detailed plans that can be used to show residents their choices

Rough cost estimates of each design plan

Useful techniques:

Synectics
Roleplaying
Brainstorming

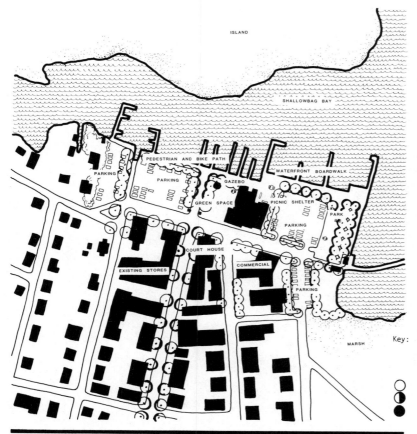

With a spectrum of plans and the cost-benefit charts, residents can evaluate the proposals before construction. In Manteo, the Dispersed, Cultural, and Performing Arts Town was the near unanimous choice of the users because it maximized the benefits with few costs. The community directed the designers to make changes in the final plan to protect local stores and further integrate the facilities.

Key:

Low relative benefit to community	○
Moderate relative benefit to community	◐
High relative benefit to community	●
Low relative cost to community	○
Moderate relative cost to community	◐
High relative cost to community	●

MANTEO ON SKIDS

RELATIVE COST-BENEFIT OF MANTEO PRELIMINARY PLANS

Cost		Benefit
○	Lifestyle preservation	● 7
○	Sacred structure preservation	● 6
◐	Village character enhancement	○
◐	Separated parking provision	○
●	Tax base increase	○
●	Property tax increase	○
●	Tourist expenditure	○
●	Tourist experience	○
◐	Integration of public-private facilities	○
◐	Local store protection	● 9

Cost		Benefit
◐	Accessibility of facilities	◐ 8
●	Diversity of stores	○
○	Prices suitable for local people	●
○	Environmental protection	●
○	Reliance on volunteerism	● 10
●	Provision of jobs	○ 1
●	Street paving and sidewalks	● 2
●	Playgrounds for children	○ 5
●	Recreation for teenagers	○ 4
●	Low income housing increased	○ 3

157

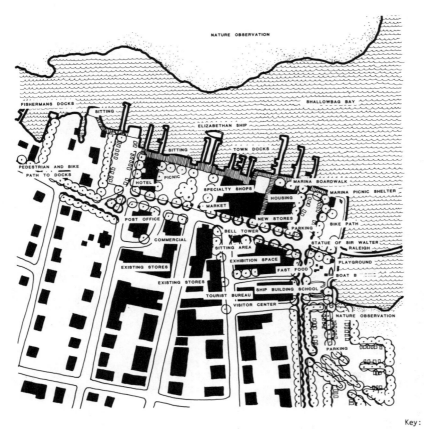

NATURE OBSERVATION

SHALLOWBAG BAY

FISHERMANS DOCKS

SITTING

ELIZABETHAN SHIP

TOWN DOCKS

SITTING

PEDESTRIAN AND BIKE
PATH TO DOCKS

MARINA BOARDWALK

HOTEL   PICNIC

SPECIALTY SHOPS

MARINA PICNIC SHELTER

MARKET   HOUSING

POST OFFICE   NEW STORES

PARKING   BIKE PATH

COMMERCIAL   BELL TOWER

SITTING AREA   STATUE OF SIR WALTER
RALEIGH

EXISTING STORES   EXHIBITION SPACE

PLAYGROUND

EXISTING STORES   FAST FOOD

BOAT B

TOURIST BUREAU   SHIP BUILDING SCHOOL

VISITOR CENTER

NATURE OBSERVATION

PARKING

Key:
Low relative benefit to community ○
Moderate relative benefit to community ◑
High relative benefit to community ●
Low relative cost to community ○
Moderate relative cost to community ◑
High relative cost to community ●

TOURIST   TOWN   MERCANTILE   CENTER

RELATIVE COST-BENEFIT OF MANTEO PRELIMINARY PLANS

Cost		Benefit
●	Lifestyle preservation	◑ 7
◑	Sacred structure preservation	◑ 6
○	Village character enhancement	●
●	Separated parking provision	○
○	Tax base increase	●
○	Property tax increase	◑
○	Tourist expenditure	●
○	Tourist experience	●
○	Integration of public-private facilities	●
●	Local store protection	○ 9

Cost		Benefit
●	Accessibility of facilities	◑ 8
○	Diversity of stores	●
●	Prices suitable for local people	○
●	Environmental protection	○
○	Reliance on volunteerism	● 10
○	Provision of jobs	● 1
○	Street paving and sidewalks	● 2
○	Playgrounds for children	● 5
○	Recreation for teenagers	● 4
○	Low income housing increased	● 3

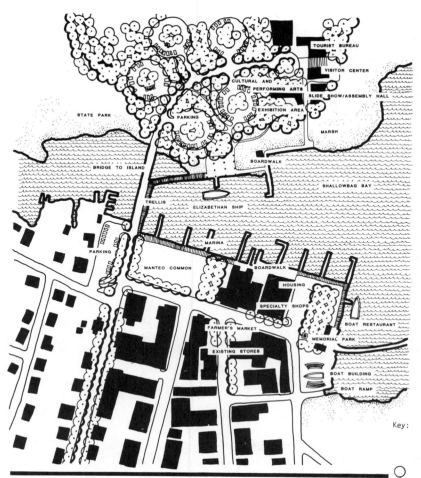

Key:

Low relative benefit to community   ○
Moderate relative benefit to community   ◑
High relative benefit to community   ●
Low relative cost to community   ○
Moderate relative cost to community   ◑
High relative cost to community   ●

DISPERSED CULTURAL AND PERFORMING ARTS TOWN

RELATIVE COST-BENEFIT OF MANTEO PRELIMINARY PLANS

Cost		Benefit		Cost		Benefit	
◑	Lifestyle preservation	●	7	○	Accessibility of facilities	●	8
○	Sacred structure preservation	●	6	○	Diversity of stores	◑	
○	Village character enhancement	◑		◑	Prices suitable for local people	◑	
○	Separated parking provision	●		○	Environmental protection	●	
○	Tax base increase	●		◑	Reliance on volunteerism	●	10
○	Property tax increase	◑		○	Provision of jobs	●	1
○	Tourist expenditure	◑		○	Street paving and sidewalks	●	2
◑	Tourist experience	◑		○	Playgrounds for children	●	5
○	Integration of public-private facilities	◑		○	Recreation for teenagers	●	4
◑	Local store protection	◑	9	○	Low income housing increased	●	3

159

STEP TEN: EVALUATING COSTS AND BENEFITS BEFORE CONSTRUCTION

Having set neighborhood goals, a gestalt, and detailed performance criteria, it is easy to write a list of evaluation standards by which the designer and residents can judge the alternative plans before construction. In some cases, it may be possible to use the performance criteria from step seven just as they were written. In other cases that list may be expanded. Frequently, there will be 100 or more specific criteria that the designer can use to make preliminary judgments with the help of several neighborhood leaders. The designers must be careful not to advocate a single plan but fairly evaluate the costs and benefits of each, suggesting when parts of plans could feasibly be combined to obtain more benefits. Then the designer and a designated neighborhood committee or planning board should reduce the evaluation list to about twenty-five of the most important factors. (More than this will make public discussion and feedback difficult.)

We used a neighborhood forum to evaluate the spectrum of plans with Manteo residents. After a detailed presentation of each of the alternative design plans, we divided into groups of six to eight people, with a design-team member as facilitator, and each person used the list of criteria to evaluate each plan. This activity was followed by a discussion of the costs and benefits of the plans, and we sought consensus about what plan to pursue from each group. Minority reports were encouraged when there was disagreement. If there are serious conflicts, role playing may shed new light on the situation for the residents; if conflicts persist, it is likely that a design plan is an inappropriate solution at that time.

Then the entire group reconvened, and a resident presented the small-group, cost-and-benefit evaluations. After further discussion, the residents took a vote directing the designers to develop one plan in more detail.

In light of the feedback from the meeting (a local newspaper may print the plans and evaluation cri-

Before construction, a modified plan should be distributed in the neighborhood through local newspapers or fliers. Construction documents consistent with resident resources can then be drawn to transfer the project to local people.

A	Living–Learning Center
B	Performing Arts Center
C	Elizabethan Ship
D	Anglo–American Folk Festival
E	Beach
F	Bridge
G	Exhibits
H	Town Launch
I	Inn
J	Sacred Lot
K	Sacred Buildings
L	Sacred Tree
M	Sacred Gate
N	Boardwalk
O	New Housing Commercial Condominiums
P	Jule's Park
Q	Sacred Statue
R	Boat Building Center
S	New Housing–Commercial
T	Infill Buildings

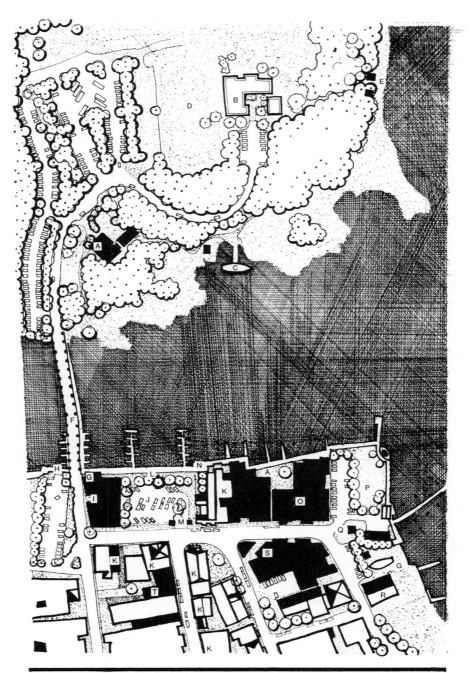

MANTEO VILLAGE PLAN

teria to receive feedback from additional neighborhood residents), the designers should change any of the performance standards and accompanying hypotheses about how the plan is expected to function. This will allow the project to be evaluated after construction and will facilitate informed modifications to the plan when changes are necessary.

What the designer should gain from step ten:

Clients who are well aware of the trade-offs necessary
A well informed evaluation of the plans by residents
A directive to complete one course of action
Consensus about one plan or well-educated splinter groups
A list of evaluation criteria that residents can use to monitor the project over time

The role of the users in this step:

To evaluate the costs and benefits of the alternative plans
To publicly discuss the trade-offs
To direct a course of action

Useful techniques:

Neighborhood forum
Newspaper survey
Role play

STEP ELEVEN: TRANSFERRING RESPONSIBILITY

After changes are made in the plan and approved by community leaders, a flyer with the final design should be circulated in the neighborhood. Where no design alternative is chosen or guidelines are established instead of an immediate physical change, the flyer should include that information. Be sure to state how the residents' use patterns influenced the outcome, particularly neighborhood idiosyncrasies that inspired design details.

Up until this point, the plan has been speculative and the designer has had a major responsibility for the work. Now that responsibility must be transferred to others. The projects must be implemented. Traditionally, this required working drawings, specifications, contract documents, and a bidding process, but neighborhood activism, scarce resources, and fiscal conservatism have stimulated new possibilities that often require creative neighborhood implementation strategies. Usually, implementation will be in somewhat disjointed and incremental stages; this must be planned in advance.

Although we prepared contract documents for the open-space improvements in Manteo, they consisted of over a dozen separate projects that could be done by volunteers. The Lions Club, for example, designated the construction of a part of the boardwalk as a community-service project. This required us to divide the neighborhood improvements into small, manageable projects and describe the construction process simply enough for local groups to be able to do the building.

As a general rule, the more responsibility the neighborhood accepts, the better. The designer must be certain that the procedure will lead to the desired end and that the policies necessary for the new neighborhood spaces to work are implemented. At that point, the designer should have transferred all of the responsibility for the project to the community group or appropriate agencies.

What the designer should gain from step eleven:

Working drawings and other documents needed to realize the project
Policies to support the plan
Design guidelines to support the plan or direct other development
Citizen awareness of the final plan and course of action
Transfer of the responsibility for implementation, maintenance, and programs to neighborhood groups or local government

Neighborhood activism, scarce resources, and fiscal conservatism have stimulated creative means of implementing neighborhood improvements. In Manteo, the Lions Club and local contractors completed a portion of the waterfront park as a community service project.

The role of the users in this step:

To approve the final plans

To accept a procedure for implementation

To assume responsibility for implementation and follow-up of the project

STEP TWELVE: EVALUATING AFTER CONSTRUCTION

Postconstruction evaluation is relatively easy if the neighborhood has set goals and the designer has carefully recorded the gestalt, the performance criteria, the hypotheses about how the project is to perform and the cost-and-benefit tally sheet. If these are made public, neighborhood residents can constantly monitor the effectiveness of the physical changes and progress towards their goals. They can pressure local officials or establish neighborhood work groups if expected progress is not made, and they can initiate informed changes to the plans as goals or local situations change. In addition, the designer can learn much from postconstruction evaluation if the

Your opinions are important to determine

How Are Things in Manteo?

These questions are part of the Town's efforts to develop plans for the future that reflect your concerns and needs. Please fill this out and return it to Town Hall with your water bill. If you have a problem, come by Town Hall and someone can read you the questions or clarify them.

1. What kind of house do you live in? (circle one)
    A. single family
    B. duplex
    C. mobile home

2. How long have you lived in Manteo? (circle one)
    A. less than 6 months
    B. 6 months to 1 year
    C. 1 year to 5 years
    D. 5 years to 10 years
    E. over 10 years

3. Do you own or rent your home?
    A. own home
    B. rent home

4. Using these steps, please circle the one that best describes Manteo right now as a place to live, "0" being the worst possible place to live and "7" being the best place to live.

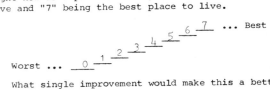

5. What single improvement would make this a better place to live?

6. How does tourism benefit you personally? (circle all that apply)
    A. more money
    B. job
    C. more stores
    D. more things going on
    E. no personal benefit
    F. other (please list)

7. What do you consider to be the good things about tourists being in Manteo?

8. Do you think there were more tourists in town this season than the year before? (circle one)
    A. more
    B. about the same
    C. less

To evaluate the project, Manteo sends this questionnaire to residents each year asking specific questions about how the design is affecting them. Not only can users correct mistakes, but designers can learn from them if postconstruction evaluation is systematic.

9. During this past summer did you have any special problems because of tourists in Town? (if yes, please list)

10. Did you have a hard time putting your boat in, parking, or getting to stores? If there were any problems please list them specifically.

11. Were you inconvenienced in any way because of tourists in Town? (if yes, please list)

12. Have you been bothered by traffic passing by your house this year?
    A. yes
    B. no

13. If it required increasing your property taxes, would you favor spending public money in Manteo for any of these? (check yes or no)

	yes	no
A. street paving and maintenance		
B. sidewalks on Highway 64/264		
C. a playground for children		
D. a recreation program for teenagers		
E. recruitment of industry		
F. downtown parking		
G. a youth center		
H. low income housing		
I. bicycle lanes		
J. a recreation program for adults		
K. recruitment of stores downtown		
L. vocational training		
M. a boardwalk on the waterfront		
N. provide more job opportunities		
O. removal of billboards on the highway		
P. plant trees along major streets		

14. Would you like to be more involved in planning Manteo's future?
    A. yes
    B. no
    If yes, please list: Name _____
    Telephone _____
    Address _____
    Area of Interest _____

Another method of postconstruction evaluation is careful observation to note where the design is not working well. This, too, can provide information necessary to make design or maintenance changes.

hypotheses have been recorded, as the case studies in the next chapter indicate.

The technique we used in Manteo for postconstruction evaluation was an annual survey to assess the impact of community improvements and tourism. The survey is mailed by the city government with the October water bill each year, the results are tallied, and a public hearing is held by the Planning and Zoning Board to discuss modifications that are needed in the neighborhood plan. This survey has provided ongoing evaluation.

What the designer should gain from step twelve:

New knowlege from testing hypotheses about how a space was expected to perform
Specific information to corroborate or dispel archetypes or develop theories of idiosyncrasies

A means of advising neighborhoods about changes that need to be made in a plan

The role of the users in this step:

To continuously evaluate the effectiveness of the plans as implemented
To initiate modifications

Useful techniques:

Questionnaires
Interviews
Observations

THINGS FOR YOU TO DO

The following exercises will clarify the issues raised in this chapter. Some will check your understanding of the material; others will help you articulate your own values or give you insights into neighborhood-design issues. You may do these exercises alone, but I would suggest sharing them with others.

1. Distinguish between an archetype and an idiosyncrasy as used in the design of neighborhoods.

2. How do you go about uncovering the gestalt in your design work? How could you make this process more effective?

3. Draw your complete neighborhood-design process. Mark on your drawing what you consider the strong and weak steps in your process. Reflect on this drawing for several days. Then make a list of ways to strengthen your weaknesses.

4. Carefully observe for several days a small space that you frequent. Then draw the activity setting for its use. Be sure to include spatial and socio-psychological details.

5. Why is it important for residents to see the costs and benefits of various plans instead of a single plan.?

6. What are the advantages of postconstruction evaluation for the residents? For the designer?

7. Try this design process on a project you have to do. How is it different from your own process? Modify this procedure to accommodate your own style. This is important because the steps shown here illustrate only one way of incorporating user patterns and idiosyncrasies into design. There are lots of other ways.

6

Case Studies

In recent years, an increasing number of neighborhood-design projects have incorporated the social factors, skills, techniques, and policies outlined in the previous chapters. It should be helpful to observe their application in a variety of case studies. In this chapter, twelve case studies are presented. In each, the designer attempted to provide a more socially suitable neighborhood space, and most of the projects were designed by hypothesis so they could be evaluated in terms of success. In addition, each study was a vital part of a community-development process. When taken as a whole, the case studies represent a range of neighborhood open space from formal community centers and open-space systems to quasi-legal, self-help efforts. They show, as well, the different roles designers may play from traditional practitioner, to laborer of love, to technical advisor.

After these projects were selected, each was visited, and during this time extensive interviews, observations, and questioning of both the users and the designers took place. (For a detailed explanation of the original selection process, follow-up visit, and method of data analysis, refer to the first edition of *Neighborhood Space* published in 1975.) In each case summary, a unique social factor, of particular relevance to the neighborhood design, is discussed. Although this factor's effect on the design process and on the resultant form and use of the space has been emphasized, other influential social factors have existed in every case. The simplified studies do serve, though, as concise examples of the applied value of the political concept of neighborhood, the concept of user needs, and the user-needs techniques.

DESIGN BY HYPOTHESIS

Jacob Riis Plaza, New York City

Jacob Riis Plaza signaled a new era of social responsibility in design. Although completed twenty years ago, without user input, it is notable as an early attempt to design by hypothesis.

At Jacob Riis Plaza, Paul Friedberg first systematically applied social information that he had discovered through observing one of his earlier projects. Two years before, on the Carver House project for the Housing Authority of the City of New York, Friedberg learned some specific things about how people used the site.

1. By using pieces of traditional equipment interconnected with each other, the idea of a "linked" play system was developed.
2. The sand area was more heavily used than any other play area at Carver House.
3. The formal sitting areas were unused.
4. The Carver House amphitheater served as a community gathering center.

Friedberg hypothesized that these considerations were relevant to the design of Jacob Riis. "It was by intuition, a certain amount of experimentation and observations . . . that we really got off what we call a *program* for the design considerations."[1]

The 2¾-acre plaza was intended to serve 8,000 people living in a public-housing project on the lower west side of Manhattan. The area was unsafe, and the outdoor space was unused. Resident input was limited to the observations of one person, the woman manager at the Jacob Riis Housing Project who pointed out the "givens". "Replace the basketball courts if you take them out; we need more lights and play facilities; replace the benches and save the big trees."[2] The resulting design program included six major areas: a playground, an amphitheater, a passive area, a sitting garden for the elderly, a relocated basketball court, and a street plaza. The playground was the activity focus and based on the linked-play concept.

Friedberg's arrangement of all program elements was deliberate. He tried to anticipate the needs of different age groups and to separate potential user conflicts. He also willingly evaluated his own design product to see if his assumptions proved correct.

Friedberg later found that the playground needed a separate play area for preschool children, that the concrete maze was "too much design for too little results," and that there was a need for more movement and open-ended play. Interviews with children confirmed his insights. The adults also complained that the water garden for the elderly was unsuitable. The designer's own response was similar: "The elderly wouldn't use it because we had misunderstood our user in this case."[3] The enclosed, walled-off area with a fountain in it had actually frightened off the elderly, whereas it provided an attractive hideaway for teens. These discoveries showed Friedberg the value of design by hypothesis, and he was more able to learn from postconstruction evaluation.

In spite of some problems, residents were positively affected by the development of Jacob Riis. It was hailed as the only contemporary playground in New York City, and when Lady Bird Johnson dedicated the facility, residents realized they had something unique.

Unique as well was Friedberg's design process. Intuition, plus a statement of his expectations of how the space would be used and by whom, led to suitable design. Implementation, followed by an analysis of actual uses, generated useful social-design research applicable to future design problems. Although the process was primitive by today's standards, the design of Jacob Riis ushered in the use of site-specific social information and hypothesis as a means of design.

The children who use the Jacob Riis Playground attest to the social suitability of the project. They can be observed running, climbing, jumping, sliding, and making up games, many of which are stimulated by the diversity of the environment. This project was an early attempt to design by hypothesis.

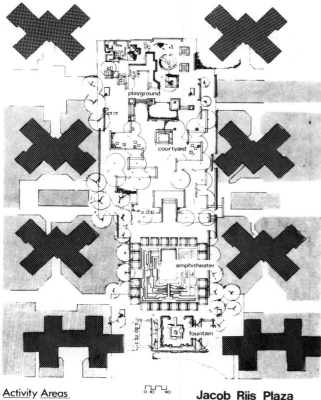

Activity Areas

Playground	Amphitheater
maze	stage
towers	seating
Courtyard	Fountain
open space	garden

Jacob Riis Plaza
for the City of New York
Housing Authority
landscape architect:
M. Paul Friedberg

ARRANGING SACRED SYMBOLS

Jule's Park, Manteo, North Carolina

Using the brick and concrete rubble from an old high school, [Jule] created a green oasis, a sacred place amidst decaying buildings along the town's waterfront . . . it is called Jule's Park, a tribute to his ongoing toil.[4]

In 1973, Jule Burrus, motel owner and town commissioner of Manteo, North Carolina, began creating his town's first park in commemoration of the American Revolution bicentennial. His desire to build the park rose out of a passion that was uniquely his own. Townspeople were skeptical; some made fun of the idea of beautifying an abandoned waterfront site. Yet Burrus withstood the criticism of his peers and community. He persevered to get the support and resources needed to fulfill his dream.

Jule's Park was inspired by a dream, not by a design. It was Burrus's dedication to that dream, combined with a lack of professional skills and standards, that led him to seek resources in an untraditional manner.

When Burrus realized he could use the rubble from the old county high school that was being demolished, he convinced a local contractor to move the rubble to the park site at no cost.[5] He then discovered that the rubble held sentimental significance for the older townspeople, most of whom had attended the school, and that this fostered sympathy for his project. Burrus decided to expand the idea of symbolic identification even further and outlined a theme for the proposed park, that of "building from ruins." This phrase was of sacred importance to most local inhabitants because of the area's history since 1584.[6]

Burrus was then able to get other people involved. A local handyman collected beach sand from nearby streets and dumped it with the high-school rubble as fill.[7] The local electric-power company contributed lamps at cost, and Burrus paid for them by getting residents to dedicate lamps as memorials to loved

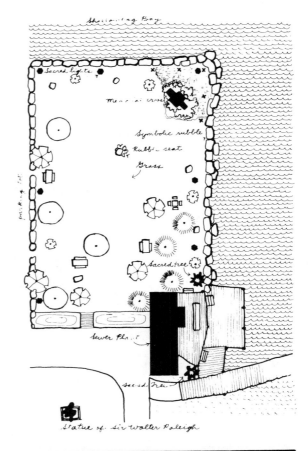

JULE'S PARK

0   20'   40'

ones.[8] A cement company, using a piece of rubble broken into the shape of a cross, erected a monument to the park's theme. Still, Burrus labored daily, doing most of the work himself with the help of one other resident.

The first phase of the project, completed in 1975, produced a landscaped lawn that was put to use immediately by residents. This enhanced the pro-

Although the park is unpolished and unprofessional to outsiders, it is meaningful to the people who built it and a vital part of the daily life of the community. Jule's Park is a collection of sacred objects designed and created entirely by users. (Photograph by Aycock Brown, courtesy of the Town of Manteo, North Carolina).

ject's visibility, and "town involvement and donations continued steadily."[9] The most prominent memorial, donated by the Women's Club, was a 20-foot statue of Sir Walter Raleigh carved from a single cypress tree. Burrus welcomed these gifts and other small-scale changes and personalizations by his fellow citizens, but he resisted modifying the park to conform with a town master plan. He was supported by other citizens who now shared his passion for the existing park and acclaimed it, already, a "perfect jewel."[10] Community support was assured when a survey indicated that Jule's Park had become more sacred than the area's churches to residents.

Some designers see the park and its rubble edge as unpolished and unprofessional. It lacks typical spatial articulation, and activity areas are not connected by material changes. Instead, the space appears to be a collection of sacred objects: a cross, a statue of Sir Walter Raleigh, memorial lamps, and nostalgic rubble. But as such, it is meaningful and sacred to the people who built the park, who maintain it, and who use it for local festivals, and religious and civic functions. Jule's Park provides designers with a model for using symbolic objects to create meaningful spaces for users. It also typifies user-originated designs that are becoming more widespread.

NEIGHBORHOOD SELF-SUFFICIENCY

Vernon Avenue Gardens, Bedford-Stuyvesant, Brooklyn, N.Y.

Though everyone interviewed recognized that the neighborhood was run down, they loved the area and wanted to continue living there. It was loving the area that encouraged them to get involved in the block association and the various neighborhood projects.[11]

Resident Hattie Carthan first organized the T & T Vernon Avenue Block Association to fight increasing neighborhood deterioration. The association's initial efforts at street beautification so impressed the mayor of New York City that he established the Tree Matching Program providing ten city trees for each one purchased by the neighborhood. The result was that hundreds of trees were planted in the area.

Encouraged by their success, in 1976, the group began planning for a neighborhood open space on a rubble-and-garbage strewn 20 by 80 foot site that was once a four-story apartment house. Their goals for the development of Vernon Avenue Garden included: improving the condition of the lot, providing a place for youngsters to learn about nature, and providing adults with a place to grow flowers and vegetables and a place to sit outside together. To achieve these goals, the block association considered property ownership paramount. They felt that a feeling of "mine" would stimulate people to build and care for the site, and that no one could ever throw them off the site. Research of the ownership was then pursued and, after some confusion, the lot was successfully purchased. One participant said, "The garden is like a church to us. It belongs to everyone in our neighborhood—and anyone else who wishes to enjoy it."[12]

The unusual garden site was designed with the special help of local assistance programs, an artist, and neighborhood children. Planning assistance came from the Cornell University Cooperative Extension Gardening Program. Cornell selected the garden as one of its "demonstration" sites and contributed manpower, soil, tools, and seeds to the project. The Magnolia Tree Earth Center's Youth Employment Program supplied summer youth workers. The Sanitation Department cleared the land, and a local artist designed a children's mural and produced it with the help of neighborhood children. This provision of free resources and technical advice enabled the block association members (mostly female) to organize local residents to assist with the development of the garden.

The completed garden became an important gathering place for the neighborhood, especially for youths and adults. It was used for sitting, parties, local art projects, and seminars for kids on planting and urban ecology. Essential to the project's success was the enforcement of a "locked entry" policy; entry to the site was possible only when a block member was there to unlock the gate. This allowed the group to set rules regarding use and to control maintenance, curb intruders, and limit potential vandalism.

The project's success did create ongoing management concerns, but the neighborhood had consistently shown an ability for making decisions and resolving problems. For these reasons, the residents' efforts exemplify neighborhood cooperation and self-sufficiency.

The Vernon Avenue Garden effort is typical of an increasing number of quasi-public neighborhood spaces that are arising where local governments cannot afford traditional open space. In such projects, initiated and controlled by neighborhood residents, there is a growing opportunity for designers to assume new and complementary roles as technical assistants.

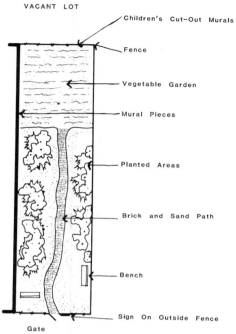

VACANT LOT

Children's Cut-Out Murals

Fence

Vegetable Garden

Mural Pieces

APARTMENTS

Planted Areas

Brick and Sand Path

Bench

Sign On Outside Fence

Gate

VERNON AVENUE GARDEN

0   10'   20'

NORTH

This neighborhood open space was an exercise in self-sufficiency from buying the land, to designing the layout, to building the garden. Designers must assume new roles when assisting such efforts as the Vernon Avenue garden. (Photograph by Mark Francis)

EXPRESSING INDIGENOUS VALUES

Dennis Chávez Park, Albuquerque, New Mexico

The proposal for the 1-acre, bowl-shaped site included Spanish dance platforms, a theater in the natural amphitheater, a place for puppet shows and movies, places for role playing after performances, and a place for craft fairs and community get-togethers. These activity settings, unique to the ethnic groups in the neighborhood, were to be linked together by a series of adobe towers and wooden sculptures built out of regional materials.

The character of these elements, described for The Total Environmental Play Area of Dennis Chávez Park, conveys a distinct image of a people, a place, and a culture. The project setting was, in fact, in adobe country on the fringe of the John Marshall neighborhood of Albuquerque, New Mexico. Of the people involved, 71 percent had Spanish surnames and 26 percent were black. The primary design objectives for this neighborhood project were to create a community focal point and a children's play area. These objectives were realized by combining a variety of suitable cultural activities, artistic and imaginative play spaces, and the use of indigenous materials. The project succeeded in giving a distinct identity to the area through its expression of local culture and community values.

The Total Environmental Play Area was the joint project of artist Julie Graham, wood sculptor Max Chávez, Model Cities planner Steve Marcus, and architect Channell Graham. Julie Graham's idea was to develop a neighborhood space to expose children to city experiences and to create spaces for children to use their imaginations—tunnels, bridges, caves, places contoured to fit kids' sizes.[13] But neighborhood residents were skeptical of the idea and generally mistrustful. They were extremely poor, many living on a family income of less than $3,000 per year. Adults were also politically reserved. To draw the residents into the discussion, a model of the proposal was presented to more than twenty different groups and their feedback was encouraged.

However, significant neighborhood involvement was not achieved until later, during the construction process. Julie Graham and a group of neighborhood teenagers did the adobe work through Willing to Work, a program to teach high-school dropouts construction techniques. A private contractor did some of the heavy work, and Max Chávez built the wooden towers. The result was a bold contrast of dark wood and light adobe towers set against a background of green.

The community's overall response to the park was conflicting. The adults valued the special functions permitted by the design—modern dances, Spanish dances, craft fairs—and wished for more community happenings. The park brought in prestigious groups and aided in the development of local talent. But at the same time, adults complained that only children used the facility frequently and that the elderly were noticeably absent. The reasons cited were the lack of shade (several large trees were cut down to accommodate the new design) and the park's location in a remote area.[14] Children, too, were upset over the loss of traditional play equipment, removed because it conflicted with the plan.

In spite of these criticisms, The Total Environmental Play Area was conceived with sensitivity to the needs of local users, and their particular social and cultural preferences are clearly reflected in the space.

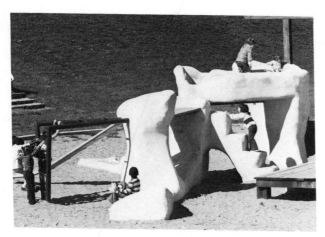

Dennis Chávez Park, built from local wood and adobe-type material and designed to provide a cultural center for the ethnic groups in the neighborhood, is an expression of indigenous values.

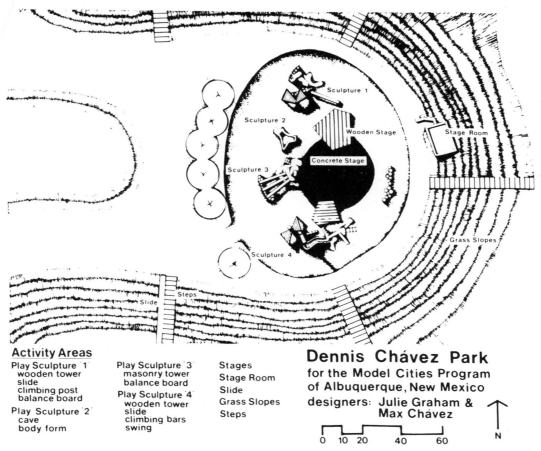

Activity Areas

Play Sculpture 1
  wooden tower
  slide
  climbing post
  balance board

Play Sculpture 2
  cave
  body form

Play Sculpture 3
  masonry tower
  balance board

Play Sculpture 4
  wooden tower
  slide
  climbing bars
  swing

Stages
Stage Room
Slide
Grass Slopes
Steps

Dennis Chávez Park
for the Model Cities Program of Albuquerque, New Mexico
designers: Julie Graham & Max Chávez

0 10 20 40 60

N

SOCIAL CLASS DETERMINES ACTIVITIES

Kingwood Forest Park, Raleigh, North Carolina

The goal was to maximize user involvement assuming that the people would be able to articulate their real needs and produce a socially suitable neighborhood space.[15]

When the residents of the all-black Kingwood Forest neighborhood first asked the city to provide a park in their community, they got nothing but a bureaucratic runaround from the Raleigh Recreation Department. H. B. Pickett, then president of the Homeowners' Association, had already acquired the land for a park by persuading the developer of a lower-middle-income suburb to donate a 4-acre site to the city. Yet the city continued to plead a lack of funds and caused an additional 2-year delay in development.

Pickett turned to The New Landscape, a university-based advocacy group, for alternative planning assistance, and Willie Denning, a student designer with The New Landscape, established a design process for Kingwood Forest Park. His process is a model of how to design with people to determine neighborhood-activity preferences. Denning started by developing a preliminary program based on the results of extensive interviews and questionnaires administered by neighborhood leaders. Using this program, he drew five alternatives that were discussed at a series of eight neighborhood meetings. These meetings, well advertised by the local media, were regularly attended by adults. However, no teenagers were invited to participate until the designer pointed out that teens would be a major user group. The Homeowners' Association then scheduled a teen social where Denning met with seventy-five teenagers to discuss the design plans. A month later, the teens met again and agreed on their priorities for the design.

These meetings gave Denning information on the physical settings that various users required. In addition, he discovered the need to consider which groups of people other groups wanted, or did not want, to

share in activities. For instance teens had a preference for coed activities, and both boys and girls said they would use the facility only if members of the opposite sex were there.

Six months after the design process had begun, three different programs existed for the site: the teenagers', the adults', and the city's. Nearly 100 residents attended a meeting with hopes to resolve

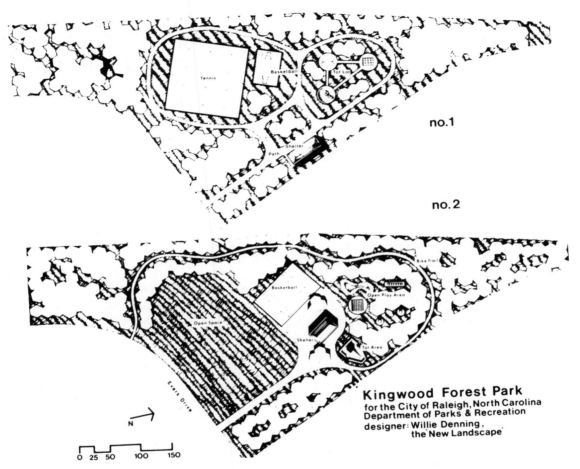

no.1

no.2

Kingwood Forest Park
for the City of Raleigh, North Carolina
Department of Parks & Recreation
designer: Willie Denning,
the New Landscape

The plan adopted by the neighborhood residents (number 2) excluded the tennis courts proposed by the city and expanded the basketball area that was more important to local teenagers.

The intensive use of the basketball courts attests to the success of the changed plan.

the differences. It was immediately apparent that the city's plan, especially the inclusion of tennis courts, was inconsistent with neighborhood priorities. The teenagers argued that two basketball courts would be more suitable than one basketball court and two tennis courts. They felt that anyone "rich" enough to play tennis could drive to the existing courts several miles away.

After several hours of debate, an older man suggested that only the teenagers, as the primary users, should vote on the plan. They did, and they voted overwhelmingly in favor of their own plan, which included four basketball goals, a shelter for hanging out, a children's play area and a big, informal open space. The result was a park that fit the special needs of the lower-middle-class residents. The one failing of the project was its location in a remote section of the neighborhood. As a result, the park was neither a focal point nor convenient to users. This points out the possible danger of developing "leftover" land for neighborhood space.

DESIGN FOR LEARNING AND PLAYING

Washington Environmental Yard, Berkeley, California

The space was a desert of asphalt, so typical of many school-yards. But by asking people what they liked about the Yard, what they wanted to change, etc. . . . the Yard is becoming a place where community and school can meet.[16]

Washington Environmental Yard has become a national standard for excellence in the integration of learning and play in a neighborhood-school environment. It involved the unique transformation of a 1½-acre, barren, asphalt playground into a spatially diverse and imaginative play environment. The yard was the result of efforts by planner Robin Moore, school principal Herb Wong, and environmental education consultant Mary Jefferds. They included not only the school but the surrounding neighborhood in planning the Environmental Yard. Their process involved meetings with teachers, a survey of children's preferences in addition to those of teachers and parents, setting up a "drop-in house" to get feedback from the entire neighborhood, and daily observations and on-site interviews to see how the Yard was being used. Moore hypothesized that children needed a variety of settings ranging from large social gathering spaces to private niches where kids could escape.

The cumulative data of user preferences corroborated Moore's hypothesis about diversity: users wanted a wide variety of spaces, interfaces, and activities. These included a natural resource area, an open space, a garden, a neighborhood-meeting space, a preschool corner, and a place for children to sit, read, and talk. Safety and appearance from the street were other concerns. The observations also revealed subtler preferences—for instance, existing basketball courts were symbolically owned by a group of older black children, which indicated that basketball courts were a necessary part of the Yard.

Moore developed a flexible master plan based on the users' criteria, concerns of the staff, and his own ideas about child play. As the plan proceeded, community yard fests were held, teachers began to use the Yard as a classroom resource, a garden was started, murals were painted, hills, forest and pond replaced the barren asphalt, and workshops were held on conservation, water supply, and gardening. When asked what he did most often in the Yard, one eight-year-old boy replied: "I do math, water the garden, fix up the dirt, plant my own garden, and play kickball."

A child can still play traditional paved-court games, but in a matter of minutes he can be hidden away in a Redwood grove or catching fish in a marshy pond. Today the Yard, a diverse spatial and tactile resource, is used by artist-educators throughout the city for innovative programs.

In the early years, the Yard plan lacked public support because the idea was a radical departure from other schoolyards in Berkeley. But today, the Yard is supported by the city, the school board, and a neighborhood group, Friends of the Yard, now responsible for most of the maintenance. The space has become a neighborhood focal point, the site of frequent street fairs and special neighborhood rituals.

One unresolved controversy concerning the Yard's appearance remains. The design was intended to be permanently incomplete and open ended, acknowledging that change would be part of a dynamic, highly used space (especially one where personal creativity was permitted). Some designers, nonetheless, have criticized the Yard for its unfinished, unprofessional appearance, and some adults even say the ponds look like cesspools. Such perspectives are not shared by the children who use the Yard. To them, the flexible and indeterminate qualities are both appealing and challenging; in the Yard, children are in adventureland.

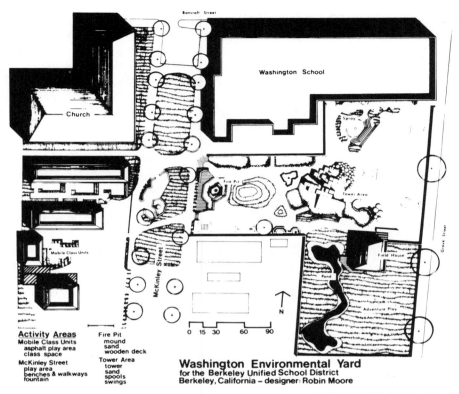

Activity Areas
Mobile Class Units
asphalt play area
class space

McKinley Street
play area
benches & walkways
fountain

Fire Pit
mound
sand
wooden deck

Tower Area
tower
sand
spools
swings

Washington Environmental Yard
for the Berkeley Unified School District
Berkeley, California – designer: Robin Moore

Washington Environmental Yard was designed as an educational resource for an elementary school. By providing a rich variety of settings and materials, it encourages creative play and learning where a child can build his own place or test his skills.

DESIGNING FOR NEIGHBORHOOD POWER

Putnam Gardens, Cambridge, Massachusetts

The problem was choosing a site that fit the patterns of the neighborhood activities. By locating the play area for preschool kids in the court, we were able to get parental supervision from the apartment windows above. This has been a great success.[17]

Residents of the Riverside neighborhood faced a major decision when they secured $40,000 of open-space improvement money. This decision concerned the location of the most critical link in their developing system of neighborhood space. "How should the money be used?" became the topic of monthly meetings among the black working-class residents. Dozens of local groups and city agencies took part in the site-selection process, which involved an almost 2-year analysis of their open-space system. Because of the lengthy site-selection process, residents learned a lot about city government and gained confidence to participate in city politics.

The Cambridge Community Development Section[18] prepared design plans and sketches for each alternative the neighborhood proposed, and these were evaluated by residents at their monthly meetings. It was the Riverside Planning Team, under the direction of Sandra Graham, which finally decided on the location and primary use. The team concluded that the critical space in the system was Putnam Garden's inner court, and that a place for preschool children was needed most.

This site-selection process exemplifies the facilitation of neighborhood control and power. Designer input was subordinate to the residents' decision-making authority.

After the selection of the ¾-acre project site, a series of neighborhood forums were held in Putnam Gardens to determine the design program. Residents wanted (1) an area for preschool children that included swings, a water spray, climbing equipment, a seesaw, and a slide (children also requested a tower clubhouse and a sandbox); (2) sitting areas for parents and teenagers watching small children; and (3) sitting and game areas for elderly people near

their clubhouse. Alternative design schemes were then developed. The designer used large plans so residents could write their feedback directly onto the plans. This technique revealed some specific user preferences. Residents wanted bright colors and powerful lights for safety, and they signaled approval for the designer's ideas of combining play equipment into a continuous movement of play and of building everything to children's scale.

Other less obvious needs also became evident. Because the supervision of small children was done by older sisters, activities for the sisters also needed to be included. In addition, the competitive life-style of the children needed to be accomodated by the design to reduce conflict. This was achieved by the design of "multispaces" rather than a single large space and created maze-like places allowing for small-group and private activities near each other, eliminating the domination of a single large space by one group.

During and after construction, a number of significant events occurred. For one, the contractor allowed the children to do small jobs on the project. The children not only learned a great deal but came to feel the project was their own. As a result, while lack of maintenance and vandalism characterized other city playgrounds, Putnam Gardens was cleaned almost daily. This was attributed to resident pride in the project and, equally, to the personal care of Sal Rossini, the housing-project maintenance man.

Another positive event was the election, two years later, of Sandra Graham to the Cambridge City Council. She became an outspoken, black-community advocate and proof of the neighborhood's effective use of the design process to develop local power.

By locating the tot lot in the interior court of the housing project, the designer facilitated parental supervision from above. Parents often call from the windows or lower snacks to children playing below. More importantly, the neighborhood gained power in the process.

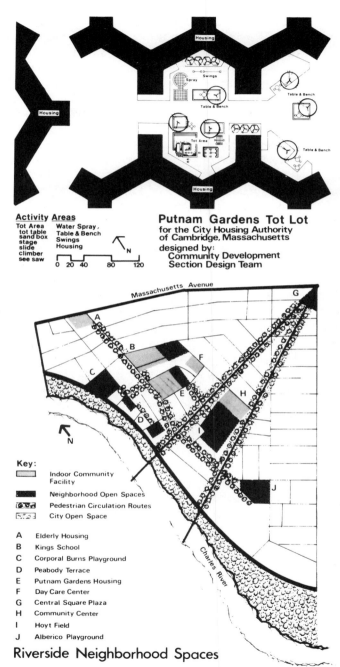

Activity Areas

Tot Area	Water Spray,
tot table	Table & Bench
sand box	Swings
stage	Housing
slide	
climber	
see saw	

0   20   40   80   120

N

Putnam Gardens Tot Lot
for the City Housing Authority
of Cambridge, Massachusetts
designed by:
Community Development
Section Design Team

Key:

▢ Indoor Community
     Facility
▮ Neighborhood Open Spaces
▨ Pedestrian Circulation Routes
▦ City Open Space

A   Elderly Housing
B   Kings School
C   Corporal Burns Playground
D   Peabody Terrace
E   Putnam Gardens Housing
F   Day Care Center
G   Central Square Plaza
H   Community Center
I   Hoyt Field
J   Alberico Playground

Riverside Neighborhood Spaces

The Putnam Gardens Tot Lot is one component of an informal
open-space system that links the entire Riverside neighborhood.

TERRITORIALITY AND SAFETY

Dana Park, Cambridge, Massachusetts

It is the only public neighborhood space so you had all these groups competing for a place. The conflicts between the teen gang, the elderly, and the small children were the worst. The idea was to resolve these conflicts by including all of the social isolates throughout the process. The final design reflects this, but the conflicts were worked out by the groups themselves as they participated in the planning process.[19]

"It doesn't make any difference what you do to improve Dana Park," said Big Richie, leader of the ill-reputed Dana Park Gang, "but unless you put in basketball courts where we can play at night, the whole place will be trashed."[20] Thus, he pointed out the major issue confronting park designers: how to resolve the conflicting space-and-activity demands of aggressive teens (adamant about the need for lighted basketball courts and a hang-out area) with those of the elderly (who wanted safe and separate seating areas) and small children (who needed a play area near their adjacent school site, yet away from the gang). The gang's dominant presence in the area was responsible for the others' desire to be "safe and separate." By asserting such preferences, each group described a need for their own respected territory.

These considerations became foremost in the design process. The design team provided neighborhood organization and design and political-strategy skills, but the team insisted that the neighborhood facilities be designed with the users making the major decisions in open neighborhood forums. At the meetings, appropriate city officials provided technical input,[21] but they similarly left the decisions to forum participants. The first action of the forums was to clarify the diverse needs of the user groups, and the priority needs of the gang, the elderly, and the children were recognized. In addition, there was consensus for a free-play paved area and a big, open-grass area. The presentation of alternative plans commenced when a user-needs consensus was reached.

A tense confrontation arose one day because of a break in the ritual of neighborhood forums. Since the elderly were afraid to attend night meetings, a special meeting was called for the Senior Citizens Organization. The teens considered this move exclusionary and crashed the meeting. Fortunately, the tension was short lived and soon the gang and elderly were discussing alternatives; in fact, the ideas presented in this irregular session led to the final design program. A teenager suggested that the foot traffic be rerouted around the edges to create a big, grass space in the middle of the park with sitting areas on the edges and that another walk-through be provided so the elderly could avoid the gang hangout. The gang made it clear that their hangout should remain where it was, convenient to the school and street where they worked on their cars. A senior citizen suggested the use of mounds to screen out the street if their sitting areas were near the street.

The resulting design did reduce tension between various user groups. The involvement of users throughout the design process, gang members in particular, was probably responsible for the park's success. In addition, the use of consensus problem solving and the recognition of various territories and use patterns was essential.

A teenager suggested that the circulation be rerouted around the edges to create a big, grass space in the middle of the park with sitting areas for observers on the edges. This reduced the conflicts between the elderly and the teenagers, who wanted to play open-space games.

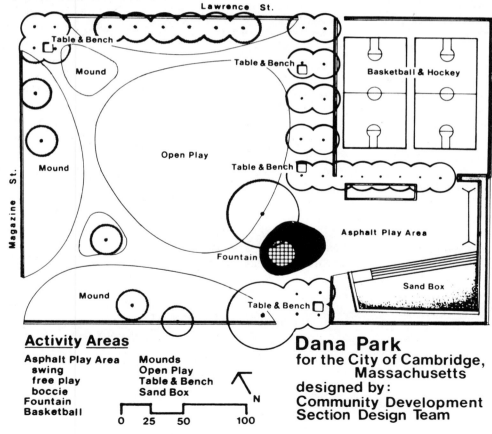

Activity Areas

Asphalt Play Area	**Mounds**
swing	**Open Play**
free play	**Table & Bench**
boccie	**Sand Box**
Fountain	
Basketball	

Dana Park
for the City of Cambridge, Massachusetts
designed by:
Community Development
Section Design Team

DESIGNING WITH STATUS OBJECTS

Redwood School, Salt Lake City, Utah

In Salt Lake City, wealthy people live up in the hills, the poor people in the flats. So it was important to get some mounds, some really big hills. They became a status object by providing for the same kinds of activities that go on in the wealthy sections. I think the hills are important to the neighborhood.[22]

When he began the design for the Redwood-Chesterfield neighborhood, volunteer architect Von White entered a process fraught with complications. He was immediately branded as a county representative by residents who were hostile towards agency functionaries. The residents were poor, white, skeptical, and frightened. Although 77 percent owned their own homes, housing values were the lowest in the city, an indication of the residents' severe economic deprivation.

Another complication was that the Neighborhood Council[23] was in turmoil because of infighting. White found the only point of consensus to be that the neighborhood badly needed a place for children to play and families to picnic. This was corroborated by a survey taken several years earlier in which 650 residents indicated a preference for a park as a priority neighborhood improvement, although many residents were in disagreement over the best location.

White tried to resolve the conflict over location by selecting three alternative sites: the Redwood School site and two others along the Jordon River. The river sites, although preferred by the neighborhood, were eliminated because they required additional aquisition funds. The school site, chosen by default, remained unacceptable to some residents. It was not only inconvenient to cross Redwood Road to get there, but the road lacked a safe crosswalk. The benefit of this site was, however, that the neighborhood school and community Office of Economic Opportunity center already formed a focal point that could be enhanced by the park.

White's preliminary plans were for a 3¼-acre park adjacent to these neighborhood facilities. It included a picnic pavilion near existing baseball diamonds and play facilities for children. In addition, White included major regrading to provide hills in the otherwise flat terrain for sledding, viewing, and imaginative play. The inclusion of hills was significant—they provided a status object for the community.

The hills exemplified the designer's understanding of important social-class factors and the concept of status objects and symbolic space.

Unfortunately, plan implementation only led to new frustrations. Residents complained when low-priority elements were eliminated because of budget limitations, and other constructed elements, such as the trees and family picnic pavilion, were immediately vandalized. But the kids loved the traditional play equipment and the hills. The hills, which were popular and heavily used, greatly increased the diversity of children's activity, a primary goal of the project. But it is interesting that equally unfavorable attitudes emerged in regard to the hills. A few council members were concerned that the hills harbored illicit teenaged behavior, and the school principal wanted to flatten the hills.

Such unpredictable controversy characterized the residents' response to all phases of the park project, and they felt their facility was still inferior to parks in other neighborhoods. The conclusion must be that deeply rooted community frustrations were not relieved by the development of the neighborhood park. The designer's sensitivity to the hills as status objects was outweighed by the symbolism of a site many didn't want and inequitable treatment by officials. This is an important, if painful, lesson for designers; you can't separate design from community development.

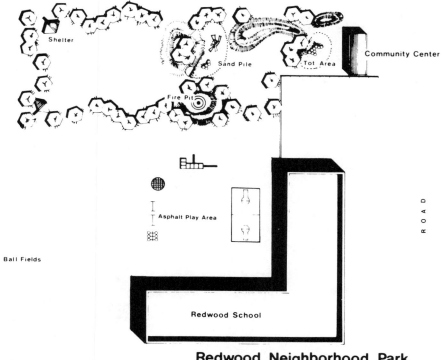

Shelter

Sand Pile

Tot Area

Community Center

Fire Pit

Asphalt Play Area

ROAD

Ball Fields

Redwood School

Activity Areas

Asphalt Play Area	Sand Pile	Community Center
seesaws	cave	Ball Fields
basketball	rocks	Tot Area
swings	climbing trees	Fire Pit
climbing bars	mound	

Redwood Neighborhood Park
for Salt Lake City, Utah
designers: Assist, Von White

0   25   50   100   150   N

The Redwood School playground provided hills, caves, and trees that broke the monotony of the flats, provided stimulating places for children to play, and created a much-needed status object.

USERS DEFINE QUIET

Grove-Shafter Park, Oakland, California

The design was exceptional in the use of what is generally conceded as unusable neighborhood space. Very few projects have had such strict guidelines for safety, aesthetic appeal, physical comfort, and psychological comfort. The space so adequately satisfied these needs that noise from the freeway overhead became a secondary factor.

Upon completion of the Grove-Shafter-MacArthur Freeway through Oakland, three irregular parcels of land were left beneath the belly of the freeway. A city official realized that to plant these areas in the usual manner would be a waste since Oakland was severely lacking in open space, and he proposed that the sites be made into a neighborhood park to serve the surrounding, predominantly black working-class neighborhood. The West Oakland Planning Committee agreed, and the city helped to acquire the land from the state.

The work of the principal designers, Advocate Design Associates, Inc., was complicated by the desires of the planning committee. Some wanted the projects to have a strong visual impact "like a piece of sculpture" or wanted brightly colored flowers year round. Others wanted a passive, quiet, peaceful, aesthetic feeling in the park. The designers respected these preferences while dealing with the major design constraints imposed by the site. Sitting areas were located under the freeway for maximum safety and psychological comfort. The group-activity areas had to be located at least 30 feet from the overhead structures to protect users from flying objects. Close attention to noise and carbon-monoxide level further reduced the usable activity area, but the final range of spaces to be selected was the most comfortable.

The final design for the first phase of development (consisting of two parcels equaling 2½ acres) provided typical neighborhood-park facilities. The design took into account activities for every age group in the immediate vicinity of the park—tots,

Included in the first phase of development were several children's play areas which had to be carefully located to provide maximum safety within the limits of the overhead freeway.

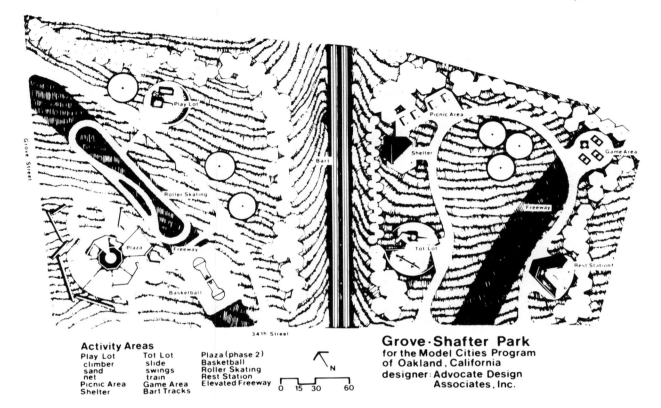

Activity Areas

Play Lot	Tot Lot	Plaza (phase 2)
climber	slide	Basketball
sand	swings	Roller Skating
net	train	Rest Station
Picnic Area	Game Area	Elevated Freeway
Shelter	Bart Tracks	

0 15 30   60

N

Grove·Shafter Park
for the Model Cities Program
of Oakland, California
designer: Advocate Design
Associates, Inc.

teenagers, young adults, and senior citizens. The built elements included a family picnic area, a sitting and game area, a paved bike and roller-skating rink, a basketball court, several children's play areas, and a rest station.

In spite of its potentially deafening location, Grove-Shafter was frequently referred to as "a very quiet park." The park had been carefully designed to minimize the noise, or one's perception of noise,

from the freeway. Success was evident in a user's remark that he came daily "to think, to get away from alot of noise."

The user's concept of quiet seems to be related to the "noise of other people." In comparisons of Grove-Shafter to nearby Mosswood Park, users said Grove-Shafter was quieter because there were fewer people and one was less likely to be bothered or robbed.

RECLAIMING NEIGHBORHOOD NATURE

Strawberry Creek Park, Berkeley, California

In the early 20th century, the creeks of Berkeley were envisioned as the feature of an open-space network stretching from the coastal hills, through the town, and ending at the bayshore marshland. The concept was to use creeks to delineate growing neighborhoods.

Today the majority of Berkeley's creeks are buried in culverts; their locations are unclear and their earlier presence mere speculation on the part of local residents. Yet in an old, flatlands neighborhood of the city, once nicknamed Irish Gulch, a creek restoration is near completion. It was during the preliminary planning for a neighborhood park that designer Doug Wolfe realized he could reveal a culverted portion of Strawberry Creek that ran beneath the proposed park site. He began calling the neighborhood open space Strawberry Creek Park, and the idea quickly engaged widespread support from citizens throughout the city.

The community's action symbolizes a recently growing value that creeks and natural water courses be an integral part of the neighborhood landscape and of the city dweller's experience. In addition, the reclaimed stream gives a unique identity to the neighborhood park. It further illustrates the potential of reclaiming land previously used for other purposes as community open space. In this case, the site had consisted of a street and an abandoned railroad yard.

The narrow site, almost 2 blocks long and ¼ block wide, was typical of an old Santa Fe freight yard. Because of the length, the design organizes the space into two distinct subareas that are separated by a wide pedestrian path formed by a street closure. One section focuses on the creek and is naturalistic with fields, mounds, and native plants and emphasizes strolling, seating, and gathering spaces for the elderly and families. The other section houses active court sports. The variety in activity settings is suited to the neighborhood, which is ethnically and economically diverse. But the separation of active and passive uses was essentially to accommodate the specific needs of the elderly and teens, who were viewed as primary and conflicting user groups. A senior-citizen home is adjacent to the site and another elderly housing facility is a short walk away. Teens come from the Berkeley Youth Alternative Center, located next to the street closure, from West Campus Junior High 1 block to the west, and from a nearby subsidized-housing project.

At this point, it is difficult to assess the technical success of the restoration. The erosion-control mechanisms, riprap formed out of concrete chunks from the demolished creek culvert, and check dams will be monitored along with the water quality. But the project does respond to new user demands to reclaim abandoned open space and to restore natural waterways in urban neighborhoods. This project is especially important because it signifies a reversal of the historic trend in many communities to culvert natural streams for health and safety reasons.

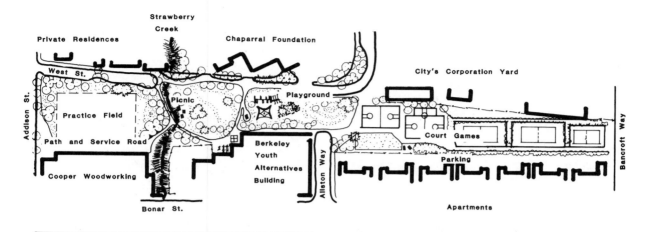

STRAWBERRY CREEK PARK

The unearthing of the previously buried Strawberry Creek was hailed by Berkeley residents as ushering in a new era in which nature will be reclaimed as part of neighborhood open space. Residents Edward Levingston, Marcia McNally, Mark McDaniels, James Sloan, and Michael Porter delight in the opportunities provided by a natural environment. (Photographs by Sandy Wendel)

DESIGNING FOR NONCONSUMPTIVE VALUES

Village Homes, Davis, California

Environmental designers should remember that their designs are not only parts of the human habitat but symbolic message systems as well, with power to affect resource consuming behavior . . . the medium may also be a message of conspicuous nonconsumption.[24]

Future scenarios, characterized by resource depletion, energy and food scarcities, social alientation, and environmental degredation, prompted Michael Corbett to design Village Homes, a 70-acre neighborhood in Davis, California. Developed between 1972 and 1980 as an alternative to traditional high-technological and energy-consumptive community systems, the project is internationally recognized as a model solar community.[25] It is exemplary, as well, because it responds to the newly expressed needs of middle-class Americans to live more self-sufficiently. The neighborhood spaces Corbett delineated reflect these needs and include shared open-space commons, community gardens and orchards and vineyards interspersed throughout the community.

Designing for a nonconsumptive life-style gives the community a unique visual and spatial character. There are over a dozen different solar technologies exhibited in the homes on south-facing roofs and walls. To accommodate solar demands, lot orientation needed to be primarily north to south, and, consequently, major streets run east to west. Circulation plans emphasized bike and pedestrian paths and a minimization of streets. As a result, 6-foot-wide paths were designed between groups of houses in lieu of normal sidewalks. The relationship of homes to open space was also distinguished by a reversal of the normal middle-class neighborhood pattern: fenced private yards are on the street side while a "common strip" occupies the space between back lots. This strip is collectively managed by the homeowners and is, moreover, an essential component of the

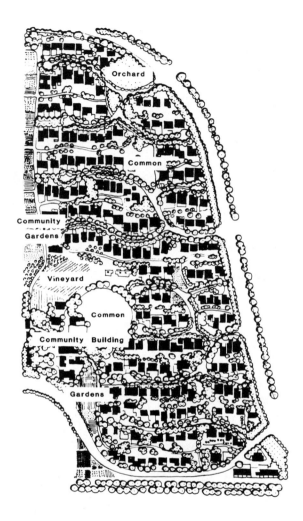

VILLAGE HOMES
Michael Corbett, Designer

The open space of the Village Homes neighborhood provides an orchard, community gardens, a vineyard, and common, multi-purpose open space. It expresses the values of the users for a less consumptive life-style. (Photograph by Mark Francis)

natural drainage system that was designed with the belief that steady soil infiltration is preferable to rapid storm-water discharge. The drainage design required that lots be graded away from streets, directing water into shallow swales that run through the common backyard areas. These swales then carry water slowly to larger collector channels that are landscaped like seasonal streambeds. The result is a natural landscape enhanced by a seasonal water element.

The absence of vast, private lawn areas has fur-ther reduced water consumption. Groundcovers, shrubs, and edible landscapes were promoted instead of lawns. Homeowners have integrated vegetable gardens into patios and play areas, while wild cherries grow freely along the drainage channels.

Although many of these design features are a significant departure from accepted subdivision layout, Village Homes seems to satisfy the needs of the residents to live more modestly and to express non-consumptive values in their community environment.

NOTES AND REFERENCES

1. From an interview with M. Paul Friedberg, October 24, 1973.
2. From an interview with M. Paul Friedberg, October 24, 1973.
3. Friedberg indicates that this is a basic problem in the playground-design field today—getting hung up on a design and not really understanding how that design is going to perform.
4. Billie B. Harper, *Implementation of a Youth Center in Manteo, North Carolina,* unpublished paper done for LAR 611, North Carolina State University, 1981, pp. 3-4. See also the Heritage Conservation and Recreation Service, *National Urban Recreation Study* U.S. Dept. of Interior, Washington, D.C., 1978.
5. Harper, *Implementation,* p. 342.
6. Harper, *Implementation.* The town is near the site of the Lost Colony, England's first colony in the New World that survived from 1584-1587. By 1590, the Colony had been deserted and no one knows what happened to the settlers. After the Civil War, a freeman's Colony that had been established nearby was obliterated. Then twice in the 1900s, most of the town burned. All these events made the "building from ruins" theme appropriate.
7. Harper, *Implementation,* pp. 4-5.
8. Harper, *Implementation,* p. 5.
9. Harper, *Implementation.*
10. *"Our Answers," The Coastland Times,* March 24, 1981, p. 4.
11. Mark Francis, Lisa Cashdan, Lynn Paxson, *The Making of Neighborhood Open Spaces* Center for Human Environments, City University of New York, New York, p. 114.
12. Francis, *The Making of Neighborhood Open Spaces,* p. 117.
13. From an interview with Julie Graham, May 13, 1973, Albuquerque, N.M.
14. This is a negative factor not only at Dennis Chávez but also at Grove-Shafter Park, Redwood School, and Kingwood Forest. The location in an interaction node or focal point for convenience seems to be a primary factor in the frequent use of neighborhood space.
15. From an interview with Willie Denning, July 31, 1973, Raleigh, N.C.
16. From an interview with Robin Moore, May 2, 1973, Berkeley, Calif.
17. From an interview with Ed Washington, Cambridge, Mass. 1972.
18. See the description of the Community Development Section in the evaluation of the Dana Park case study.
19. From meeting notes, Cambridge Community Development Section, Cambridge, Mass., 1971.
20. From meeting notes, Cambridge Community Development Section, Cambridge, Mass., 1971.
21. Several important technical considerations were included in the most important design criteria. The fact that snowplows had to get through the park became a critical factor in the final design.
22. From an interview with Von White, May 17, 1973, Salt Lake City, Utah.
23. Redwood-Chesterfield was one of seven Model Cities Neighborhoods.
24. Robert L. Thayer, Jr., "Conspicuous Non-Consumption: The Symbolic Aesthetics of Solar Architecture," *Optimizing Environments: Proceedings of the Eleventh Annual Conference of the Environmental Design Research Association,* Roger R. Stough and Abraham Wandersman, eds., Environmental Design Research Association, Washington, D.C., 1980, p. 182.
25. Michael N. Corbett, *A Better Place to Live: New Designs for Tomorrow's Communities,* Rodale Press, Emmaus, Pa., 1981, 164p.

Epilogue

The neighborhood movement has reshaped our processes for designing local communities. Planners have replaced outmoded techniques with participatory methods that contribute to neighborhood control and the expression of local idiosyncracies. Designers now share the job of creating community spaces with users. Collectively, lay people and professionals are giving form to their ideals of deliberative democracy, community responsibility, and personal development.

But the ideal that has motivated neighborhood designers for over two decades, environmental justice, is far more difficult to achieve. Powerful special interests benefit from environmental injustices of inaccessibility, exclusion, and unequal distribution of neighborhood resources. Class-based insecurities reinforce the injustices. As a result, suburban neighborhoods still isolate mothers from jobs, and designers still concentrate on environments for middle- and upper-income clients, excluding minorities, undesirables, and the poor whose neighborhoods continue to have unsuitable housing, second-class facilities, and inadequate services. Designers who are compelled by social conscience to overcome these inequities find themselves in the midst of a gentle class struggle against environmental oppression. It is a struggle that requires professional skill and commitment. It is a struggle I support.

In moments of great expectation, I hope that the theories, methods, and techniques presented in this primer will provide the tools needed for planners and designers to fight environmental injustices. In moments of lesser expectation, I hope that the book will contribute to the design of more socially suitable neighborhoods and will support deliberative democracy and local self-sufficiency.

My wish is that both my great and lesser expectations be realized.

Index

About the Author

RANDOLPH T. HESTER, JR. teaches community design at the University of California, Berkeley. He is a graduate of North Carolina State and Harvard universities with degrees in sociology and landscape architecture. In varied roles from community organizer, planner, designer, and researcher to elected official, he has focused on grass-roots control of the community development process to promote socially suitable and equitable environments. He worked for three years with Cambridge, Massachusetts, neighborhood groups in a successful effort to save their communities from the Inner Belt freeway.

In Raleigh, North Carolina, he established a city-wide citizen participation program that developed neighborhood plans based on local goals; he conceived and implemented a multimillion dollar open-space plan that rectified past class and racial discrimination in providing public parks; he organized a grass-roots effort to stop freeway construction that led to an alternative, low-cost transportation plan for the city; and he worked for ten years to realize a neighborhood rehabilitation plan for Chavis Heights, a black community that had been scheduled for urban renewal clearance.

In 1975, Hester developed a plan with citizens in Aurora, North Carolina, that prevented a multinational corporation from mining the community and he most recently completed an economic recovery plan for Manteo, North Carolina, that preserved the sacred structure of the neighborhoods. That plan won both the National Trust for Historic Preservation and the Virginia Dare awards.

In addition, Hester's projects have won awards from the Society of Technical Communication, the All-America City award, a national award for design excellence from the American Society of Landscape Architects, and the Outstanding Extension Service Award at North Carolina State University.

Hester has written numerous books and articles on participatory planning and community design including *Community Goal Setting* with Frank Smith (1982, Hutchinson Ross Publishing Company, Stroudsburg, Pennsylvania). He is married to Marcia J. McNally and has one son, Nate.